Marine Tropical Aquarium Guide

Marine Tropical Aquarium Guide

Marine Tropical Aquarium Guide

by Frank de Graaf
Curator, the Artis Aquarium

Photographs by
A. van den Nieuwenhuizen

Translated by
Dr. Joseph Spiekerman (The Netherlands)

Distributed in the U.S. by T.F.H. Publications, Inc., 211 West
Sylvania Avenue, PO Box 427, Neptune, NJ 07753; in England by
T.F.H. (Gt. Britain) Ltd., 13 Nutley Lane, Reigate, Surrey; in Canada
to the pet trade by Rolf C. Hagen Ltd., 3225 Sartelon Street, Mon-
treal 382, Quebec; in Canada to the book trade by H & L Pet Sup-
plies, Inc., 27 Kingston Crescent, Kitchener, Ontario N28 2T6; in
Southeast Asia by Y.W. Ong, 9 Lorong 36 Geylang, Singapore 14; in
Australia and the South Pacific by Pet Imports Pty. Ltd., P.O. Box
149, Brookvale 2100, N.S.W. Australia; in South Africa by Valid
Agencies, P.O. Box 51901, Randburg 2125 South Africa. Published
by T.F.H. Publications, Inc., Ltd., the British Crown Colony of Hong
Kong.

Table of Contents

Front cover: *Amphiprion   ocellaris*
Back cover: *Chaetodon   ephippium.*
Photo by Allan Power.

Black Angelfish, *Pomacanthus arcuatus*, juvenile form.

Black Angelfish, *Pomacanthus arcuatus*, adult form.

Introduction

In recent years the tropical marine aquarium has enjoyed a growing popularity among aquarists. In spite of this growing interest, home saltwater aquariums are still comparatively rare, and knowledge of how to keep them is still difficult to acquire. Why this discrepancy? The explanation seems to be that the marine aquarium is still shrouded in mystery, as if it were something reserved for the exceptionally gifted hobbyist. Today, however, keeping marine fishes in the home aquarium is no longer an impossibility. A saltwater aquarium is certainly not much more difficult to maintain than a freshwater one. It does, however, require a different technique, and therein lies the problem. To put it briefly, a marine aquarium can only be maintained in first-class condition if the aquarist can effectively control the artificial habitat of his charges. But such control presupposes knowledge of what goes on—and what is liable to go wrong—in the aquarium.

The present book seeks to fill a long-felt need by presenting the necessary theory in a form readily understandable to the non-professional aquarist. If the reader will familiarize himself with the subject matter of this volume, the marine aquarium will keep few secrets from him. He can also find quick answers to many of his questions in the handy summaries at the end of several of the longer, more detailed chapters. Although the book was written for tropical marine aquarists, the theory and practice discussed in the first five chapters hold for cold, unheated saltwater aquariums as well. Therefore aquarists specializing in North Atlantic and subtropical (Mediterranean) fishes can also benefit from it.

This book reflects the present state of our knowledge of marine ichthyology. It is in large part based on the author's 16 years of experience with the Artis Aquarium in the Amsterdam Zoo, Holland. Since our knowledge of the processes occurring in saltwater aquariums is growing all the time, it is quite possible that some points will have to be revised within the next few years.

The author has endeavored to write this book for beginning as well as for advanced hobbyists. This has proved a difficult undertaking, which he hopes has been successfully accomplished.

Part A: Theory and Practice

I Sea Water in Nature

Almost all the problems encountered in maintaining saltwater aquariums occur because the composition of sea water in an aquarium changes, slowly but surely, due to the presence of its inhabitants. These changes in the composition of the water make it impossible, after a certain time, for the water to support animal life at all. Therefore, in order to understand the problems, the aquarist must first study the conditions under which the animals live in their native habitat. Once he knows the environmental factors that govern the lives of marine animals, he can endeavor to simulate these conditions in the aquarium.

In general, because most of the fishes and invertebrates that we keep are from coral reefs, we will concentrate on that type of habitat.

The Coral Reef

Coral barriers and reefs extend all around the world in a broad belt on both sides of the equator. They are found in the Indian Ocean and the Pacific, along the numerous islands of Indonesia, in the Red Sea, along the coast of Brazil, and in the Caribbean. All in all, corals cover an area of some 2,000,000 square miles. The corals composing the reef formations are the skeletal remains of polyps, tiny animals related to sea anemones that live in colonies. The individuals in these colonies propagate by continually putting forth new buds. Each individual surrounds itself with a tiny calcareous home, so the colony is growing all the time. This is the way coral islands—some of them 30 miles across, and reefs and barriers as great as 1,200 miles long and 100 miles wide (Great Barrier Reef, Australia)—have come into being.

Build-up of the Reef

The polyps that build the corals require a very special habitat. The temperature of the sea water must remain between 68° and 82°F (20°–28°C) all year round. The water must be fairly shallow, at most 90 to 130 feet. The oxygen content must be high, and the water in constant motion. Also, the water must not contain floating mud particles or large amounts of bacterial detritus or decomposing organic matter. Those species that have built the coral masses are found only in regions where all these conditions exist. The non-reef-building coral species, which are solitary or live in small colonies, can survive under altogether different conditions. For this reason it is possible to encounter solitary coral species at great depths in the colder oceans, and other coral species in subtropical seas like the Mediterranean, where they form small colonies. No major reef formations are found in these regions, however.

Constant Change

In addition to the above-mentioned environmental factors, we must point out one more extremely favorable characteristic of the coral habitat. The sea water surrounding the coral reefs forms part of the huge water mass of the world's oceans. (Over 70 per cent of the global surface, or 140,000,000 square miles, is covered with water.) Because the water surrounding the coral reefs is an ever-moving part of this huge water mass, the coral reefs provide a very stable habitat. Whenever, for some reason, there are changes in the composition of the water, these are rectified by mingling with the vast surrounding churning water mass. The water of the oceans is in constant, restless motion and never stagnates, at least not in the surface layers. As a result, any changes in the coral reef habitat will be very small and of short duration. Adverse conditions never continue long enough to affect the reef fauna. This means that coral fishes and other reef animals are never exposed to oxygen shortages, to dangerous concentrations of carbon dioxide or waste matter, or to abrupt and major fluctuations of temperature, acidity and the like. As a result, coral fishes have never developed adaptation or defense mechanisms enabling them to survive unfavorable environmental factors, because such unfavorable factors simply do not exist.

In this respect, they differ greatly from their freshwater relatives, most of which have adaptive mechanisms that enable them to survive under a variety of widely differing conditions.

We have pointed out, however, that salt water in an aquarium inevitably changes as a result of the presence of the animals living there and eventually becomes quite different from natural sea water. This, combined with the very limited adaptive powers of coral fishes, is the source of the problems encountered in keeping these fish in captivity. These two basic ideas must always be borne in mind by the marine aquarist.

Chemical Composition Research

Our present-day knowledge of the chemical composition of sea water is based on the pioneer work done by the British *Challenger* expedition in the years 1872 to 1876. This research vessel, manned with a staff of scientists, roamed the world's oceans for more than three and a half years, collecting information about the ocean and its denizens. This marked the beginning of systematic scientific exploration of the oceans. The results of this gigantic undertaking have been laid down in 50 publications, which to the present day form the solid foundation of our knowledge of marine water. When the thousands of water samples collected had been analyzed and compared, the surprising discovery was made that the composition of sea water is the same in almost every corner of the globe. That is, the same principal components were found

Black Clown, *Amphiprion sebae*, in symbiotic association with sea anemone, *Radianthus* sp.

dissolved in the water everywhere, and these components were inevitably present in the same relative proportions, although the total concentrations might differ a little from one place to another.

Stable Ratios

Subsequent research has fully confirmed the *Challenger's* findings. Because of the stable ratios of the salts present in sea water, it is possible to determine the concentration of one or more components and then work out those of the others by means of formulas. But there are exceptions. In areas near river mouths, for example, or in more or less landlocked seas, coastal lagoons, tide pools and the very deep ocean troughs, different conditions may prevail. But these exceptions are not important for the practical maintenance of our marine aquarium.

Salinities

The most striking characteristic of sea water is its high salinity,

Black-Banded Triggerfish, *Rhinecanthus rectangulus.*

which in the open oceans averages 35 grams of salt per liter (4.67 ounces per gallon). Not all seas are equally saline, though. Higher salinities are found in sea areas connected with the oceans by narrow straits that impede rapid water exchange. Total salinities in the Mediterranean, for instance, range from 5.02 to 5.37 ounces per gallon. The Red Sea, which not only has a narrow connection with the Indian Ocean, but is also subject to a high rate of evaporation due to hot and dry desert winds, has higher total salinities than any other regular sea area—over 6.1 ounces of salt per gallon. Whenever any part of a sea is entirely closed off from the rest of the oceans and there are no freshwater discharges into it, the salinity will, as a result of evaporation, rise to a point where normal vegetation and animal life are no longer possible. For example, because the Dead Sea has been cut off from any ocean water for a long time, its salt content has risen to 33 ounces per gallon. The salinity of ocean water is expressed by the symbol "S" and is usually measured in proportion per thousand: ‰. A salt content of 35 grams per liter (4.67 ounces per gallon) may be written S 35‰.

The coastal areas from which our coral fishes originate show fairly large differences in salinity.

Table I—Salinity

Red Sea	40 gram/liter
East Coast of Africa	32–35 gram/liter
Ceylon	30–34 gram/liter
Singapore	30–32 gram/liter
Caribbean Sea	35 gram/liter
Florida	34–35 gram/liter
Philippines	30–34 gram/liter
Sea of Java	32 gram/liter

The specific gravity (or density) of sea water is directly dependent on its total salinity. The more salts dissolved in the water, the higher the specific gravity, and vice versa. The temperature of the water also affects its density. We shall come back to this subject when we discuss salinity determination in the aquarium (page 96).

Chemical Composition

The principal salts which, dissolved in ocean water, make up its salinity are (in descending order of concentration): sodium chloride ($NaCl$), magnesium chloride ($MgCl_2$), magnesium sulfate ($MgSO_4$), calcium sulfate ($CaSO_4$), potassium sulfate (K_2SO_4), calcium carbonate ($CaCO_3$), and potassium and/or sodium bromide (KBr, $NaBr$). (Of course, salt water does not contain, e.g., K_2SO_4, but K^+ and SO_4^- KCl and $MgSO_4$ give exactly the same solution as $MgCl_2$ and K_2SO_4 after dissolving.) In addition to these, many other compounds are found in sea water, frequently in minute concentrations. The presence of more than sixty different elements has been demonstrated, and probably more will be found as more sophisticated techniques of analysis become available. Elements occurring in minute quantities are called trace elements, several of which have been shown to be of great importance biologically. A few are known only from the tissues or blood of invertebrates or from algae.

In sea water, the concentrations of these substances are so low that their presence can not, or can only with great difficulty, be demonstrated by chemical methods. Certain organisms are capable of filtering off these minute quantities and storing them in their body tissues. Such substances include nickel, molybdenum, zinc, vanadium, cadmium, titanium, thallium, germanium and chromium. The following table shows concentration factors for some of these trace elements in different algae. The numbers indicate how many more times the metal is concentrated in the algae than in the sea. For example, there is a thousand times more nickel in the algae *Fucus spiralis* than in the surrounding water.

Table II—Concentrations of Trace Elements in Algae
(after Black and Mitchell, 1952)

Algae species:	Nickel	Zinc	Vanadium	Titanium
Fucus spiralis	1000		300	10,000
Fucus vesiculosus	900	1100	60	2000
Fucus serratus	600	600	20	200
Ascophillum nodosum	600	1400	100	1000
Laminaria digitata	200	1000	20	100

The blood of several invertebrates contains 0.15–0.25 per cent copper, whereas in sea water its concentration is no more than 0.001 to 0.002 milligrams per liter. The vanadium content of Ascidians (a type of sea squirt) is about 0.05 per cent of their dry weight; in sea water the concentration of the element is no more than 0.003 milligrams per liter. Later we shall come back to trace elements and see what role they play in the lives of marine animals and plants.

Sea water also contains dissolved gases, among which oxygen and carbon dioxide will concern us most. In addition, there are small quantities of argon, krypton, neon and xenon. In spite of its complexity, sea water has two important characteristics: it has a homogeneous composition and it is stable. Thus we find a high and constant dissolved oxygen concentration in the surface layers, particularly of those areas inhabited by the tropical fishes usually kept in a marine aquarium. Sea water, as compared with fresh water, has less capacity for absorbing oxygen because of its high content of other dissolved substances. At a temperature of 68°F it can dissolve only 5.35 cc per liter, whereas fresh water of the same temperature is saturated at 6.57 cc per liter. As the temperature rises, even less oxygen remains dissolved, so that at 86°F a liter of sea water contains only 4.50 cc of oxygen.

Table III—Elements Dissolved in Sea Water
(in Milligrams per Liter)

Chlorine	18980	Cl
Sodium	10561	Na
Magnesium	1272	Mg
Sulphur	884	S
Calcium	400	Ca
Potassium	380	K
Bromine	65	Br
Carbon	28	C
Strontium	13	Sr
Boron	4.6	B
Silicon	0.02–4.0	Si
Fluorine	1.4	F
Nitrogen	0.006–1.0	N
Aluminum	0.12–0.5	Al
Rubidium	0.2	Ru
Lithium	0.1	Li
Phosphorus	0.001–0.1	P
Barium	0.05	Ba
Iodine	0.05	I
Zinc	0.01–0.05	Zn
Arsenic	0.01–0.02	As
Manganese	0.002–0.02	Mn
Copper	0.001–0.02	Cu
Lead	0.005	Pb
Selenium	0.004	Se
Cesium	0.004	Cs
Uranium	0.002	U
Molybdenum	0.0015	Mo
Thorium	0.0005	Th
Cerium	0.0005	Ce
Silver	0.0004	Ag
Vanadium	0.0003	Va
Lanthanum	0.0003	La
Yttrium	0.0003	Yt
Nickel	0.0001	Ni
Scandium	0.00004	Sc
Mercury	0.00003	Hg
Gold	0.000006	Au
Radium	$0.2{-}3 \times 10^{-10}$	Ra

Thallium, cadmium, titanium, germanium, cobalt, tin, indium, antimony, bismuth, tungsten and chromium are also present in smaller amounts.

It is possible for sea water to dissolve oxygen in excess of its normal concentration; however, high concentrations are not stable and the excess will pass back into the atmosphere readily, particularly if the water is in motion. Oxygen concentrations, even if they are higher during the day, usually drop to 100 per cent during the night, since the daytime excess is mainly due to oxygen production by phytoplankton (microscopic plant life).

In tide pools and rock pools with luxuriant algal growths, periods of low water accompanied by intense sunlight will result in oxygen saturation values far in excess of 100 per cent because of the action of the algae, while the pH will sometimes rise to 10 or over. This is caused by a combination of things. The calm water does not encourage an exchange of gases between the atmosphere and the water; at the same time, the algae are giving off oxygen and absorbing carbon dioxide, causing the pH to rise to values over 9.0. Such conditions are not likely to occur on the coral reefs, where most of the aquarium fishes we are concerned with originate, although supersaturation up to 110–120 per cent often occurs.

The constant saturation of the surface water with oxygen is brought about by the rapid diffusion process in the ever-changing thin top layers. As a result, the sea water down to a considerable depth is also constantly saturated, as fresh water is being carried to the surface all the time.

Carbon dioxide (CO_2), which is dissolved in sea water from the atmosphere or given off as a respiratory waste by marine organisms, undergoes a number of changes, as shown in the following diagram:

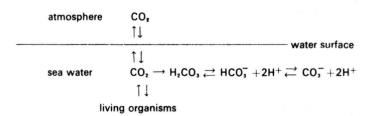

Black-Spotted Boxfish, *Ostracion tuberculatus*.

Carbon dioxide is dissolved in water either as CO_2 or H_2CO_3 (carbonic acid). Carbonic acid disintegrates into hydrogen ions (H^+) and bicarbonate ions (HCO_3^-). The bicarbonate ions eventually dissociate into carbonate ions ($CO_3^=$) and hydrogen ions (H^+). All these are so-called equilibrium or reversible reactions —that is, they move forward or are reversed according to prevailing conditions.

In most sea water, and certainly on the coral reefs, carbon compounds are normally present in the form of hydrocarbonate ions and carbonate ions. There is very little dissolved carbon dioxide (0.18–0.44 cc per liter); in fact, the amount of carbon chemically combined in the hydrocarbonates and carbonates is at least a hundred times greater than the amount of free carbon dioxide.

pH and CO_2

Because there is so little free carbon dioxide in sea water, it is quickly exhausted in areas with high algae concentrations, thus forcing the algae to turn to the hydrocarbonates to fuel the photosynthetic process. This causes the precipitation of carbonates and a resultant increase in pH to values as high as 10. This may occur in tanks as well as in tide pools at low tides in nature. The excessively high pH may kill fishes and invertebrates, but vigorous aeration or circulation will prevent this.

The pH of sea water, which expresses the relative proportions of acid hydrogen ions (H^+) and alkaline hydroxyl ions (OH^-), is closely connected with the equilibrium system of the forms in which carbon dioxide is present in sea water. When carbon dioxide is decreasing, the equilibrium of the pH shifts toward the right or alkaline side of the scale, and the water becomes more alkaline. When there is an increase in dissolved carbon dioxide, the pH drops and the water becomes less alkaline (more acid). Under normal conditions the pH of natural sea water remains within very narrow limits: 8.0–8.3. A pH of 7.0 is "neutral," which means that the hydrogen ions and hydroxyl ions balance each other. When the pH is below 7.0, water is acid; when it is over 7.0, it is alkaline.

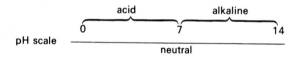

As we have seen, very little free carbon dioxide is present in sea water at pH values of 8.0–8.3, as the quantities produced by animals and plants are quickly absorbed by the algae or released back into the atmosphere. An abnormally large concentration of carbon dioxide in sea water causes a drop in the pH. Under certain circumstances, sea water can easily become saturated with carbon dioxide because, like oxygen, the gas readily dissolves in water, but unlike oxygen, it is not readily passed back into the atmosphere.

The "buffer" system must also be considered. Because of the quantities of dissolved ions, both acid and alkaline, sea water tends to remain stable, that is, to resist changes in pH. Often fairly large quantities of chemical must be added before the pH responds.

The water in the oceans, particularly around the coral reefs (which are often located in areas where surf breaks on the coasts), is always so turbulent that, barring exceptional conditions, over-saturation doesn't occur. If the sea water stagnates, however, as it does in tide pools isolated from the sea at low tide, carbon dioxide concentrations may rise to the point where the pH of the water drops rapidly. On the other hand, if there is an abundance of seaweed in the tide pools, these may use up so much carbon dioxide during photosynthesis that the pH, instead of dropping, soars to abnormal values. These processes are also encountered in the home aquarium.

Another property of sea water of special importance in the marine aquarium (as we shall find in the next chapter) is the surprisingly low concentrations of such inorganic nutrient salts as phosphates, sulfates, ammonia and nitrates. Of these, the nitrogenous compounds, ammonia (usually expressed in terms of the nitrogen molecule "N") and nitrates, will concern us most, since these are the end products of the bacterial decomposition of the proteins of dead organisms and of the excretory wastes of living ones. Since the latter are produced in the aquarium in large amounts, it is of interest to know in what concentrations these substances occur in natural sea water. The concentrations are actually extremely low—so low that it is sometimes very difficult to demonstrate their presence by chemical methods. There is a twofold explanation for this. First, any substance released into the sea is subject to a continuous process of dilution by the huge water masses. Second, the plankton algae and attached seaweeds remove these substances from the sea water as they are formed, by using them as nutrients. Since only tiny amounts are available, these substances more than any others impose limitations on growth, particularly that of plankton algae. Indirectly, this in turn imposes a limit on animal plankton, which feeds on phytoplankton. As a result, the concentrations of plankton in nonpolluted sea water are comparatively low, so the water is crystal clear.

When organic pollution makes the water richer in nutrients, there may be plankton population explosions which can color the water and make it cloudy—a well-known phenomenon on some of our coasts, but one which under normal conditions never occurs in coral reef areas. The concentrations of organic sub-stances in sea water from which the inorganic compounds are eventually formed are similarly very low: 2-5 mg per liter (including 1.2–2 mg of organic carbon and 0.2 mg of organic nitrogen—nitrogen in proteins—per liter). But however small its concentrations, organic matter, in the form of enzymes, vitamins, antibiotics, amino acids, amines, organic dyes and several other substances, plays a very important role in sea water. The precise role of these substances in marine life is largely unknown, but their absence from synthetic sea water may be the reason many delicate forms of life, such as invertebrate larvae, cannot *live. Synthetic sea water becomes a viable medium for these organisms only after some freshly collected natural sea water has been added.

One of the waste products of fishes is ammonia. It is also a by-product of the decomposition of protein. In coral reef water, ammonia is limited to concentrations of 0.000–0.090 mg N per liter, nitrites (intermediate products in the conversion of ammonia to nitrates) to 0.000–0.400 mg N per liter and nitrates to 0.000–0.250 mg N per liter.

Another characteristic of natural sea water, particularly in the open oceans of the tropics, is the extremely small number of bacteria. Although the nutrients available in natural sea water can support millions of bacteria per cubic centimeter, the actual number is generally no more than 10 to 200 bacteria. In coastal waters, in bottom layers, and particularly in mud, these numbers are a little higher; so there must be factors in natural sea water that keep down the number of suspended bacteria.

One of these factors may be the absence of a suitable substratum to which they can attach themselves, as bacteria find it less easy to propagate when free-floating. Although in sea water they will attach themselves to such things as plankton organisms, these are, as a rule, present only in relatively small numbers. When a substratum is introduced into sea water, or when ocean water is brought into contact with sand and glass in an aquarium (which amounts to the same thing), there may be a population explosion of millions upon millions of bacteria. The rapid propagation of bacteria on a substratum is partially due to the adsorption of organic substances to solid surfaces—the bacteria can find more concentrated food there.

In addition to the absence of a substratum, the fact that plankton organisms feed on bacteria keeps down their numbers. Other agents which act to reduce the excessive growth of bacteria are the bacteriophages and the recently discovered predatory bacteria

Black-Spotted Moray, *Gymnothorax tesselata* (*favagineus*).

present in both fresh and salt water. (The first species described was *Bdellovibrio bacteriovorus*.) Predatory bacteria bump into other bacteria, larger than themselves, and then digest the disabled ones by secreting protein-disintegrating enzymes. How important a part predatory bacteria play in keeping down bacteria populations and whether they can live in aquariums is as yet unknown. But all the factors mentioned so far do not account for the scarcity of bacteria in the open water of the world's oceans. So it is assumed that open ocean water contains an unknown substance, or perhaps substances, that kill bacteria or impede their growth. Certain iodine compounds and chlorine compounds have been suggested. Whatever the causes, the bacteriocidal or bacteriostatic quality is lost when sea water is heated or stored in containers. Another factor in keeping down the number of bacteria in natural sea water, at least in the surface layers, is the intense tropical sunlight, mainly because of the sterilizing effect of ultraviolet rays.

Motion

The last important characteristic of the natural marine habitat is the continuous motion of the water. This turbulence, which is very intense around the coral reefs, is important not only for the exchange of gases between water and atmosphere, but also for the well-being of living organisms. In water every object, alive or dead, is surrounded by a thick or thin layer of stagnant water. In moving water it is thin; in still water it is comparatively thick. Animals and plants must pass oxygen and carbon dioxide through this "mantle." Other metabolic wastes must also pass through, if they are not to affect the organisms. Obviously, the thicker the mantle of stagnant water, the more it will impede these processes. All animals living in the turbulent waters around the coral reefs are naturally surrounded by a thin mantle, which permits unhampered respiration, ingestion and elimination. This factor merits careful consideration, as we shall see in subsequent chapters.

Summary

We have thus surveyed the main characteristics of the natural reef habitat and shall conclude this chapter by reviewing them briefly.

Sea water has a stable composition, any changes being slight and of short duration. All vital elements are constantly present in the necessary concentrations (although experiments in aquariums indicate that many species grow better in water enriched with trace elements). The oxygen content in sea water is always high, for example, while the carbon dioxide content is always low. Organic substances are present in small amounts, as are the inorganic compounds produced from them by the action of bacteria. The pH is constant within the 8.0–8.3 range. The number of bacteria is surprisingly small. The water is in ceaseless motion. The coral reefs present an ideal habitat for countless species, some of which exist in incredible profusion. It is this last factor that leads to what is, in effect, the only adverse characteristic of the coral reef habitat: permanent overcrowding; each individual must fight continually for its territorial rights and food. Predators of many kinds either inhabit the reefs or visit them regularly in search of prey. The struggle for life is fierce and unceasing, as the

Black-Tailed Humbug, *Dascyllus melanurus.*

scars on many coral reef fishes testify. But despite cutthroat competition and ever-present predators, the coral reef habitat is an ideal environment, and this is what makes it difficult to keep its denizens in captivity. They have become so conditioned to their stable environment that, as we have remarked before, they are fastidious to the point of being spoiled. Never having been exposed to adverse environmental factors in their native habitat, they have not been forced to develop protective mechanisms and are conspicuously lacking in adaptive powers. Fortunately for us they do possess some minimal adaptability, which does make it possible to keep them in well-tended aquariums. Even so, what little adaptability they have responds rather slowly.

It should be evident by now that we must never expose coral fishes to abrupt and major changes in their environment, and that we must in fact provide them with an environment resembling their natural habitat as closely as possible. Of course, it takes a great deal of work to do this, for as soon as sea water containing marine life ceases to be part of the immense oceans, it begins to change and eventually loses the peculiar life-supporting characteristics of natural marine water. The exact nature of these changes will be discussed in the next two chapters, as well as how best to control the process.

In this section, we have exaggerated to make a point here and there, for while the coral reef habitat is stable, it is not always quite so stable as we have maintained. During the frequently prolonged periods of tropical rain, there is inevitably a certain amount of disruption in the off-shore coral reef habitat. The rain water dilutes the surface layers, causing a temporary drop in total salinity. Drainage water and suddenly swollen rivers carry silt and other foreign matter far out into the sea. The intense sunshine may be absent for considerable periods. Last but not least, tropical gales will sometimes lash the water into such wild fury that even the reefs are damaged. These, of course, constitute only temporary changes in the habitat, but they are bound to affect the marine fauna adversely. Observations have shown that, during prolonged spells of sunless weather, coral fishes are more prone to skin diseases. During hurricanes their mortality rate may rise steeply. In the wet season, when the water becomes turbid, many fishes temporarily abandon the reefs and migrate to more favorable localities in deeper water.

II   Sea Water in the Aquarium

What we have said about the chemical complexity of marine water might lead the reader to conclude that nothing but natural sea water will do for his aquarium. Fortunately this is not true. For quite some time now it has been possible to make synthetic sea water of such high quality that even the fastidious coral fishes accept it. (In fact, the advent of synthetic sea water marked the first major breakthrough in home aquarium keeping.) Where periodic water renewal—so essential to the fishes' health—used to pose almost insurmountable problems to anyone not living near the ocean shore, synthetic salt mixes have finally solved this problem. Even aquarists living in coastal areas often prefer to use synthetic sea water, because in many areas sewage and polluted river water have contaminated our inshore waters so that they are no longer a good source for the aquarist. This is not to say that synthetic sea water is altogether preferable—it is still true that there is nothing to beat absolutely pure natural sea water.

Natural Sea Water

Sea water should be obtained as far as possible offshore—since the water of the open oceans contains far fewer impurities—and at high tide while the wind is blowing inland. At any other time undercurrents will dislodge a good deal of organic matter from the bottom, and what we want is water with the smallest possible content of organic matter. When the sea water has a brown or brownish green tint from the explosive growth of phytoplankton, we should not use it for our aquarium. (This occurs particularly in spring.) Most of the plankton algae will die en route to or in the aquarium, making for water that is less suitable for our purpose because of the relatively large amounts of organic matter released by dead algae. Even sea water which seems perfectly clear should be filtered through a fine sieve to remove any suspended dirt and plankton organisms. Older manuals state that natural sea water is preferable to the synthetic product because it introduces plankton organisms into the aquarium, but, bacteria aside, plankton organisms seldom survive in the confined space of a home aquarium.

Synthetic Mixes

The ready-to-use artificial salt mixes that fish dealers and pet stores carry are of such high quality, as a rule, that the modern aquarist need not bother buying the various salts from a drug store to mix them himself. However, a formula is given in the next chapter for those who still prefer to make their own.

Both natural and synthetic sea water have their advantages and disadvantages, as indicated here:

NATURAL SEA WATER	SYNTHETIC SEA WATER
chemically complete	chemically incomplete
all trace elements present	trace elements not all present
contains growth-promoting substances	may impede growth
harmful microorganisms may be present (particularly disease germs)	harmful microorganisms absent
useful bacteria present	useful bacteria absent

Because the absence from synthetic sea water of certain substances present in natural sea water might cause deficiency symptoms in aquarium inhabitants and impede the growth of algae, a number of indispensable trace elements are added to most ready-to-use salt mixes. We shall return later to a discussion of these. The occasional failure of synthetic sea water to promote satisfactory growth may also be due to the absence of certain vitamins and other organic substances. In general, this failure will disappear after the aquarium has been running for some time and there has been a fair amount of algal growth.

The absence of harmful microorganisms from synthetic sea water is a major advantage, however, for if we use natural sea water we must always watch out for disease germs. Absolute certainty on this score can only be obtained by sterilizing the ocean water; a less foolproof method is to store it in the dark for some weeks. (See Chapter III.)

Synthetic sea water is almost sterile; thus, bacterial fermentation processes do not get underway at once in a newly set-up aquarium filled with synthetic sea water. This is reflected mainly in the rapid accumulation of ammonia in the water, which may cause a sudden high mortality rate among the fishes. In order to introduce the necessary bacteria into synthetic salt water, we can add either a small quantity of water from a well-established aquarium, or some natural sea water, or even an infusion of good garden soil, which contains the same useful bacteria as natural sea water.

Salinity

At this point, we shall make only a brief remark about the salinity to be maintained in the aquarium. Although salinities vary in the seas and oceans, and in the tropics, where our aquarium fishes originate, their value is generally 34–35‰. While marine animals, particularly fishes, are not very susceptible to changes in total salinity so long as these are not abrupt, we should avoid extreme fluctuations. Regular checks and water replacement are therefore necessary. The optimal salinity seems to be 34–35‰, the value prevailing on the coral reefs. On the other hand, tropical marine fauna thrive even at values between 30 and 32‰, and there are indications that certain skin parasites do not bear

Blue Devil, *Pomacentrus coeruleus*.

Blue King Angelfish, *Pomacanthus annularis*.

up well under such conditions. However, there is still too little evidence in favor of a somewhat lower salinity for us to recommend the lower concentration unreservedly. For the present, 34–35‰ seems to be the safest figure.

Differences from Sea to Aquarium

We have repeatedly said that, whether natural or synthetic, salt water in an aquarium undergoes a number of changes until it no longer resembles natural ocean water. Exactly what happens, and what causes the changes?

First, evaporation causes a constant increase in the total salinity, since only pure water evaporates and the salts are left behind. This process must not be allowed to continue unchecked, as the salinity may become too high for the animals and algae. Moreover, the higher the salinity, the less oxygen the sea water can hold.

Never replace evaporated water with sea water but with chlorine-free tap water warmed to the temperature in the tank. (The British call this "topping up"—to fill a partially full tank to the brim. It is an expression Americans could usefully adopt.) Tap water frequently contains varying amounts of free chlorine, which may be very harmful to some fishes. Sea water is lost during cleaning operations, siphoning, etc., so check the salinity regularly. We will discuss the proper procedures in the next chapter.

Organic Compounds

In the sea there is a closed cycle of certain chemical compounds, with animals, bacteria and algae maintaining an equilibrium.

To do justice to the complex processes occurring in the bacterial decomposition of organic substances, we would need a whole volume, for scientists have not yet fathomed them in all their complexities. Fortunately, the aquarist needs no more than a "simplified" approach. A measure of insight into the marine-chemical processes occurring in the aquarium will enable him to see the why and wherefore of such techniques of aquarium maintenance as filtration, aeration, ozonization, etc.

The plant-like organisms which build organic substances from non-organic compounds are called *producers*; the animals which cannot produce organic materials themselves and must obtain them directly or indirectly by eating plant forms are called *consumers*. The bacteria which convert excretory wastes and the remains of dead organisms to non-organic compounds are called *reducers*. When producers, consumers and reducers are in balance a biological equilibrium prevails in the water.

SCHEMATIC REPRESENTATION OF THE BIOLOGICAL EQUILIBRIUM

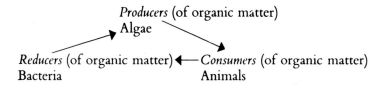

Such an equilibrium obtains in the oceans (at least in most localities, although there are exceptions, particularly temporary ones). As a result, the concentrations of all kinds of substances neither increase nor decrease, since they are involved in a continuous cycle—apart from a certain loss of organic and non-organic matter that sinks down into deep troughs. In the home aquarium, however, this kind of equilibrium between animals, bacteria and algae is unattainable for several reasons. First, the number of fishes per gallon of water far exceeds that in the oceans, and the production of organic substances is correspondingly greater. Second, the salt water aquarium (unlike the freshwater aquarium) can never sustain a sufficient growth of algae to absorb all the substances produced by bacteria. As a result, the aquarium water will gradually accumulate far greater concentrations of all sorts of substances than sea water does. While the presence of algae can slow down this process, it cannot altogether eliminate it unless the hobbyist is satisfied to keep just one or two fishes swimming among luxuriant growths of algae. But in most cases, that is hardly what he wants. In the final analysis the problems with aquarium water all stem from the fact that it is not part of the vast water masses of the oceans.

The major changes occurring in aquarium water in the presence of animals and plants result from bacterial decomposition of nitrogenous organic compounds. These substances are present in

Blue Squirrelfish, *Myripristis adustus*.

the shape of proteins and breakdown products of proteins
released by the metabolic processes of plants and animals. We
shall therefore confine our discussion to the decomposition of
these substances and bypass the decomposition of carbohydrates
and fats. For the convenience of the reader we include two charts
(pages 59 and 60–61) to which he can refer.

The nitrogenous organic compounds given off in the aquarium
consist, first of all, of those proteins which the aquarist himself
introduces into the water. Even with the most scrupulous attention
to feeding the fishes, some food particles will remain uneaten.
These particles then settle on the bottom among the decorative
materials and are decomposed by bacteria or sucked into the filter
system to undergo decomposition there. Second, proteins are
released into the water by dying and dead organisms. The death
of a big fish will naturally lead to a big increase in these substances,
but smaller amounts are set free all the time whenever any kind
of microorganism or algae dies off. Finally, our fishes excrete
relatively large amounts of undecomposed proteins, considerably
more, in fact, than do their fellows in the wild. This is due to the

peculiarities of the fishes' metabolism plus the fact that aquarium fishes, in spite of their reduced energy requirements, are generally overfed. They have a slow rate of digestion, and partially digested food is passed out of the intestinal tract when they ingest fresh food. In the ocean this will seldom happen because the fishes there have to hunt continually for their food, seldom finding enough at any one time to fill them up. Also, in their natural state they are less likely to go on feeding when they are satiated. In an aquarium the more strongly developed competitive urge will make even a satiated fish eat as soon as it sees other fishes feeding. Other factors, too, are likely to affect the digestion of aquarium inhabitants, which are of necessity less active than they would be in their natural state. Their environment is sheltered; there is no need to scurry away from enemies, to defend their territory, to use up energy in a strenuous food hunt, etc. In addition, slow feeders are often housed side by side with more voracious species; this compels the keeper to overfeed the latter in order to be sure that the slow feeders get enough. The same thing happens when we combine surface dwellers with bottom species.

Blue Surgeonfish, *Paracanthurus hepatus*.

In addition to the unnatural quantities of wastes due to captivity, fishes excrete several other metabolic compounds. In decreasing order of importance, fishes excrete ammonia, trimethylamine-oxide, urea, uric acid, amino acids, creatine, creatinine, and a few less important nitrogenous organic compounds. Excretion takes place mainly through the gills. Marine fishes produce little urine: two to four cc/kg/day in contrast to freshwater fishes, which may produce 300 cc/kg/day. This striking difference is due to the fact that the body fluids of marine fishes contain fewer salts than the surrounding ocean water. As a result, through osmosis they lose water to their environment all the time, so it is essential for them to conserve body fluids by passing out any waste products with only a minimum amount of water. To make up for their loss of water, marine fishes drink a lot of sea water, the salts of which pass out through the gills. The small quantities of urine produced by marine fishes are highly concentrated.

Invertebrates, too, give off nitrogenous compounds, the principal one again being ammonia; other excretory wastes are urea, amino acids, amines, etc. The amounts of nitrogen given off are considerable. The beach crab (*Carcinus moenas*), for example, passes out 44 mg of nitrogen/kg/day, 38 mg in the form of ammonia nitrogen. A medium-sized octopus (*Octopus vulgaris*) passes out an average of 25 mg of nitrogen a day, half if it in the form of ammonia, 15 per cent as urea and 20 per cent as amines. Unfortunately, no such precise figures are available for any of the tropical marine fish. Saeki (1964), however, assumes an average of 30 mg of nitrogen/100 gr/day, 25 to 50 per cent as ammonia. Of course, the amounts given off depend strongly on diet and feeding techniques, water temperature and the peculiar characteristics of the species.

All these compounds must undergo rapid bacterial decomposition if the water is to remain a healthy environment.

When proteins are released into the water, they are broken down primarily by three species of bacteria: *Bacterium coli*, *Bacterium proteus* and *Bacterium subtilis*. By secreting enzymes outside their cells, these bacteria break down the proteins, first into peptides and then into amino acids, the "building blocks" of protein molecules. This process may cause serious problems in the aquarium because, as a by-product of their own metabolism, the bacteria secrete certain substances, the so-called bacterial toxins, which are dangerous for fishes and invertebrates in even

Blue-Banded Sea Perch, *Lutjanus sebae*.

relatively small concentrations. Normally this is not a problem, since it is rare for excessive amounts of proteins to become suddenly available to the bacteria. The danger does exist, however, whenever a larger animal dies and begins to decompose, or when so much live food is offered that not all of it is eaten before it dies. Under these circumstances so much toxin may be produced within a short time that all the aquarium inhabitants may be adversely affected or even killed. Such conditions are particularly liable to occur in an overcrowded tank, where it is difficult to feed sparingly, or in aquariums with inadequate filter systems.

Fortunately, these three species of bacteria are not found in aquarium filter systems, apparently because conditions there do not suit them; if they *could* live in the filters, their toxic products would constantly be released into the aquarium, with dire consequences. They *are*, however, always present in the tank itself, on and in the bottom soil, on stones and corals, on the glass and even on and in the mucoid skin of our fishes. To prevent toxic effects from these bacteria, the hobbyist must be careful not to have dead organic matter accumulate in the aquarium.

Blue-Spotted Boxfish, *Ostracion lentiginosum*.

Scrupulous cleanliness, correct feeding techniques and daily checks to make sure there are no dead animals tucked away in dark corners are absolutely essential.

For practical purposes, the amino acids which are produced (via a peptide stage) in the first phase of protein decomposition, and which are also passed out by the animals (especially echinoderms and crustaceans), can be divided into a few main groups. Of the 20 amino acids which can theoretically be released into aquarium water, the so-called aliphatic group without heteroatoms is of little importance, since it is non-toxic and has no effect on the water.

A second group, the sulfurous amino acids, are of greater importance, since they have strong reductive properties. If these are present in relatively large amounts, they can lower the ratio of reducing compounds to oxidizing compounds in the water (redox potential). It is not necessary to go too deeply into detail; it is enough to say that a high redox potential (normal in open sea water) means that many oxidizing compounds are present. Then oxygen saturation presents no problem; all the decomposition processes are normal, and algae grow well. When the redox potential is low (a situation not normally found in open ocean water), all kinds of dangerous processes may occur in the tank; the water can not be adequately saturated with oxygen, and the normal growth of algae is interrupted. If oxygen is scarce or absent, certain bacteria produce hydrogen sulfide from the sulfurous amino acids; this is very toxic and can react with iron to form ferric sulfide. These processes may occur if the substrate sand is particularly deep. It will show black stains of ferric sulfide and when stirred will give off the characteristic hydrogen sulfide smell of rotten eggs. Stirring such a thick sand layer may have fatal consequences for the aquarium inhabitants, and experienced aquarists have always warned, "Leave the sandy bottom of a marine aquarium strictly alone." Nowadays we avoid thick layers of sand or rinse the sand upwards with filtered water. (See Chapter III.)

A third group of amino acids, the cyclic or aromatic amino acids, have slightly reductive properties, but they are easily oxidized by bacteria. An intermediate phase in this process produces phenols and cresols. Phenols in particular are toxic even in small quantities, but, in turn, are easily oxidized, producing dyes. Because dyes do not undergo further bacterial decomposition, they accumulate in the water. It is partially due to them that the water turns first yellow and then yellowish brown. Protein colloids can also make the water yellow.

Amino acids are broken down by various bacteria into amines, many of which are volatile and escape into the atmosphere. The presence of large amounts of volatile amines may cause the tank to smell of overripe fruit or onions. This smell should be regarded as a signal that amines have accumulated and that the decomposition of organic matter is not proceeding properly. The trouble usually can be traced to the fact that certain species of bacteria that normally further decompose the amines have died off, perhaps because antibiotic drugs have been used in the tank. Or the accumulation of amines may be due to such an excess of organic matter that the available bacteria cannot carry through the decomposition process at their usual rapid pace. For example, there may be a dead animal lying in some dark corner of the tank.

One group of amines is toxic and, when present in large

quantities, may poison the fishes' blood. Under normal conditions, however, this never occurs, because the quantities formed in an aquarium are broken up, again by bacteria, into organic acids and ammonia before they reach danger level. The former present few problems in the aquarium, unless they are present in fairly large quantities. If that is the case, they may cause a temporary drop in the pH. Normally, bacteria quickly break the acids down into carbon dioxide and water.

Ammonia, the first non-organic product of bacterial decomposition, is in turn oxidized by special bacteria (*Nitrosomonas*) to produce nitrite. Finally, still other bacteria (*Nitrobacter*) oxidize the nitrite into nitrate. Nitrate marks the end of the decomposition of nitrogenous organic matter. All the bacterial processes mentioned thus far can proceed adequately only in the presence of sufficient oxygen.

If there is not enough oxygen in the water to enable the bacteria to do their work properly, the decomposition process may proceed on altogether different lines, as the decomposition of proteins will produce amino acids, which are again, but now only partially, broken down into ammonia, fatty acids and carbonic acid; but some of the amino acids undergo decomposition by "anaerobic" bacteria and produce such substances as hydrogen sulfide, indole and skatol. All of these are odorous, but the last two are largely responsible for the stench resulting from these decomposition processes (fermentation). Should this occur, the water can become highly toxic, but there is never any danger of anaerobic fermentation if plenty of oxygen is circulated through the tank. However, bear in mind that the oxygen-poor or anaerobic conditions can occur not only in the water, but even more frequently in overly thick substrates, in filter wadding packed too tightly, under stones and corals or in any other place where the water can stagnate. It is also possible that under anaerobic as well as reductive conditions, dyes (formed by the oxidation of phenols) will revert to phenols. The production of large amounts of these dyes could, in a short time, produce a toxic concentration of phenols.

Another real possibility is that nitrate will undergo reduction to ammonia, with the intermediate production of such highly dangerous compounds as nitroxyl and probably hydroxylamine. Apparently the reduction of nitrate to ammonia is often interrupted during the process. (For a more complete chemical picture, see the chart on pages 60–61.)

We must add a few words about the substances formed during the bacterial decomposition process. Some of these compounds are no more than interim products, that is to say, if decomposition proceeds unhampered, they are present only briefly in the water. In stronger concentrations, however, they can become harmful even during their relatively short existence. Examples of this dangerous compound are phenols, some amines, ammonia and nitrite. Even under aerobic conditions ammonia may accumulate fairly readily when there is a sudden rise in the amount of organic matter being decomposed, and this, combined with the ammonia the aquarium animals normally excrete, may overwhelm the system. When ammonia accumulates, further oxidation through nitrite to nitrate is seriously impeded. Even if the concentration of ammonia is no more than 0.2 to 0.3 mg/liter, sensitive fishes may experience respiratory troubles. A concentration of as little as one milligram per liter can be fatal. The first symptom of ammonia poisoning in fish is rapid respiration, but that in itself is not sufficient to support a positive diagnosis of excess ammonia, since such things as oxygen shortages, an excess of carbon dioxide or certain parasites on the gills can also cause respiration increase. We shall come back to this point in our discussion of diseases.

When the pH drops, ammonia changes into the far less toxic ammonium compound. The following table shows the relative proportions of the two substances at different pH values at 20°C:

pH Value	% Ammonia (NH_3)	% Ammonium (NH_4OH)
6	0	100
7	1	99
8	4	96
9	25	75
10	78	22
11	96	4

As we have seen, pH in the marine aquarium has a tendency to drop. Although this means a reduction in the amount of toxic ammonia, marine fish cannot cope with low pH values. A pH of

Cardinalfish, *Apogon nematopterus*.

around 7 is a safeguard against ammonia poisoning in the freshwater aquarium, but a seawater tank always requires a pH of over 7.8, a precariously high level. In a tank with a low pH, water changes or pH correction by chemical means may cause the conversion of non-toxic amounts of ammonium to ammonia. Even a rise in pH from 7.5 to 8.5 increases the concentration of ammonia about ten per cent, which may be enough to kill sensitive specimens. Therefore, any water renewal should be carried out slowly and gradually, and chemical pH correction should similarly never be done abruptly. Furthermore, such activities should be suspended whenever there is reason to suspect that there are relatively high concentrations of ammonia—that is, after feeding or filter cleaning. The toxicity of the ammonia varies, not only according to the amount present, but also according to a possible oxygen shortage or excess carbon dioxide saturation. Both enhance the toxicity of the ammonia, which becomes acute for some species earlier than for others and for young specimens before older ones.

Finally, the general state of the animals' health naturally plays an important part. Undernourished, sick or overfed specimens will be affected by far smaller amounts of ammonia than will healthy ones. Ammonia poisoning plays a greater role in the seawater aquarium than has hitherto been suspected. Particularly in newly set-up tanks, where the bacterial decomposition process is not yet fully established, overfeeding or overcrowding may easily lead to the formation of toxic concentrations of ammonia. The sudden death of certain species in a tank where other species apparently continue to thrive may be due to ammonia poisoning.

A recent theory about the relative degrees of toxicity of ammonia and ammonium in ocean water contends that in sea water strictly chemical processes convert ammonia into ammonium chloride (NH_4Cl), and that it is in fact wrong to refer to the ammonia content of sea water. According to this theory, the ammonium ion in sea water is just as toxic as ammonia. If this is true, we may as well forget the above table and strive all the harder to keep down the ammonia-ammonium complex in the aquarium.

As we have seen, bacterial activities reduce ammonia (and also ammonium and ammonium chloride) to nitrite. Nitrite is relatively harmless with a danger threshold of about 20 mg/liter for fish and a considerably lower one for invertebrates. In a well-regulated tank, nitrite values will, as a rule, be limited to a few tenths or hundredths of a milligram per liter. Only in filters and under circumstances in which large amounts of organic matter suddenly decompose (dead animals, inadequate hygiene) may harmful concentrations possibly accumulate. Normally, however, nitrite is speedily oxidized to nitrate by bacteria. A simple test to determine the nitrite content of the aquarium water is available nowadays. The aquarist is now able to check the efficiency of his biological filter system regularly.

Once it was believed that nitrate, which slowly accumulates in the tank to values many times higher than ever found in the oceans, was a principle cause of toxicity. This is most certainly not true. Nitrate values of over 1,000 mg/liter have been measured in properly maintained tanks with no sign of discomfort to the fishes. But high nitrate values do become dangerous when oxygen-poor or anaerobic conditions obtain. The reduction processes that then set in produce highly toxic amounts of nitroxyl, hydroxylamine and ammonia. Alternatively, nitrate reduction will stop at nitrite, which might then accumulate in toxic concentrations. Acclimated specimens can stand nitrate values of far over 500 mg/liter if concentrations have risen slowly. Newly imported marine tropicals are somewhat more sensitive; amounts of 400 to 500 mg/liter are apparently harmless for them, although it is wise to keep near the lower limits at first. How to protect newly imported specimens from exposure to high nitrate values will be discussed in Chapter VI.

The point at which a nitrate concentration of around 500 mg/liter is reached depends on many factors, such as: size of the population, characteristics of the species (voracious or slow feeders), size of the specimens, capacity of the tank, feeding technique and maintenance. With so many factors involved, every aquarium is a law unto itself as far as water changes are concerned. To stay on the safe side, we may adopt this rule of thumb: replace one third or one fourth of the water every four to six weeks; if the tank is overcrowded, or there are large fishes in the tank, change one half of the water. As for invertebrates, there are species that show signs of discomfort or die at much lower nitrate concentrations (80–200 mg/liter). Here again we do not know whether it is the nitrate that is to blame or perhaps one of the organic compounds accumulating at the same time. Nevertheless, nitrate can serve as an indicator of deteriorating conditions. Tanks that also house invertebrates require more intensive water changes—perhaps one half every four to six weeks, again depending on the size of the population, the efficiency of the biological filter, etc.

pH

Along with nitrates, the pH of water is an important indication of its quality. If, in spite of proper ventilation and aeration, the pH tends to drop too quickly, replacement of the water is necessary. The pH is affected not only by carbonic acid and high concentrations of nitrate but, indirectly, also by the phosphates that accumulate in the water as the end product of the decomposition of organic matter. Phosphate ions accumulate in the water until the solution has attained saturation. Then they start precipitating as magnesium phosphate and calcium phosphate, removing these elements from the water. As a result, the buffering power of the sea water (the ability of the water to resist pH changes) decreases, and the pH can drop more quickly. We can counteract this process by adding ground seashells to the filter system. The phosphate will then react with the calcium and magnesium of the shells, so no calcium or magnesium will be removed from the water.

Nowadays, instead of ground seashells, coral sand can be used in the filter system. Coral sand of good quality consists primarily of calcium and magnesium compounds that are fairly soluble. Carbonic acid readily dissolves calcium from the coral sand to form calcium hydrocarbonates. In this way, coral sand regulates the pH of the water even more effectively than ground shells do. Coral sand can also be used for the bottom cover, particularly if a reversible undergravel filter is used. While not desirable, a normal undergravel filter can also be used with coral sand. The decomposition processes appear to proceed quickly and completely in coral sand, although further research is needed to confirm this.

In the next chapter we shall see how pH measurements, which we have shown to be an important aid in controlling the quality of the aquarium water, can easily be made.

Nitrogen and Algae

Nitrates, phosphates, sulfates and even ammonia—many algae species absorb the latter in preference to nitrates—together with other substances, are indispensable nutrients for algae; promoting an optimal growth of green algae will thus help remove many such substances accumulating in the tank.

Several species of algae, particularly diatoms (incorrectly called "brown algae" by aquarists) and the blue-green algae, can even absorb organic nitrogenous compounds. The diatoms frequently act as pioneers in newly set-up aquariums, where they grow mainly on the bottom, covering it with a brown coating. The presence of diatoms or of blue-green algae is an indication of poor illumination, since both need little light. This is particularly true of the blue-green algae, which can adapt their pigmentation to the available light. The presence of either blue-green algae or diatoms is also an indication that the tank is fouled—that is, that the normal bacterial balance is upset. This is substantiated by the fact that blue-green algae also survive many adverse environmental factors, such as a low redox potential, low oxygen content, low pH and high hydrogen sulfide concentrations. Luxuriant growths of blue-green algae should therefore put us on our guard.

The presence of green algae, on the other hand, is an indication that everything is shipshape, since their growth is impeded by an excess of aromatic amino acids and phenols as well as a low redox potential.

The Role Played by Algae in the Aquarium

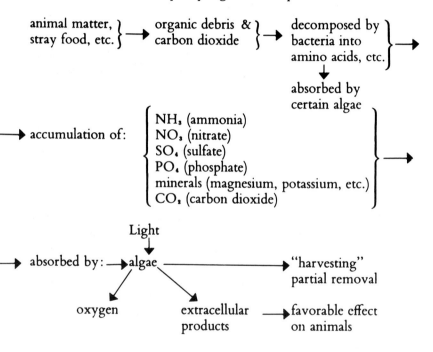

Finally, the excess algae must be harvested (partially removed). This is necessary from time to time to prevent the algae from suffocation due to overcrowding, for when they die off, all the substances they had integrated into their cells are released, and we are no better off than before. Therefore, by harvesting algae we remove organic substances from the tank. As an alternative to promoting the growth of algae in the tank, we can run the water

Cherubfish, *Centropyge argi*.

over an algae filter hanging outside the tank. This technique will be described in Chapter III.

Other Effects of Algae

In addition to absorbing organic substances and thus keeping the tank water healthy over a longer period of time, algae play yet another role. By giving off certain substances (extra-cellular products), as shown on the chart, algae considerably influence and improve the general condition of fishes and invertebrates. Perhaps the vitamins (e.g., B_{12}) and trace elements present in the cells of algae have a tonic effect on animals eating them, or perhaps it is the antibiotic substances given off by the algae. At any rate, it is a fact that in tanks that contain luxuriant algae growths or have an algae filter, fishes hardly ever get sick, and show a better growth rate. The same effect can be obtained by placing untreated pieces of dead coral in the tank. The skeletal remains of these dead corals have a green color from the algae living in the outer calcareous layer of the coral. Since these algae cannot be eaten (except by parrotfishes, which bite off and digest sizable chunks of the coral), the favorable effect on the water and the animals is almost certainly due to organic substances formed by the algae and passed out into the water. In any case, algae are virtually indispensable in the marine aquarium.

Theoretically it is possible to remove nitrates from the tank with denitrifying bacteria (see the diagram on page 61), but its practical application in aquariums is still so difficult that we shall not describe the technique. Incidentally, denitrifying bacteria often multiply in the filters, even under aerobic conditions, resulting in a certain loss of nitrogen (Kawai *et al.*, 1964). Even well-oxygenated filter systems show a loss of nitrogen, especially if they have not been cleaned for some time. With regular cleaning, a nitrate equilibrium can be maintained in the tank at about 400–500 mg/liter.

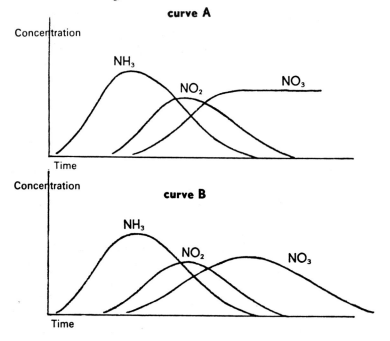

Schematized curves show nitrification after introducing a measured quantity of organic matter into an experimental tank.

Curve A shows nitrification in the absence of algae. Curve B shows nitrification in the presence of algae that developed in the tank during the experiment. This curve shows clearly that the amount of nitrate does not remain constant, as it does in curve A, but decreases gradually, due to absorption by algae. In curve B, the amount of ammonia is smaller, too, as some of it is absorbed by the algae.

Clown Labrid, *Coris angulata*.

If nitrate is not to blame for the gradual fouling of the tank water, what is? We can not answer with certainty. It is not the phosphates and sulfates, for experiments have shown that these become toxic only at very high concentrations. It appears reasonable to assume that the culprit is an organic substance (or substances) produced during the decomposition of organic matter that can not be broken down by bacteria and therefore accumulates simultaneously with nitrates.

Recent work published by Dr Yu, working at New York University, has proved that fishes do indeed give off a filterable material, which in concentration is toxic. One of the most interesting features of this material is that its toxic effects are restricted to the species which produces the substance and to closely related species. It has little or no effect on unrelated fishes, which, of course, produce their own self-specific toxins. In practice this seems to mean that an aquarium can support more fishes if the species are mixed.

Sea water that gradually turns yellow or yellow brown (from, among other substances, the oxidation products of phenols) is toxic for sensitive fishes and especially so for invertebrates. When these dyes are removed, the water loses at least some of its toxicity.

Clownfish, *Amphiprion percula.*

The yellow dyes are of organic origin, for they can be removed by an activated charcoal filter. The organic dyes also have a growth-impeding effect and some of them can perhaps be classed among the so-called inhibitors (also called "pheromones"), which are produced in the tank water by innumerable organisms.

At this point a note of caution must be injected about the effect of light on the growth of useful bacteria. *Nitrosomonas*, which oxidize ammonia to nitrite, and *Nitrobacter*, which convert nitrite into nitrate, are hampered by light of wave lengths below 4,500 angstroms. *Nitrobacter*, in particular, are very susceptible to short wave blue light but also to natural daylight. If the filter system, where these bacteria must perform their useful task, is exposed to strong light, accumulations of ammonia and nitrite may result. *Nitrobacter* are also more sensitive than *Nitrosomonas* to a low oxygen content and high ammonia concentrations. We must take these facts into consideration when constructing our filters, in order to avoid accumulations of harmful substances.

Filters

In our theoretical discussion of the chemistry of the marine aquarium, we have mentioned filters repeatedly, but not yet explained why filtering is necessary.

If all of the decomposition processes were to take place in the tank itself, these would lead to undesirable concentrations of bacteria, which would cloud the water and use up oxygen needed for our fishes. (One gram of actively growing bacteria in sea water uses up an average of 30 cc of oxygen per hour at 72°F, while marine animals use up only 0.002–1.0 cc oxygen per hour per gram of living tissue at the same temperature!) Also, all the harmful intermediate products would be formed in the immediate vicinity of our animals. Last but not least, the tank itself offers no adequate substratum for bacteria. For all these reasons we must try to move the decomposition process to a place outside the tank, that is, to the filters. (See Chapter III.)

As it is clear that we can not hope to move all waste matter to the outside filter in time, a bottom cover must be provided in the tank suitable for those bacteria whose presence is a necessary supplement to the filtration process. As we have seen, this cover must never be thick (unless water flows through it) to prevent anaerobic conditions from developing there. This small precaution will save you many headaches later on.

When the tank and filter system are newly set up, there will not be sufficient bacteria at first to cope with a large amount of organic detritus; in fact, if the tank is filled with synthetic sea water, it will be almost sterile. By adding some water from a properly functioning aquarium or an effusion of garden soil, the right bacteria can indeed be provided, but not necessarily in the right numbers and the right proportions of different species. To attain such an equilibrium, essential for proper and speedy decomposition of organic detritus, the aquarium and filters must be allowed to "mature." This process requires not only time but also a source of organic matter on which the bacteria can feed. To provide this, place a small number of inexpensive fishes in the tank, or drop in small bits of organic matter such as pieces of clam or mussel—the kind to be used as food for the inhabitants later on. At a water temperature of 68°–75°F, maturation will take from 10 to 14 days.* At first there may be so many bacteria that they make the water milky. This need not worry the aquarist, for this explosive growth of bacteria will soon drop back to normal proportions. We must stress that during the maturation period, the aquarium and filter system must operate exactly as if the animals had already been introduced into the tank. Neither the protein skimmer nor the ozonizer are to be used during this period, since these devices, respectively, remove and burn organic matter without the intermediation of bacteria.

While the filter sand is "maturing," the various populations of bacteria attain their maximum densities in the same stages as during the decomposition process. Thus the ammonia-forming bacteria develop first, followed by the nitrite-producing species, while nitrate-forming bacteria develop much later. Kawai *et al.* (1964) found in their experiments that while the nitrite-forming class attained its maximum density in the filter sand after one month, the nitrate-producers did so only after two months.

In the course of the numerous decomposition processes which take place in the aquarium, the bacteria release large amounts of carbon dioxide while using up a great deal of oxygen. Carbon dioxide dissolves readily, forming carbonic acid, which is very difficult to remove. This is at least partially responsible for the drop in pH. In the oceans very little carbon dioxide can be present in the water at the prevailing pH of 8.0–8.3.

Strong aeration is one dependable way of removing excess carbon dioxide. A second is by arranging the filter return (which is richest in carbon dioxide and poorest in oxygen) in such a way that the water flows back in a thin layer. This will insure the release of a great deal of the carbon dioxide. This is not really necessary if the outflow is run over an algae filter, for if sufficient algae are present, they absorb nearly all the carbon dioxide.

A third way of dealing with the excess carbon dioxide produced in the aquarium filters is by providing these with a source of calcium. Carbon dioxide can combine with calcium to produce calcium hydrocarbonates (see page 43). The use of ground sea-shells or coral sand in the filters provides a cheap and harmless

*After two weeks the maturation process, while not complete, will have advanced to the point where a few more fishes can be placed in the tank. The entire process may take up to three months.

method of disposing of excess carbon dioxide and insuring a high pH.

If these measures remove carbon dioxide effectively, the pH will remain high, and if the water is sufficiently oxygenated, the fishes' gills will move slowly, indicating a very low rate of respiration. If—despite aeration, coral sand, ground shells and an algae filter—the pH remains too low (its value should be somewhere between 7.8 and 8.5, preferably over 8.0), chemical correction or a water change is required.

Earlier in this chapter we discussed the differences between tank water and natural ocean water. One last important difference is the oxygen content. In natural marine water, oxygen is always present in maximum concentrations (at least in those areas where our tropical fauna originate). In a marine aquarium, on the other hand, large amounts of oxygen are consumed in the respiratory processes of animals and algae, and in bacterial decomposition. We have shown that the water should be rich in oxygen in every corner of the tank; so the aquarist must see to it that all the oxygen consumed is immediately replaced. This can be done first of all by aeration, i.e., by pumping air through the water. There are still many aquarists who believe that the stream of tiny air bubbles releases oxygen into the water. This is only partially true. The bubbles rise to the surface so quickly and their contact with the water is so brief that during their actual passage the bubbles give off only a little oxygen while taking up the carbon dioxide. Actually, the oxygen–carbon dioxide exchange takes place mainly at the surface. It is fairly easy for oxygen molecules from the atmosphere to penetrate the uppermost layer of the water, and for excess carbon dioxide to return to the atmosphere. The thicker the water layer, the slower this diffusion process. Now, the stream of bubbles produced in aeration carries water continuously from the lower parts of the tank to the surface and surface water to the deeper parts. This assures a constant exchange of gases between the tank and the atmosphere (see Figure 3, page 71). Obviously, the greater the rate of water movement, both up and down, the better the water will be oxygenated. Optimum results will be obtained by a broad band of air bubbles rising to the surface.

An often debated point is whether these bubbles should be large or small. Before we consider this question, we must consider

Eight-Banded Butterfly,
Chaetodon octofasciatus.

another point. The exchange of gases with the atmosphere is impeded by waves. When we aerate with large bubbles, we produce a strong vertical current in the tank, but this results in a good deal of surface turbulence. On the other hand, if we have a stream of small bubbles, there are no waves, but the water circulation is reduced. The best solution, therefore, lies in multiple strong streams of small bubbles. One positive side effect is that many of the small bubbles tend to float in the water for some time before bursting at the surface. These bubbles are in contact with the water for a considerable time, thus allowing them more time to exchange gases.

In connection with aeration we must warn the reader of a frequently forgotten fact. Although aeration will expel it from the water, carbon dioxide is a "heavy" gas that tends to concentrate just above the water surface if it cannot escape easily. As a result, as much carbon dioxide might be washed back into the water as is expelled from it. The reflector hood on top of the tank should therefore be ventilated to allow the carbon dioxide to escape. Glass covers should never seal off the tank hermetically.

For the proper exchange of gases at the water surface, it is essential that any film of dust, scum or oil that forms, promptly be removed. This can be done by carefully laying a sheet of newspaper over the water surface and drawing it off before it is completely soaked with water. The scum and other dirt will adhere to the paper, leaving the water surface perfectly clean.

Aeration will, at least in theory, maintain a balance between the gases in the water and in the atmosphere, with the saturation percentage at 100 or a little over.

The oxygen content of sea water depends on its temperature and total salinity. As these rise, sea water can hold progressively less oxygen in solution. This is why it is important to avoid unnecessarily high temperatures and salinities. The following table shows the oxygen content (100 per cent saturation) at different temperatures and salinities.

Table IV—Oxygen Concentrations

Temperature			Oxygen in cc's per liter		
		Salinity	32.5 ‰	34.3 ‰	36.1‰
		Chlorinity	18 ‰	19 ‰	20 ‰
°C	°F				
10	50		6.52	6.44	6.35
15	59		5.93	5.86	5.79
20	68		5.44	5.38	5.31
21	70		5.35	5.29	5.22
22	72		5.26	5.20	5.13
23	73		5.17	5.11	5.04
24	75		5.09	5.03	4.95
25	77		5.00	4.95	4.86
26	79		4.92	4.86	4.78
27	81		4.83	4.78	4.70
28	82		4.75	4.69	4.62
29	84		4.66	4.60	4.54
30	86		4.58	4.52	4.46

If a great deal of algae is growing in the tank, their oxygen production may cause a temporary rise in oxygen saturation to over a hundred per cent. Aeration will rapidly put an end to this by driving off virtually all the excess. Careful measurements show that in marine tanks strong aeration with small bubbles produces a saturation percentage of 100 to about 108 per cent.

As we have seen in the previous chapter, water circulation, so essential for maintaining the correct mixture of gases in the tank water, also serves another important need. Aquarium animals, with few exceptions, originate from coastal areas, where they live in turbulent water—frequently even in surf. In water that is moving sluggishly, a mantle of virtually stagnant water forms around the organisms, hampering their respiratory and excretory processes. The thicker the mantle, the more seriously these processes are impeded. While fishes, by moving swiftly, can, to a degree, make the mantle thicker or thinner, this is hardly possible for invertebrates that are fixed in place, and not at all for algae. Therefore, effective water circulation in the aquarium serves the important need of keeping the stagnant mantle around animals and algae down to a minimum. Thus we find algae growing first and fastest near air bubbles, where the water movement is greatest, as well as in the siphon tubes where the water is fast-flowing. Invertebrates like to take up a position close to the bubbles. Sea anemones often keep moving around until they have found a spot where the water is moving fast. Many invertebrates become more active in moving water, while some species (e.g., hydroid polyps and some sponges) cannot even live in stagnant water. Experiments have shown that carbon dioxide assimilation by seaweeds is slowed down in stagnant water and accelerated in flowing water (Gessner, 1955).

All that has been said so far about the changes in aquarium water can be traced back to bacterial activity. Although this activity (decomposition of organic substances) is completely natural, as we have repeatedly stressed, even a minor disruption of the tricky balance can have serious consequences for the aquarium inhabitants. Marine aquarium experts have anxiously searched for ways to eliminate this dangerous dependence on bacterial decomposition. Two technical devices have recently become available for which we have great expectations. The simpler and less dangerous is a device popularly called a protein skimmer, the construction of which will be discussed in the next chapter. The protein skimmer works on the principle that if air is bubbled through sea water containing organic matter, froth bubbles form at the surface and do not burst immediately the way foam bubbles do in water containing no impurities. The bubbles formed in foul water have a brownish color. Because of certain physical properties of these bubbles, organic substances accumulate around them. In the protein skimmer normal, rapidly disappearing foam is separated from the "protein froth" and the latter removed from the aquarium. This is a simple and excellent method of attacking the fouling of tank water at the source.

Persistent bubbles will form at the water surface when the surface tension is lowered. Among the substances which lower surface tension are water soluble proteins, organic acids, and hydrophilic colloids (e.g., peptones). As soon as these get into the water, e.g., after feeding, a quantity of persistent foam is produced.

When at that moment a substance is added to the aquarium water that increases the surface tension, foam formation immediately decreases or stops. This happens when we feed fresh flesh or hacked worms to aquarium inhabitants; it is the plasma-proteins in the blood that raise the surface tension of the water.

Another purifying method, which is more expensive as well as more difficult to handle, utilizes ozone. Ozone is an active form of oxygen with an extra oxygen atom. Atmospheric oxygen is O_2, ozone is O_3. The extra oxygen atom can not adhere to the ozone molecule for long, separating from it in the water. As a single atom, oxygen has a strongly oxidative action—in other words, it is capable of "burning" all kinds of organic substances. If we bubble ozone through tank water, organic waste products will be burned—*without bacterial activity*—producing ammonia and other compounds. In this way we avoid all sorts of problems and risks inherent in bacterial decomposition.

Unfortunately, it is impossible to prescribe so many milligrams of ozone per gallon of tank water, as the dosage depends entirely on how much organic matter has to be "burned." Too much ozone in the tank will harm the animals, and it may even be noxious to humans if it escapes from the tank. Moreover, we still need bacteria in the aquarium, since ozone cannot oxidize ammonia to nitrite although it can convert nitrite to nitrate. Ozonizing the tank water may produce a large temporary accumulation of ammonia harmful to the animals.

Diseases can not be cured by ozonizing the water because the concentrations required are harmful or even lethal to sick fishes. The next chapter, again, will explain how best to use ozonizers.

In the wild, marine tropicals are used to extremely low numbers of bacteria. In contrast, aquarium water contains large numbers of bacteria—that is, large populations of relatively few species. These may be not only useful bacteria, but also disease germs— for example, blood-destroying bacteria—and sensitive species react adversely. Bacterial problems generally occur in tanks that do not function properly, particularly if they lack an abundant growth of algae or an algae filter, so it may be useful to sterilize the water returning from the filter. For this, ozone or ultraviolet light can be used. Sterilization techniques will be covered in the next chapter.

Up until now we have been discussing the most important

Emperor Angelfish, *Pomacanthus imperator*.

changes which can occur in aquarium water. We have spoken only of the direct toxic effect of certain substances formed in the aquarium once they attain dangerous concentrations. However, lower concentrations of toxic substances, while not lethal, can also harm animals, for it gradually undermines their health and reduces their resistance to all kinds of diseases. This is a theory that has never been proved, but experience and observation point that way. Tanks with inadequate filtration or which are over-crowded always contain relatively large amounts of all the harmful substances enumerated above, including such substances as phenols, which are normally present only for a short time. In tanks like these the animals grow slowly, they lack color, their skin is lusterless, they are prone to infectious diseases and their life span is relatively short. Algae, with the exception of diatoms and blue-green algae, do not thrive there either. On the other hand, in uncrowded tanks with proper filtration dangerous substances are present in small amounts and for a short time only, and these symptoms simply do not occur there. Even in tanks that are well-filtered but crowded, heavy temporary production of intermediate compounds such as phenols, amines and ammonia will occur some time (two to three hours) after large amounts of food are offered. Such bottlenecks in the disposal of organic matter must, of course, be avoided.

Summary

The marine aquarium compared with the open oceans

1. The actual absolute bacteria count increases; on the other hand, the number of *species* decreases.

2. The end products of bacterial decomposition increase (nitrates, phosphates, sulfates).

3. The ammonia content rises.

4. There is an accumulation of organic substances which can not be further broken down by bacteria, causing among other things the water to turn yellow or yellowish brown.

5. The pH tends to drop.

6. The oxygen content tends to drop.

7. The carbon dioxide content tends to rise.

8. Under anaerobic conditions toxic substances are formed.

9. A sudden increase in the amount of organic matter (uneaten food, dead animals or algae) may disrupt the bacterial decomposition processes; this will result in accumulations of phenols, amines, ammonia, nitrite, etc.

10. Evaporation may cause an increase in salinity.

To deal with these changes

1. Scrupulous cleanliness and sparse feeding, to keep down the amount of organic wastes in the tank.

2. Filtration, to concentrate and accelerate the bacterial decomposition processes outside the tank.

3. Effective aeration to ensure a high oxygen and a low carbon dioxide content as well as to maintain water circulation.

4. Periodic partial water renewal to remove excess accumulations of organic and inorganic substances.

5. Promotion of algae growth to slow the accumulation of various inorganic substances.

6. Regular addition of fresh water to maintain the proper salinity.

7. The use of a protein skimmer to remove organic wastes.

8. The use of ozone to eliminate the hazards of bacterial decomposition.

9. Sterilization of the filter outflow to curb the spread of disease germs and to cut down the number of bacteria in the tank.

The techniques by which to implement these measures will be covered in the next chapter.

SIMPLIFIED DIAGRAM OF THE BACTERIAL DECOMPOSITION OF NITROGENOUS ORGANIC MATTER IN THE ABSENCE OF OXYGEN (ANAEROBIC DECOMPOSITION)

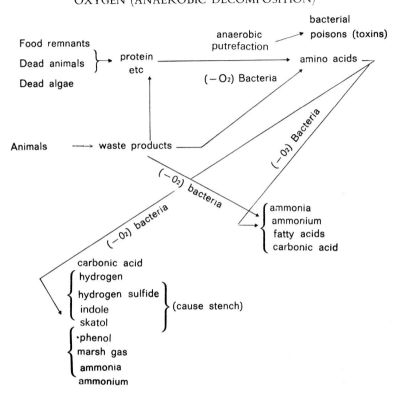

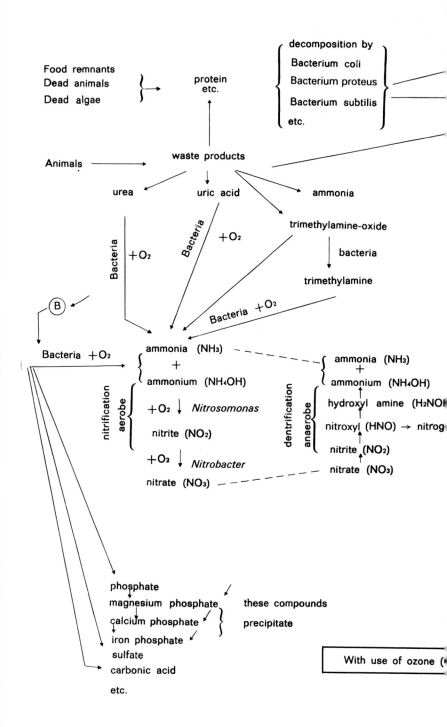

Food remnants
Dead animals
Dead algae
} → protein etc.

decomposition by
Bacterium coli
Bacterium proteus
Bacterium subtilis
etc.

waste products

Animals →

urea   uric acid   ammonia

trimethylamine-oxide

bacteria

trimethylamine

Bacteria +O₂

Bacteria +O₂

(B)

Bacteria +O₂   ammonia (NH₃)   ammonia (NH₃)
                          +   +
                    ammonium (NH₄OH)   ammonium (NH₄OH)

nitrification aerobe   +O₂ ↓ Nitrosomonas   dentrification anaerobe   hydroxyl amine (H₂NO)

                    nitrite (NO₂)   nitroxyl (HNO) → nitrog

                    +O₂ ↓ Nitrobacter   nitrite (NO₂)

nitrate (NO₃)   - - - - - - - -   nitrate (NO₃)

phosphate
magnesium phosphate   these compounds
calcium phosphate   } precipitate
iron phosphate
sulfate
carbonic acid   With use of ozone (●

etc.

60

DIAGRAM OF THE BACTERIAL DECOMPOSITION OF NITROGENOUS ORGANIC MATTER (AEROBIC DECOMPOSITION).

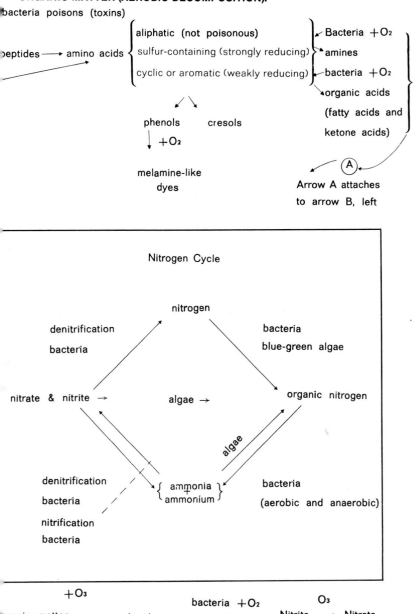

bacteria poisons (toxins)

peptides ⟶ amino acids

- aliphatic (not poisonous)
- sulfur-containing (strongly reducing)
- cyclic or aromatic (weakly reducing)

↙ ↘
phenols   cresols

↓ +O₂

melamine-like
dyes

↙ Bacteria +O₂
↗ amines
↙ bacteria +O₂
↘ organic acids
(fatty acids and
ketone acids)

(A)

Arrow A attaches
to arrow B, left

Nitrogen Cycle

nitrogen

denitrification
bacteria

bacteria
blue-green algae

nitrate & nitrite →   algae →   organic nitrogen

denitrification
bacteria

algae

bacteria
(aerobic and anaerobic)

nitrification
bacteria

{ ammonia }
{ ammonium }

+O₃

bacteria +O₂   O₃
organic matter → ammonia etc. ⟶ Nitrite ⟶ Nitrate

61

III   Preparing the Marine Aquarium

The Aquarium Itself

In the preceding chapters we have presented the theories behind the techniques of marine aquarium maintenance. As we have repeatedly pointed out, unless the aquarist knows how to control his artificial marine habitat, he will not be able to keep a saltwater home aquarium, since a biological equilibrium does not evolve unaided.

In choosing the material for a marine aquarium, the hobbyist must be extremely careful. Because of its high salinity, salt water acts very aggressively on many substances, particularly metal. As a result, metal salts (chlorides, sulfates, etc.), which can be very toxic to fishes and invertebrates, may form in the water. In selecting the materials that will come into contact with water, the guiding principle should be that any material that has not undergone extensive testing under actual aquarium conditions is suspect until proven harmless.

Asbestos cement tanks are very suitable for our purposes; these are on the market in various standard sizes or can be made to order in practically any shape. Their great advantage is that they are completely and permanently impervious to salt water. They have only one drawback, and that is of an esthetic nature: they are rather unsightly, and only the front panel is glass. The appearance can be improved, however, with a wooden cabinet frame for the front, or the tank can be built into a wall or cupboard, which will go a long way toward masking its unsightliness. The drab, grey interior can be enlivened with non-toxic epoxy waterproof paint or covered with slabs of shale or flagstone, or the walls brightened with a coat of colored cement.

Asbestos cement which has not been in contact with sea water gives off certain toxic substances, and these can bring the pH level up too high. Therefore, soak the tank with tap water in which a few handfuls of common salt have been dissolved. Change the solution every other day and give the walls a thorough scrubbing; repeat the procedure about five times. A tank with a colored cement coating must also be soaked, but one treated with epoxy paint need only be washed down with lukewarm water.

To be absolutely thorough, fill the tank with a mixture of water and common salt and let it cure for a few days.

The front panel in an asbestos cement aquarium must be set in with silicone cement. If the inside of the tank is not painted, we must still put a coat of paint on the cement edge around the glass pane.

Sometimes asbestos tanks are somewhat porous, so that after a while the outside becomes encrusted with salt. A coat of paint on the inside will prevent this, but it is not really necessary because even a porous tank will never leak.

Another, faster way to detoxify asbestos cement tanks, as well as cemented back walls and built-in rocks, is to add $\frac{1}{2}$ to $\frac{3}{4}$ ounce of 25 per cent phosphoric acid per 25 gallons of tap water, stirring constantly. To avoid discoloration, do not pour the phosphoric acid near the rocks or back wall. When the phosphoric acid has been added, the water will become clouded, and after about twenty-four hours the milky substance will precipitate to the walls and bottom. Then siphon off the water, remove the white material, refill the tank with water and pour in the phosphoric acid. The clouding of the water will now be considerably less. Repeat the procedure after 24 hours. No precipitate will form, as a rule, the third time around, so after a thorough scrubbing the tank is ready for use. If, however, there is still a precipitate, repeat the procedure every 24 hours until there is no longer any reaction.

If, for esthetic reasons, an asbestos cement tank is not desired, the common type of metal frame tank used for freshwater aquariums must be used, but the iron frame must be thoroughly insulated from the sea water. Epoxy paints can again be used for this purpose; these make it possible for the aquarist to treat the frame himself. He can also use spreadable plastics, which are on the market under several names and provide even greater security. For good results, follow the package directions closely and, in particular, remove any rust or grease from the frame. A coat of primer is usually necessary.

It is even better to have the frame treated with plastics applied at high temperatures. This treatment will make the frame permanently impervious to sea water. (Epoxy paint coats generally must be renewed every few years.) On the other hand, the plastic (or hard rubber) coating must be applied in a factory, and this makes it relatively expensive. But this type of aquarium

Forcepsfish, *Forcipiger longirostris.*

frame really pays for itself, because it requires absolutely no maintenance.

There are two other ways to protect the metal frame. The parts that suffer most from contact with salt water are the top edges and the bottom. By having the top edges turned outward instead of inward, splashing water and condensation moisture are prevented from reaching the metal edges. This also makes it possible to have the glass sides extend well above the edges. If the tops of the glass panes are protected with U-shaped plastic sleeves, the glass cover can rest on the side panes. In this way hardly any water will ever touch the metal edges.

In the United States, most aquariums are made of high-quality stainless steel. However, even the very best stainless steel will eventually be corroded by sea water. Secondly, stainless steel at the weld point loses virtually all of its noncorrosive properties. Considering these factors, a stainless steel tank is not the most desirable to use.

Enameling the frame is not adequate either. If a chip of enamel should be knocked off, rust will spread underneath the enamel coating and force it off the frame.

A recent development is the hard plastic frame. In smaller sizes these appear to be satisfactory, but for larger tanks plastic frames are inadequate, because they lack the necessary rigidity. In the future, synthetic materials will undoubtedly come to play an ever-greater part in the manufacture of marine tanks. Today large tanks of lucite (perspex) or plexiglass are being made; they are non-toxic and completely impervious to sea water. However, they are expensive and scratch easily.

It is also possible to make tanks from sheets of plate glass welded together with special cement. These tanks are attractive and priced competitively with other types on the market. Considering its advantages, this type is certainly the marine tank of the future.

Tanks can even be made of wood, which gives them the appearance of a glorified box with a glass front panel. The wood is covered on the inside with non-porous synthetic material such as polyethylene glass fiber foil.

Not only the tanks, but the filter systems and other equipment as well, must be completely impervious to salt water. Plastic, glass or asbestos cement filters cause no trouble.

Four-Eye Butterfly, *Chaetodon capistratus*.

Now a few words about the shape of the aquarium are in order. With the exception of the three-sided tank made of asbestos cement, the only tanks on the market are of the traditional rectangular type. But there is no reason why we should not depart from the standard pattern and have a frame constructed in the shape of a hexagon, a pentagon or even a delta.

If asbestos cement or concrete is used, an illusion of depth can be created by making the back convex and simultaneously flaring it out toward the top. Because they must be made to order, these models tend to be expensive.

A question frequently asked by beginners concerns the size of the aquarium. The dimensions of the marine aquarium are indeed of greater importance than those of the freshwater aquarium. As a general rule, the bigger the tank, the better. This is based directly on the theory discussed in the previous chapter. The larger the water mass, the more gradual the changes; because of the greater dilution, peak concentrations of the various bacterial decomposition products occur less easily than in a small tank. On the other hand, a big tank also has a severe drawback. If complications necessitate a complete water change, the aquarist is faced with the problem of how to make or obtain a large amount of sea water on very short notice. A large tank also requires a large filter system and a pressure pump for water circulation. On the other hand, a home aquarium should not be too small, for even a minor mishap will have an immediate catastrophic effect. The golden mean is somewhere between 40 gallons ($36 \times 16 \times 16$ inches) and 110 gallons ($60 \times 20 \times 20$ inches). Within this range all sorts of variations in dimension are possible, but for an effective exchange of oxygen and carbon dioxide at the water surface, as well as for effective water circulation, the depth of the tank should not be greater than its width. Shallow tanks are easier to keep in prime condition than tanks with a high water level. The length of the tank should also match an available size of fluorescent tube if that type of light is used.

Materials for the Tank

All equipment in the tank—air tubes, air lifts, siphons, etc.— should, if at all possible, be made of plastic or other synthetic material. Not all plastics are suitable, however, for many kinds contain "mollifiers," chemicals to keep the plastic pliant. These mollifiers often dissolve in the water with toxic effects. A simple toxicity test can be carried out by placing the plastic in hot water. If, after soaking a few hours, the plastic still gives off a "chemical" smell, the plastic is probably toxic and should not be used. Plastic air tubes generally contain mollifiers, which will dissolve slowly, making the tube hard in the long run. For this reason they should not be used *under* the water (particularly not in small tanks). Silicone tubing is completely harmless, but relatively expensive. To carry the air from the tube to the bubbler, use a piece of celluloid tubing. Rubber tubes are hardly ever impervious to sea water and so will decompose sooner or later; it is better not to use any rubber tubing at all.

Artificial Sea Water

The next consideration is water. Tap water can be used, except in localities where its total hardness is over 15° DH (German hardness). Tap water in these areas should be diluted with distilled water, or distilled water used alone, in order to avoid an excessive concentration of calcium. Always use water distilled in glass vessels, never in copper or zinc. Rain water is sometimes used, but is unreliable, especially near big cities and factories, because it may contain large numbers of harmful substances from the polluted atmosphere. Tap water which contains too much copper can be very dangerous. Water drawn through new copper mains may contain up to one mg of copper per liter, but the copper content will diminish rapidly if the tap is run hard for some time. Swimming pool test kits will give you the level of copper in your water, or you may send a sample to your local water board for testing. In any case, if you are in doubt, run the water at least ten to fifteen minutes before using it.

The free chlorine added in a great many cities to the municipal supply by the local water board is much more dangerous, but can be eliminated by filtering the water through activated charcoal or aerating it well for several days. It is all right to use fluoridated tap water, since water boards add a dosage of about one mg per liter, that is, the same as the concentration found in natural sea water. If fluoridated tap water is used, leave out the potassium fluoride in the following seawater formula.

To make 26 gallons (100 liters) of sea water, take 24½ gallons (90 liters) of fresh water and dissolve in it the following:

2765.0 grams common table salt, NaCl
706.0 grams magnesium sulfate, $MgSO_4.7H_2O$
518.0 grams magnesium chloride, $MgCl_2.6H_2O$
69.7 grams potassium chloride, KCl
14.3 grams sodium bicarbonate, $NaHCO_3$
10.2 grams potassium bromide, KBr
3.5 grams sodium carbonate, Na_2CO_3
2.6 grams boric acid, H_3BO_3
2.5 grams strontium chloride, $SrCl_2.6H_2O$
0.4 grams potassium fluoride, KF
0.01 grams potassium iodate, KIO_3

In one separate liter of fresh water, dissolve 154 grams of calcium chloride, $CaCl_2.H_2O$; when both mixtures have become perfectly clear, pour one into the other, stirring constantly. Finally, add water to this mixture until the right salinity has been obtained, checking frequently with a hydrometer.

The pH of the salt water thus obtained should be between 9.0 and 8.5. Before using the water in the aquarium or putting animals in, aerate it throughly for 48 hours and filter it through charcoal. If water is needed immediately, neutralize any free chlorine present by adding one gram of sodium thiosulfate for every 26 gallons (100 liters) of water and stirring well. After five minutes add 5 cc of 15 per cent hydrogen peroxide for every 26 gallons, again stirring well. To make absolutely sure, the water can then be run through a fresh charcoal filter, after which it will be ready for use.

Keep a store of concentrated salt water in carboys or polyethylene containers for emergencies. To prepare this, dissolve the same amount of salts as in the first formula above, but in only 2½ gallons (10 liters) of tap water. The proportions in the second part of the formula remain the same. Store the two solutions separately in the dark. In an emergency simply mix and dilute the concentration and carry out pH and salinity checks to make sure that they are the same as that of the tank water.

The chemicals for synthetic sea water can be ordered in the pharmaceutical grade from any good drugstore or chemical supply house. The analytic grade is too expensive, and the technical grade contains impurities which may be toxic.

Whether or not trace elements (those elements present in sea water in minute quantities) should be added cannot yet be said with certainty. Their absence may have an adverse effect, particularly on invertebrates and algae. Undoubtedly, many will be introduced with the food, particularly if a variety is offered, but it is still an open question whether all of the indispensable trace elements will actually be brought in, in this way. In theory it is possible that certain ones such as iodine would still be lacking. It is dangerous to experiment with trace elements in the aquarium, since an overdose of certain metals may be toxic. However, we shall return to this subject when we discuss fish diseases.

Rather than mix his own, the hobbyist can buy ready-to-use mixes. The sea water made this way must also be aerated for 24 hours before it can be used in the aquarium. Any components that have not dissolved or that have precipitated must be siphoned or filtered out after 24 hours. Usually the commercial mixes contain a number of trace elements.

Salts should never be dissolved in metal containers such as zinc pails or tubs. If the aquarium is set up for the first time or re-organized from scratch, the tank itself can be used. Otherwise, use plastic containers. Never use pails or other utensils that have contained detergents. It is best to buy extra pails exclusively for aquarium use.

The sea salt obtained from the evaporation of sea water and sometimes offered as a mix for the aquarium is not suitable for our purposes. During evaporation in the salt pans, several important substances escape. In addition, this kind of salt often contains large amounts of impurities.

We have seen before that synthetic sea water, being almost sterile, must be "fertilized" by adding some natural sea water, some water from a thriving aquarium or an effusion of good garden soil. For the latter, take a handful of black soil (no leaf mold) and pour half a gallon of tap water over it. Stir well and allow to settle for 48 hours. Pour off the clean water carefully and after filtering, add it to the tank water.

Aeration and Water Circulation

To maintain a proper balance between oxygen and carbon

dioxide, aerate the tank water by means of an air pump, which pumps air into the tank through bubblers, also called diffusers or air stones; these break the air stream into bubbles of a proper size. There are several different kinds of air pumps on the market. Vibrator pumps will probably prove to be the most satisfactory. These operate on a "make-break" principle like an electric buzzer, but instead of actuating a clapper, a vibrating arm actuates a rubber or plastic diaphragm, which pumps air like a bellows. While the diaphragm is subject to wear, it can easily be replaced by the aquarist. This type of pump operates economically and has few moving parts to break down.

In selecting a pump, it is better to err on the side of greater capacity than lesser, because most filters also operate on air. Order two smaller pumps rather than one big pump, for one can be used for the filters, the other for aeration. If one pump fails, there is no immediate breakdown of the entire apparatus. Although one big pump with the same capacity as the two smaller ones combined will serve our purposes just as well, it requires a larger investment.

How much air is required for a particular size of tank? The ground rules are, first, that an excess of air will do no harm and, second, that air needs are relevant to the population density. Taking these factors into consideration, the requirement is about six to eight quarts of air per hour for each gallon of water. This amount will serve to aerate the tank properly and operate the filter system as well.

For larger tanks, a vibrator pump is usually not sufficient. The maximum capacity of the normally available types is about three hundred and fifty quarts of air per hour. If much more air is needed, use a small oilless compressor or a pump with a motor-driven piston. Air stones are on the market in the form of square or round air stones made from molten silica. Never use metal parts for connecting the air stone with the air tube.

As a rule, air stones will not last long, because the pores soon become clogged with algae, dirt and salt deposits. These can be soaked out in dilute hydrochloric acid. (See page 121) "Do-it-yourself" bubblers can easily be made out of limewood, beechwood or malacca cane. Cut small discs from the wood and fix these in holders tooled from plastic blocks (Figure 1), or make tapering slabs and fix these in a plastic or celluloid tube. On one side of the tube an air intake is inserted, and the device weighted down to keep it on the bottom. This method makes it possible to combine a large number of bubblers (Figure 2).

Figure 1.   Bubbler of limewood or beechwood in a plastic holder.

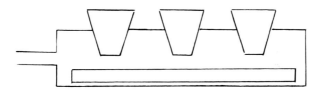

Figure 2.   Three wooden bubblers in a weighted plastic or celluloid tube.

The bubblers should be placed in the corners of the tank, not only to circulate the water throughly but also because a stream of bubbles in the center of the tank would look unnatural. For proper circulation at least two bubblers, one on either side, are recommended (Figure 3). If the tank is very long, it is almost impossible to avoid placing a third bubbler in the center, unless one is put in each of the four corners.

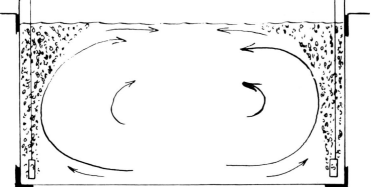

Figure 3.   Arrangement of two bubblers showing the direction of the water circulation.

In a large tank a water pump will produce more thorough circulation. The pump sucks the water from near the bottom on one end and returns it to the surface on the other end. Very effective aeration is obtained by returning the water through a multiple outlet as shown in Figure 4. The end of the spray tube is sealed off and the device is turned at such an angle that the water is returned obliquely to the surface. The pumps must, of course, contain no metal parts that come in contact with the salt water.

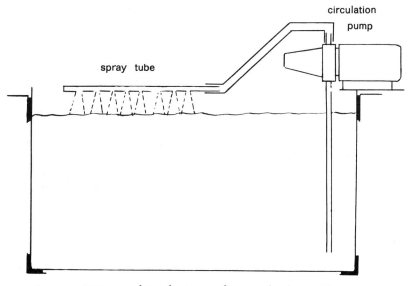

Figure 4.   Water circulation by means of a pump fitted out with a spray tube.

It is possible to aerate with oxygen–enriched air or pure oxygen, to obtain oxygen supersaturation in the tank (Gelbhaar, 1961). However, the apparatus required is cumbersome, needs a good deal of attention, and is fairly expensive to operate. Its usefulness seems limited and the method has a few snags.

First, oxygen saturation obtained by aerating with pure oxygen may disguise the fact that all is not well in the tank. Second, the fishes will quickly become conditioned to the high oxygen content, as their very low rate of respiration will show. Third, if the apparatus should break down; the animals will very soon show symptoms of severe suffocation. Proper aeration with ordinary air, combined with effective water circulation, produces the same effect as less thorough oxygen aeration, but has none if its disadvantages. Oxygen aeration actually has advantages only when normal aeration, circulation and filtering processes are inadequate.

Another technique is passing the air through a chamber filled with sodium hydroxide (soda lye, NaOH) before it enters the tank. This removes carbon dioxide. But the same drawbacks apply to this as to using pure oxygen. It, too, is a superfluous technique.

The Filter System

The theories set forth in the previous section must now be translated into equipment that is both simple and technically efficient. We have seen that it is necessary to move most of the bacterial decomposition processes to a place outside the aquarium —the filter system, which must take care of the following processes:

1. Removal of coarse and suspended detritus, the source of many of the undesirable substances in the water.
2. Provision of an adequate substrate for the needed bacteria.
3. Removal of organic substances that can not be further broken down by bacteria.
4. Automatic control of the pH.
5. Optimum removal of inorganic substances by algae ("algae filters").

Let us examine each of these points in more detail and find out the type of filter and filter medium required for each.

A filter is a separate unit connected to the tank and filled with a filter medium through which the water is circulated. The tank water is siphoned into the filter and then pumped back by means of an airlift (see Figure 5).

The siphon, the tube that brings the water from the tank into the filter, is a double bent glass, plastic or celluloid tube, the long end of which extends into the tank, the other into the filter, so that these are turned into communicating vessels. The action is started by immersing the tube upside down in the aquarium. With the tube full of water, one finger is used to close the short end. The tube is then righted, lifted and placed in the filter with

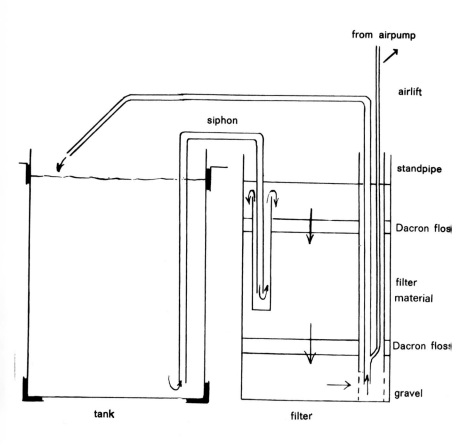

Figure 5. Diagram of a filter, showing how it is connected with the tank.

the short end still held closed. The long end should not be lifted out of the water or the water in it will run back. When water is pumped out of the filter, tank water automatically flows through the siphon into the filter to restore the level.

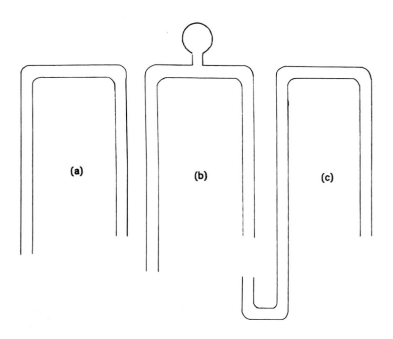

Figure 6. Different types of siphons.

Different types of siphons are shown in Figure 6. For small tanks that can easily be manipulated, the simplest type (a) is the most suitable. On the other hand, this is the most likely to clog, causing all the water in the filter to be pumped back into the aquarium. To prevent this, the vertical arm extending into the filter should be made as long as possible by having it run down into a closed cylinder placed inside the filter material (Figure 5).

For larger tanks type (b) in Figure 6 is more suitable, because a siphon with a long vertical arm is difficult to fill completely with water. The rubber bulb attachment of type (b) enables the keeper to start the siphon by simply squeezing it.

In general, the most adequate procedure is to siphon off the tank water close to the bottom. To keep small animals from being sucked into the siphon, the intake tube can be closed off with a piece of perforated glass or plastic. If circumstances make it necessary to place the intake and the bubbler close together so

75

that air bubbles rising into the siphon might interrupt the flow of water, fix an upturned attachment to the underside of the siphon tube (see Figure 6c).

The siphon tubes should not be too narrow. An inside diameter of ½ to ⅝ inches (12 to 15 mm) or even larger, depending on the size of the tank and the filter capacity, is most satisfactory.

An airlift consists of a long glass, celluloid or plastic tube bent at the top. A thin air line connects with the air pump and introduces air at the bottom. The rising air bubbles reduce the air pressure in the vertical tube, causing the water to flow through. The rate of flow depends on the length and diameter of the airlift tube, the amount of air sucked in and the pressure of the water column against which the air bubbles must rise. About seventy per cent of the airlift should be submerged.

An airlift with an inside diameter of one-half inch (12 mm) and a moderate amount of air is most efficient. It will move over 1.6 quarts of water per minute, by means of 1.2 quarts of air, if the water column through which the air bubbles must pass is about 16 inches (40 cm) high. Again, the outflow tube of the airlift should be extended to the opposite side of the aquarium so that the filtered water is returned to the tank as far away as possible from the intake.

To increase the capacity of the filter system, more than one airlift, of course, can be used. In addition, it would be wise to install at least two siphons; even if the second one is not strictly necessary, it will insure the uninterrupted functioning of the system, should the other unexpectedly clog.

The removal of coarse dirt particles suspended in the tank water—excrement, uneaten food, bottom detritus, etc.—takes place in the so-called mechanical filter (Figure 7a), which removes the coarse particles from the water passing through it, in the fashion of a fine-meshed sieve. The filter medium consists of glass or Dacron filter floss or wadded thin layers of polyurethane foam. These are packed tightly against the walls and standpipe to a depth of 2 to 2⅖ inches (5–6 cm). This type of mechanical filter must be cleaned frequently by washing the nylon filter floss or other material under the tap. In this way we remove large amounts of dirt from the aquarium before decomposition sets in. If dirt is allowed to accumulate, the mechanical filter becomes

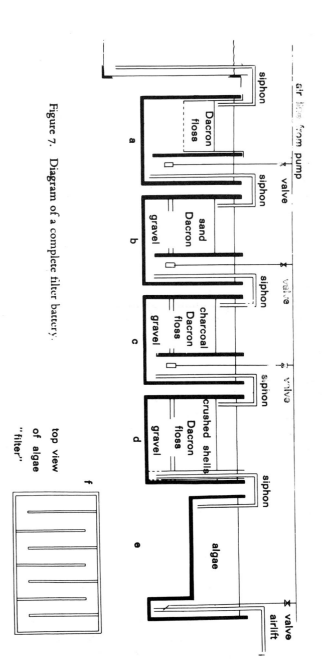

Figure 7. Diagram of a complete filter battery.

top view
of algae
"filter"

77

worse than useless, since bacteria will settle there and decompose the dirt. Cleaning the top layer of the filter medium daily goes a long way toward maintaining sanitary conditions in the tank.

The biological filter (Figure 7b) provides a substratum for the bacterial decomposition of those organic substances which, because they are in solution, have passed through the mechanical filter. The best substratum for bacteria is sand or fine gravel. Even Dacon floss may be used, although this provides less total surface area than do the other two materials. The sand should not be too fine, about ⅒- to ⅛-inch (2–3 mm) grains, because the interstices between extremely fine grains of sand are so small that they could soon fill with dirt, thus impeding the flow of water through the bed. Should this occur, anaerobic conditions may develop in the lower layer. Nor should the layer of sand or gravel be too deep, again to prevent anaerobic conditions in the lower layers. A depth of somewhat over two inches is ample if there is a large surface area, but of course the area is limited by the available space.

The size of the sand filter depends on several considerations. A small one will permit only a limited aquarium population. The larger the sand filter, the more animals that can be maintained in a given volume of water—but only up to a point. If the aquarist economizes on the sand filter, he must make more frequent partial changes of water.

According to Saeki (1964), the weight of the sand in the filter of a closed tank system should be 30 times the weight of the fishes. Following up Saeki's research, the Cleveland Aquarium formulated these ideal requirements: Every pound (450 grams) of fish requires 7.1 gallons of filter sand (27 liters) and a tank of about 100 gallons (380 liters). All the tank water must pass through the filter once every hour. This situation is not likely to be duplicated in a home aquarium, but it does serve to point out that a maximum surface area of the sand filter is essential. Because higher filtration speeds and pressures can be obtained with circulation pumps, the latter permit a sand layer deeper than two inches and a reduction of the surface area. There is a supporting layer of Dacron floss under the sand in the biological filter, and below that a layer of coarse gravel. The biologically active portion of the filter must be washed out in *salt water;* otherwise the bacteria will be killed.

The removal of organic substances that cannot be broken down by bacteria is taken care of by the third filter medium, activated charcoal (Figure 7c). This consists of small pieces of charcoal made highly porous by a special type of processing. The more porous the charcoal, the more organic matter it can absorb, or rather, adsorb. The charcoal merely retains the organic matter, but does not change it. Moreover, its capacity for adsorbing organic matter is limited. If the charcoal filter were placed before the sand filter, it would have to be replaced after a very short time (a few weeks for a sparsely populated aquarium; a few days for an overcrowded tank), and this would make the charcoal filter a costly business. Filter charcoal can only be regenerated by baking at high temperatures or by steam pressure, and that is impractical in the home. Also, old charcoal filters can become dangerous, because they accumulate organic matter, which decomposes and releases unwanted materials into the water. On the positive side, a charcoal filter which is *not* regenerated eventually becomes a biological filter. The charcoal particles create an excellent substratum for bacteria, furnishing them with favorable living conditions.

Incidentally, filter charcoal cannot remove ammonia, nitrite or nitrates. What it *can* do very well is adsorb those substances which cause the tank water to turn yellow in the course of time.

Before placing the charcoal in the filter, wash it thoroughly under the tap and then boil it for some time to expel any air from the numerous tiny pores. After this treatment the charcoal must, of course, not be allowed to dry out again, so store it under water.

The subject of automatic adjustment of the pH of the tank water was already discussed in Chapter II, where we learned that a filter containing ground seashells or coral sand could be used. On the bottom of this filter (Figure 7d) place a layer of coarse gravel, then a supporting layer of Dacron floss, and on top the ground seashells or coral sand, which can form a deeper layer than that of the sand filter. If the shells are to be effective, they must be finely ground, since the calcium of the shells is in contact with the water only at the broken surfaces.

At least some of the inorganic end products of the bacterial decomposition of organic matter will be removed in the algae "filter" (Figure 7e). This is not a filter in the strict sense, but merely a shallow basin with a good deal of overhead illumination so that a luxuriant growth of algae can develop. It should be so constructed as to insure maximum contact between the water and the algae (Figure 7f). Although a shallow basin is recommended for efficient utilization of available light, a deeper section is also needed from which the water can be returned to the tank by means of one or more airlifts.

Algae, like all green plants, manufacture their own food under the influence of light. During this process they absorb carbon dioxide while releasing oxygen. But do not overestimate the quantity of nitrates that can be removed by algae. One quart (liter) of wet green algae is equivalent to about $2\frac{1}{2}$ ounces (75 grams) dry weight and only about five per cent of that weight is nitrogen. Removing 1/300 ounce (100 mg) of nitrogen in the form of nitrates per liter of water from a 52-gallon tank would require the absorption of 200×100 mg nitrogen = 20 grams of nitrogen by the algae. That would take not quite two gallons (seven liters) of green algae. A well-populated tank produces about 50 mg of nitrogen each month, so a monthly harvest of about one gallon (3.5 liters) of algae from the filter is needed to maintain an equilibrium. This would require larger cultures than could be raised in the living room. But even a comparatively small algae filter is worthwhile, because in addition to removing nitrogen compounds, algae affect the aquarium environment favorably in other respects (see Chapter II).

Another type of algae "filter" employs an even thinner water layer (Plessis, 1964), one which optimizes the exchange of gases between the water and the atmosphere. Figure 8 shows the construction of this "thin layer" type of algae filter. The bottom and vertical edges may be made of asbestos cement or plastic. In a variant of this type the filter outflow runs over a plate of ripple glass with upright sides, slanted so that the water runs back into the aquarium. In this way the aquarium illumination is used to advantage. This method cannot replace the normal algae filter altogether, because if we use a large glass it would deprive the tank of too much light. It is, however, an elegant method of enriching the filter outflow with oxygen and removing some carbon dioxide.

The filter battery illustrated in Figure 7 may seem a formidable —and indeed extravagant—technical appurtenance, but it really is not. There are several advantages to having separate filter units. The various filter media can be cleaned and replaced at intervals, the size of each unit can be varied, and the water can be aerated on its way from one unit to the next. The aquarist who does not want so large an installation can combine several units. For example, he can combine the mechanical filter with the sand filter and the charcoal unit with the ground seashell filter. If there is no room for an algae filter, a small algae culture over the aquarium will do, or a strong light bulb placed directly over the Dacron floss covering the sand filter. The little extra on the electricity bill is balanced by the saving on the cost of heating the water.

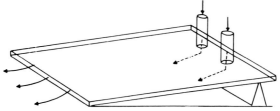

Figure 8. Arrangement for cultivating algae in very shallow water. The cleansed water flowing out of the filter system streams through the connecting pipes at the right and runs over the algae layer growing in the flat pan and into the aquarium.

If the mechanical filter is combined with the sand filter, bear in mind that the Dacron floss must be cleaned frequently, because if dirt is allowed to accumulate, a great deal of oxygen will be consumed there and consequently withheld from the sand filter.

A few refinements can be introduced to prevent deoxygenation, which is always a potential danger when using the wet type of sand filter, since the entire unit is filled with water. The "dry" sand filter, on the other hand, is placed just above the tank so that the water falling through it carries air through the filter medium, which should consist of somewhat coarser material than in the wet sand filter. A "dry" sand filter can be constructed in a comparatively low unit along the length of the tank so that the water is simply carried up by airlifts (Figure 9). This cannot be more than a few inches high, as the ability of the airlift tubes to raise water above the surface is limited. By using a small circulation pump, we can construct a filter with deeper layers (Figure 10).

The duration of the filtering process depends on the size of the aquarium population, but ideally the entire volume of water

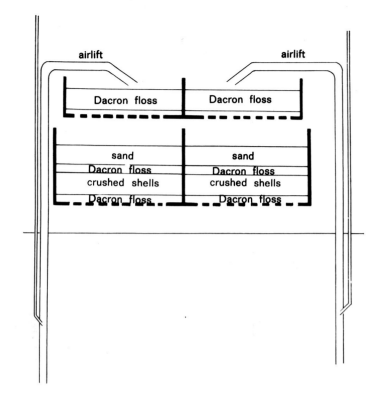

Figure 9. "Dry" sand filter combined with mechanical filter.

should pass through the filter system every one to two hours.

For small temporary aquariums such as quarantine tanks, simple inside filters can be used; these are easily made from a preserving jar or round plastic container (Figures 11, 12). However, most inside filters have a limited capacity and require frequent cleaning.

A reversible flow sand filter, though not commercially available, can be made by the aquarist (Figure 13). This is designed so that the flow of water in the bottom area is slower in the wider portion, causing the heavier particles of dirt to settle on the bottom so they can not block the filter itself. It is not necessary to disassemble the parts for cleaning. Merely close the intake and outflow and open the valve in the bottom. Now pour water on the filter, and it will run through it as shown by the broken lines, carrying off all the dirt through the drain hole.

In recent years an exceptionally good type of filter has been introduced. This consists of a filter box which hangs on the

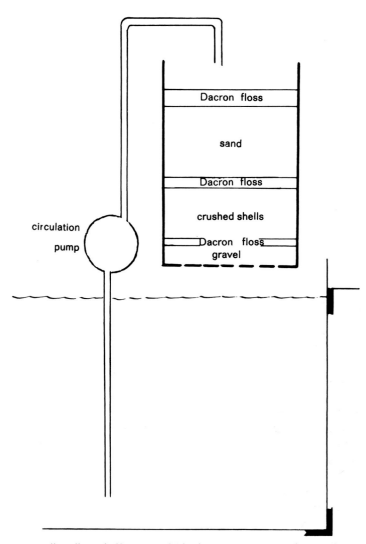

Figure 10. "Dry" sand filter, in which the water is pumped out of the aquarium into the filter with the aid of a water circulation pump.

outside of the tank. A circulation pump with a capacity of about one to ten gallons (4 to 40 liters) per minute is attached directly to this. Depending on the size of the tank, one or more filters of this type can be mounted and filled with Dacron floss, coarse

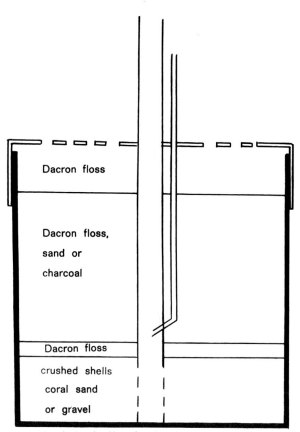

Dacron floss

Dacron floss,
sand or
charcoal

Dacron floss

crushed shells
coral sand
or gravel

Figure 1 .   Simple inside filter for the quarantine aquarium, easily made at home. The water runs through the perforated cover, and past the filter layers. The clear water, which seeps into the airlift through the perforations at the lower end, is pumped back.

sand, charcoal and ground shells. The high filtration speed will prevent anaerobic conditions.

All filter systems should operate continually. If the filters are stopped for any length of time—for example, at night—there is a real danger of almost complete deoxygenation of the filter media, since this stops the transportation of water containing oxygen from the aquarium. The bacteria in the idle filter, which continue their activities, may quickly use up all the available oxygen. Toxic substances may form under the anaerobic conditions which will then prevail; these will be carried into the aquarium when the filters are started again.

As we saw in Chapter II, a recently developed technique employs ozone; this is produced by conducting air over high-voltage electrodes, which converts atmospheric oxygen (O_2) into ozone (O_3). The quantity of ozone produced by an ozonizer depends on the humidity and impurity of the air (dry and dustfree air giving the highest yield). To make certain that the tank water is purified chemically (i.e., that all organic matter is burned

Figure 12. Inside filter for quarantine aquarium, constructed out of plastic or celluloid tubing. Water seeps in from the sides and is pushed out through the standpipe by the airlift.

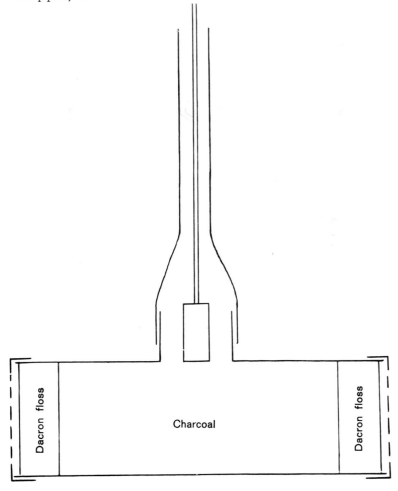

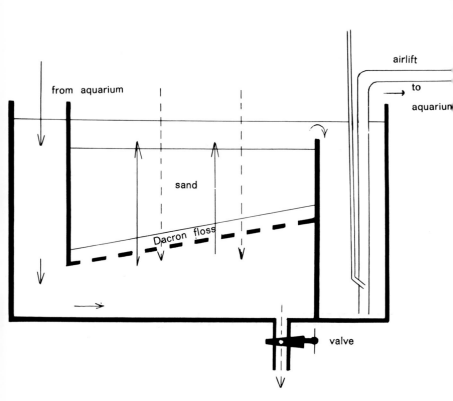

Figure 13. Scheme of a reverse-flow sand filter, which has one advantage: the coarse dirt particles carried in are deposited in the lower chamber and can be easily removed by opening the drainage valve.

completely) the water should be optimally exposed to the ozone. This ozonization should take place outside the aquarium, since ozone above certain concentrations is dangerous to the aquarium population. The ozone "filter"—or rather the ozone contact tube —operates on the principle of counterflow. The direction in which the water to be treated flows is opposite to that of the ozonized air flow. This insures close and prolonged contact, particularly if the ozone bubbler produces a broad flow of small bubbles filling the entire tube. A small quantity of filter charcoal placed at its lower end will prevent any ozone from passing into the tank water. As the ozonized water passes through the filter charcoal, a small quantity of carbon dioxide (CO_2) and perhaps even some carbon monoxide (CO) may be formed. If the return flow to the aquarium is properly aerated, these can do no harm.

Since the ozone cannot oxidize nitrogenous organic compounds beyond the ammonia stage, the ozone tube outflow must pass through a sand filter, where bacterial oxidation of ammonia through nitrite to nitrate will take place. If the ozonized water were to be returned directly to the aquarium, there would be a danger of temporary excessive ammonia concentrations there, which could have unpleasant consequences. The biological sand filter should therefore be capable of dealing with all the ammonia produced by ozonization. This may not always be possible, so there may well be hidden dangers in the use of ozone.

In the unlikely event that the ozonizer produces so much ozone that a good deal escapes into the atmosphere, causing headaches and even nausea, cover the top of the contact tube with a closely fitting gauze bag filled with charcoal. Ozonization is a difficult technique, as each aquarium has its own ozone needs, and it is impossible to give a specific formula for the amount to be used.

Geisler (1964) describes a method of assessing how much ozone to use in a given aquarium. A stock indicator solution may be prepared by dissolving 100 mg of orthotolidine in 50 cc distilled water. Pour this solution into 50 cc of a standard solution of dilute hydrochloric acid (see page 119). This should be stored in the dark in a brown bottle. If the solution turns yellow, it has degraded and should be discarded. Take $2\frac{1}{2}$ gallons (10 liters) of water from the tank and aerate in a polyethylene basin using ozonized air. Every five or ten minutes take a $3\frac{1}{3}$ ounce (100 cc) sample from the basin and pour it into a clean glass. Immediately add 5 cc (1 teaspoon) of the stock reagent. If the reagent turns the water slightly yellow within one minute, there is free ozone in the water. This means that virtually all the organic substances have been oxidized. Now calculate how long the tank water is to be ozonized in the contact tube: if, for instance, 15 minutes of ozone aeration were required for a water sample from the basin to turn yellow, a tank containing 200 liters requires 200/10×15 minutes, or 300 minutes before all the organic matter in it has been oxidized in the contact tube. In practice, this five-hour duration will mean that the contact tube must be run at a fairly high speed. The test must be conducted at a moment when a peak production of organic substances is to be expected, i.e., some time after the fishes have been fed. If the test produces a positive result after only a few minutes of ozonization, the amount of ozone is excessive. If a positive result is obtained only after a long time or not at all, then too little ozone is being used. For the present, the best solution in practice seems to lie in continuous ozonization *at relatively low concentrations.* This will at least insure that the concentration of organic waste products, which are being formed in the aquarium at all hours of the day and night, is held at a very low level. Intermittent ozonization can do no more than level peak productions of organic waste products.

Although ozonization is clearly a difficult technique, it also holds very distinct advantages, since it prevents all sorts of upsets in the chemistry of the aquarium and serves to establish a high redox potential.

When drugs are being administered in the aquarium, we must stop the ozonizer, since ozone would either negate the effect of the drugs or, worse, change their composition and possibly turn them into harmful substances. If a tank has been treated with copper sulfate, for example, copper sulfides will be present both in the water and in the filters. Ozonization could then release so many metallic ions that they might reach a toxic level.

It is better not to use ozonized air to aerate the aquarium. As we have stated before, an overdose of ozone in the water is harmful to all fishes and may even be fatal. Nor can ozone be used to cure skin infections. The amounts that would be needed to kill the skin parasites are, as a rule, harmful even to the sick fishes.

Ozone has a highly corrosive effect on rubber. Equipment coming into contact with ozonized air or water must be made of synthetic materials.

Another modern development that eliminates bacterial decomposition to a large extent is the protein skimmer discussed in Chapter II. This method, too, strikes at the root of the problem. Figure 14 shows the principle of the protein skimmer which, like

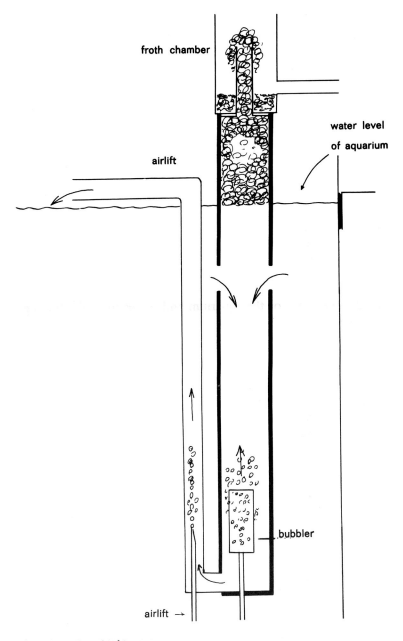

Figure 14. Protein skimmer.

89

the ozonizer, operates on the counterflow principle.* To stimulate the formation of froth in the upper part of the device, a strong stream of tiny bubbles must be emitted in such a way as to fill the entire water column. (The capacity of the skimmer must, of course, be adequate in relation to the volume of the aquarium, but overcapacity can do no harm. Even if no more froth can be formed, the skimmer continues to operate as an effective aerator.) If the skimmer is to be efficient, it must turn the water over rapidly. Otherwise, the bacteria in the tank will have time to break down a portion of the organic substances before they can reach the skimmer. It is frequently recommended in the literature that the skimmer be operated with ozonized air; this appears to be ill-founded, since ozone would oxidize proteins and other organic compounds before the skimmer had an opportunity to remove them.

The skimmer will remove other substances (through adsorption to the thin film of the bubbles), such as the organic dyes (which eventually turn the water yellow), phosphates, small dirt particles, algae spores, along with the protein colloids. There is also evidence that certain trace elements are removed.

The development of the protein skimmer is so recent that it is not yet possible to say whether it has made filtration superfluous, so for the time being it is advisable to use the device plus the regular filter equipment. The protein skimmer is a very valuable addition to the existing aquarium and should be present in every well-equipped set-up. Most protein skimmers sit inside the tank, but can also be housed outside, in an empty filter basin connected to the aquarium by a siphon and with an outflow into the filter battery. Disconnect the skimmer when drugs are being administered, or they may be skimmed off.

Many advantages are attributed to the undergravel filter. When first introduced, the rationale was that the sand on the bottom of the tank could be used as a biological filter. To this end, a perforated sheet of plastic was placed over the bottom of the tank and covered with gravel. One or more airlifts were attached to it. When these were activated, the tank water was sucked down through the sand layer, which thus became a filter. Although this technique does have certain merits, particularly with regard to the organisms living in the sand, it has not always worked well in practice. The reason is that it is impossible in the long run to insure a uniform

*The protein skimmers available in the trade are all similar to this one, but can be improved.

flow of water throughout the sand layer. Sooner or later, accumulated dirt retards the flow in certain areas, and dangerous anaerobic conditions may result. The diminished flow will also reduce the filter capacity. If, in an effort to eliminate the possibility of clogging, we reduce the depth of the sand, the bacteria may not have an adequate substratum. Then, too, the action of the inhabitants may cause the sand to shift, reducing the depth in some places. The tank water, choosing the line of least resistance, will pass through these bare areas, which means the end of effective filtration. If the undergravel filter is to work properly, the sand layer must be fairly deep, and we are back to the possibility of undesirable anaerobic conditions. Another disadvantage is that if something goes wrong with the undergravel filter, there is nothing to do but take the aquarium apart and set it up again from scratch. Many aquarists run a thin stick or even their hands through the gravel regularly, some every day. Done gently, this does not disturb the inhabitants, but does prevent caking and maintains an even grading throughout.

An even more useful method of utilizing the undergravel filter is to reverse the direction of the flow through the gravel. The outflow from the filter battery can be used to oxygenate the bottom layer and even rinse it. If enough pressure is provided, it will even wash dirt particles from the coarse-grained bottom material. Of course, it is not to be expected that in a deep sand layer ideal conditions will obtain throughout, but the great advantage over the standard undergravel filter is that this reverse flow will not bring any dirt *into* the sand. Figure 15 illustrates the reversed undergravel filter. The movable attachment to the standpipe serves to control the pressure. As the tube is turned further toward the vertical, the pressure in the standpipe will rise because less water will escape from the attachment. This kind of "filtration" is particularly useful if there are invertebrates in or on the sandy bottom.

Yet another method of water purification is the use of synthetic resins which adsorb protein colloids. There are several brands of resins on the market, but they are not yet quite foolproof, as they give off traces of phenols (0.1–0.3 mg/liter) which, added to the phenols already present in the tank, may be toxic to sensitive fishes, particularly Chaetodontidae (butterflyfishes and angelfishes). If synthetic resins could be produced that would adsorb

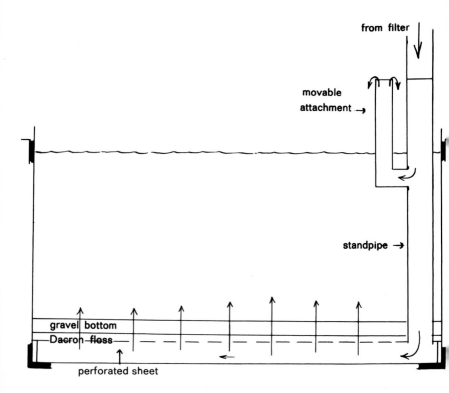

Figure 15. Reverse-flow undergravel filter. Turning the attached pipe determines the rate of flow through the bottom plate.

all the organic matter and not give off any harmful substances, they might be useful in the aquarium, particularly if regeneration of the resins proved feasible. The protein skimmer, however, appears to be a cheaper, safer and more elegant solution.

The biological filters (page 78 and Figure 7b) will, of course, release many bacteria into the filter outflow. Among these are not only the useful species not directly dangerous to fishes, but also those species that cause diseases in fishes and invertebrates (such as the *Shigella* species). These bacteria apparently find a particularly favorable environment in filters connected with overcrowded aquariums in which an abundance of organic detritus is produced.

To combat this, a technique has been developed for sterilizing the filtered water before it is returned to the tank. This is done by means of sterilizer lamps, which produce ultraviolet rays with extremely short waves. This type of light, which has a powerful sterilizing effect, is produced by the sun, but is not found on earth (being absorbed by the upper layers of the atmosphere). If water is exposed to the rays of these tubes, close to one hundred per cent of the bacteria can be destroyed or inactivated. Fungi and other microorganisms are also affected. However, since different organisms require different doses of exposure, it is impossible to sterilize the filtered water completely. Unfortunately, ultraviolet light can penetrate only an inch or two through water, so if it is to be effective, the water must flow through the tube in a thin

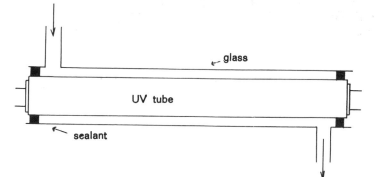

Figure 16. UV sterilization tube with water mantle.

layer. Figure 16 shows a UV sterilizing tube with a glass jacket surrounding it at a maximum distance of ⅜ inch (10 mm) fitted with intake and outflow tubes. Silicone cement should be used to seal off the opening between the tube and the jacket.

The value of this sterilizer depends on the extent to which the UV rays can penetrate the water; this, in turn, is determined by such factors as the temperature, transparency and color of the water. The higher the temperature, the greater the penetration.

The maximum useful effect of the sterilizer is obtained at 104°F (40°C). At 70°F (21°C) the useful effect has dropped by as much as 50 per cent (Herald, 1962). Since the temperature of aquarium water can never be this high, but ranges between 75° and 79°F (24-26°C), the sterilizer will have to be modified as shown in Figure 17. The UV tube is housed in a cylinder made of quartz or fluorite glass (which allows the transmission of ultraviolet rays). This, in turn, is surrounded by a water jacket made of ordinary glass. The result is that the air surrounding the UV tube is warmed to about 104°F (40°C) by the light unit, which allows the sterilizer to penetrate at maximum capacity. Unfortunately, the special glass needed for the construction of the inner jacket is very expensive, but such a modified sterilizer has considerable advantages. First, it is practically impossible for sea water to seep into the sockets of the tube. Secondly, a spent UV can be replaced very easily, whereas in the simpler construction the water jacket must be replaced at the same time.

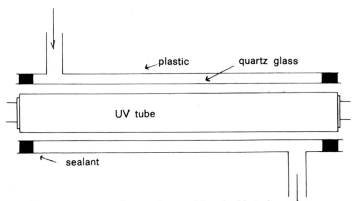

Figure 17. A UV sterilization lamp with a double jacket.

It is by no means certain that maximum sterilization is really necessary for the ordinary home aquarium; for a moderate-sized uncrowded tank the lower yield is probably adequate, and it is even possible that no sterilizer at all is needed. For larger tanks, however, a sterilizer is a valuable asset. Incidentally, the proper place for a UV unit is behind the last filter unit, where it can destroy the bacteria released by the filter battery. Moreover, colorless water free of suspended particles permits maximum penetration by the rays.

The rate of flow through the water jacket determines how long the organisms will be exposed to the ultraviolet rays. The speed at which the filters of home aquariums are normally run probably provides adequate exposure. To be quite safe, insert a plastic (ultraviolet-resistant!) coil in the water jacket.

One notorious parasite of tropical sea fishes is the ciliate *Cryptokarion irritans*, which will be discussed at some length in the chapter on skin diseases. Like several pathogenic bacteria, this skin parasite can subsist in a filter without a host. Experiments in the Artis Aquarium have shown that there is a good possibility that this parasite is destroyed with the normal sterilizer tubes. Of course, miracles cannot be expected. All the tubes can do is keep down the number of bacteria in the tank and prevent diseases from passing through the filters and attacking the fishes; they cannot cure diseases! Since the purpose of the UV tubes is to sterilize the filter outflow, they should, like the filter battery, be in operation day and night.

The sterilizer tube can also do a good job of getting rid of unicellular organisms that cloud the aquarium. To do this, disconnect the UV lamp from the filters and run the tank water directly through the sterilizer.

Unfortunately, the effective life of a sterilizer tube is comparatively short: 2,500 hours for 6-watt and 15-watt UV's, 4,000 hours for 30-watt UV's. Although the tube will not necessarily burn out after the stated number of hours, the impact of the ultraviolet light will have brought about such changes in the glass that the latter is no longer pervious to the UV rays.

Ultraviolet light, in addition to its sterilizing properties, acts as a catalyst to set up or accelerate all sorts of chemical reactions. The extent of this in the aquarium is still unknown. We do know, however, that any proteins in the water will be degraded, presumably producing volatile amines and organic nitrite compounds. Furthermore, UV rays can reduce nitrates to nitrites. However, in this reduction process, strongly reductive intermediate products are formed, which in turn retard the reductive action. For the present, it is safe to assume that under normal conditions nitrate reduction by UV light is not an important factor in the well-run aquarium, although it may indeed be in the badly fouled one. If copper sulfate or copper chloride is being administered as a drug, UV rays will reduce bivalent copper ions in solution to univalent ions, catalytically, causing such a degree of deoxygenation of the water that the fishes are forced to greatly accelerate respiration. An even worse situation arises when there are too many iodine compounds in the water, as iodates are reduced by UV light to iodides and these oxidized to free iodine. Free iodine is toxic even in small concentrations. Older seawater formulas (e.g., by Kramer and Wiedemann) prescribed so much total iodine that ultraviolet lighting was able to produce toxic concentrations of free iodine. Ozonization, which also oxidizes iodides to free iodine, has the same effect. This is why more recent seawater formulas reduce the amount of combined iodine drastically, to 0.1 mg potassium iodide.

To conclude: from our knowledge of the chemical action of UV light and ozone on sea water, it follows that neither the sterilizer nor the ozonizer should be used in the presence of any type of drug, but especially not with copper sulfate or copper chloride.

Salinity

We have seen that a certain amount of evaporation is inevitable. As water evaporates, the salinity of the water rises slowly. Now, unlike algae, the aquarium animals are not very sensitive to salinity changes, so long as these are not too abrupt. Any water lost by evaporation can therefore be replaced with an equal amount of ordinary tap water which, however, must not contain any free chlorine. To be on the safe side, allow the water to stand for 24 hours in an open basin. Of course, the water should be the same temperature as the aquarium. Besides the effect of evaporation, various maintenance operations will cause salt water to be lost, so periodic salinity checks must be carried out. With a hydrometer, determine the specific gravity (density) of the aquarium water. The specific gravity reading will give us the salinity if an appropriate table, like that on page 97, is used. Suppose that the hydrometer reading is 1.025 specific gravity at a water temperature of 76°F (24.5°C). Now draw a horizontal line from the 76°F point in the temperature scale until it intersects the sp gr 1.025 diagonal. A line drawn perpendicularly from this intersection will give the corresponding value, in this case 35‰, on the salinity scale.

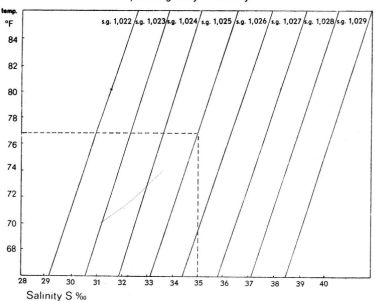

specific gravity (= density)

To obtain a very precise reading, float the hydrometer in a glass cylinder filled with water from the aquarium and find the exact value at the intersection of the water surface and the hydrometer scale (i.e., at the lowest point of the meniscus). Most hydrometers are set for a standard temperature of 59°F (15°C) or 63.5°F (17.5°C). The water in the cylinder should be allowed to cool to this standard temperature, because with rising temperatures the specific gravity will decrease. The temperature effect cannot be neglected.

Foxface, *Lo* (*Siganus*) *vulpinus*.

For the tropical marine aquarium the specific gravity should be between 1.024 and 1.025, which means a salinity of 34–35‰ at a temperature of 77°F (25°C). If a total salinity of 32‰ (see Chapter II) is preferred, the specific gravity at 77°F (25°C) should be 1.023.

Acidity or Alkalinity (pH)

In a previous chapter we saw that the pH of natural ocean water is very constant, moving within the narrow range of pH 8.0 to 8.3. In the aquarium a somewhat wider range, pH 7.8 to 8.5, is permissible, and even higher values are not necessarily harmful. The pH in the tank tends to drop because of the accumulation of carbon dioxide, the production of acids and nitrates in the decomposition of organic matter, and the removal of free calcium and magnesium from the water by phosphates; so a simple method of checking the pH is needed. An electric pH gauge, which is most accurate, is too expensive for the home aquarist. The pH-paper kit, which is often recommended, is not accurate enough and the readings are too inconsistent. This leaves only the liquid pH indicators. Hückstedt (1963) recommends the following very reliable pH indicator for salt water: to one gram of *a*-naphtholphthalein dissolved in 400 cc of 96 per cent alcohol, add 100 cc of a 2 per cent alcoholic solution of phenolphthalein. A clean test tube (rinsed a few times in the aquarium) is carefully filled with water from the tank and four drops of the indicator solution added. Depending on the pH value, the color of the indicator will change within the following range:

COLOR CHANGE	pH
almost colorless, slightly yellow	below 7.0
green	7.5–7.8
sea green	7.9–8.1
sky blue	*8.2–8.3*
dark blue	8.4–8.5
bluish purple	8.6–8.7
dark purple	over 8.7

The indicator solution can be standardized in this way: dissolve one teaspoonful of sodium carbonate in a clean glass of distilled water and aerate the solution throughly with a bubbler for 30 minutes. After aeration the solution will have a pH of 8.7, and a few drops of the indicator solution should cause a bluish purple hue.

If a pH check reveals that the pH has dropped below 8.0, the water may have lost its buffering power, that is, the tendency to resist changes in pH. The only remedy is to buffer the water back up to the correct pH of 8.3 by slowly adding a mixture of six parts sodium bicarbonate and one part sodium carbonate. Add small quantities and check the pH after each addition. When the pH has been restored to normal, add an additional level teaspoonful for every 25 gallons (100 liters) of water, which will maintain the pH at a constant level between 8.3 and 8.4 for quite a while.

It goes without saying that pH corrections should be carried out only when it is believed that there is a low ammonia concentration in the aquarium. This will probably be 24 hours after the last feeding. If the pH starts to drop again shortly after it has been corrected, it is time to renew the water, because it is useless to go on correcting the pH by chemical methods. Remember that in cases other than loss of buffering capacity, the addition of buffering mixtures treats the effect rather than the cause.

Water Renewal

A steadily falling pH is a sure sign that the water is aging. For the amateur, pH checks are really the only suitable method of determining when partial removal of the water is due, since nitrate determinations are beyond his means. Of course, the behavior of the fishes will also make it clear that the water is no longer a healthy environment. Some of the symptoms are fading colors, growing apathy, diminishing appetite and a heightened susceptibility to skin parasites and other diseases. Of course, if we adopt the rule of thumb given on page 42, conditions will never deteriorate to this extent. However, keep these points in mind: first, aerate synthetic salt water throughly for about twenty-four hours before using it; second, make certain its temperature and salinity are the same as those of the aquarium. Even if water removal is overdue and it looks as if more than one third or one fourth of the water will have to be replaced, do not rush in with large amounts of new water. It may sound paradoxical, but fishes that are used to rather poor water will react adversely if they suddenly find themselves in water of good quality, because the sudden change may upset their osmotic balance. In such a case, make the change gradually; never renew more than one third or one fourth of the total volume at one time. This will take more time and water, but it will teach the hobbyist not to fall behind in renewing the water. Too rigorous water renewal may well destroy the entire growth of algae, the useful microfauna and microflora and valuable fishes as well.

One last word about the pitfalls of water maintenance. Many aquarists believe that so long as the aquarium is crystal clear, all is well. In point of fact, sparkling clear sea water can be just as toxic as clouded, yellowish water. If there is a sudden, inexplicable high mortality among the fishes in a perfectly clear aquarium, the cause may well be poisoning by phenols, amines, ammonia or even excessive concentrations of nitrates. The clarity of the water provides no guarantee whatsoever as to its quality!

Heating the Tank

For tropical marine fauna, maintain a water temperature of 75°
to 79°F (24° to 26°C). Higher temperatures of up to 82°F (28°C)
are frequently recommended, but certainly not necessary. For one
thing, a constant temperature of 82°F (28°C) is by no means found
throughout the native haunts of our fishes. For another, such high
temperatures would make the fishes expend energy at a con-
sistently high level. They are poikilothermic creatures; that is, they
take on the temperature of the surrounding water and this, in
turn, determines the rate of speed of their physiological processes
and their activity. A higher temperature will speed up their
metabolism and cause greater activity. It stands to reason that if
the fishes are constantly maintained at this high level of activity,
they will be worn out sooner than if we moderate the temperature
somewhat. Lower temperatures mean a longer life span and
slightly reduced nutritional requirements, two factors of great
importance to us. Even coral fishes have been maintained with a
fair degree of success at still lower temperatures (70° to 72°F, 21°to
22°C) than those recommended above. Certain species will even
survive a long spell at 64°F (18°C) if they are slowly acclimated
to this temperature. However, there will be a drastic drop in
activity as well as in food consumption; and, of course, growth
will slow or even cease.

To maintain the aquarium temperature at 75-79°F (24-26°C),
use the same electrical apparatus as in the tropical freshwater tank
—glass immersion heaters and thermostats, the latter preferably
of the type that can be attached to the outside of one of the side
panels. In this way the thermostat is completely protected from
any contact with sea water. If the tank is in a normally heated
room, the immersion heater can be housed in a filter unit, so there
will be no need to camouflage the heater and its cable. Of course,
the speed at which the water circulates should be high enough to
meet the heat requirements of the aquarium. The only risk
involved in housing the heater in the filter is that if the filter
should run dry, the heater will burn out, or if the water flow is
interrupted, the water in the filter will be overheated and the
aquarium itself remain cold. Only glass (no metal) heaters
should be used. Also, the watertight casing of the cable should be
made of synthetic material rather than rubber, which will be

corroded by the salt water. If the heater is placed inside the aquarium, it should be suspended in a corner rather than lie on the bottom where bottom-haunting fishes might lie on it and get badly burned.

A low- rather than a high-wattage heater should be used so that if the thermostat should malfunction, the water will not overheat. In an average room allow about three watts for each gallon. Naturally, an immersed, easy-to-read thermometer is an absolute must in the aquarium.

Lighting

Lighting marine tanks is a thorny problem, because the cultivation of a luxuriant growth of algae automatically involves factors, many of them still unknown, other than adequate lighting. If your only object is to observe the fishes, there is hardly any problem; merely place one or more fluorescent tubes over the aquarium. The use of incandescent lighting consumes much more power and we shall therefore not discuss it. Of course, as mentioned at the beginning of this chapter, it is a good idea to buy an aquarium whose length is roughly equivalent to the size of the fluorescent tubes that are to light the tank.

A 20-watt fluorescent tube is 24 inches long (59 cm) and therefore suitable for a tank over 26 inches long (65 cm); a 30-watt tube is 36 inches long (90 cm) and so can be placed over a tank 39 inches (100 cm) long; a 40-watt tube is 48 inches (120 cm) long and can be used over tanks 56 inches (150 cm) or more in length. For more lighting, one tube for each 12–16 inches (30–40 cm) of width is actually sufficient if the depth of the water does not exceed 16 inches (40 cm). A little more light will, of course, do no harm and probably even be beneficial to the fishes, which are used to very intensive light in their native coral reef haunts.

If the aquarist wants a luxuriant growth of algae in the aquarium, more tubes are needed—in fact, as many as the width of the tank will allow. This strong lighting is necessary not primarily because marine algae need more light than freshwater species, but because other factors in the aquarium environment impede algae growth, and stronger lighting partially compensates for these. Public aquariums often use mercury arcs for intensive lighting. These are not suitable for home use because they are too expensive, take up too much room and generate too much heat. For the small home aquarium the best lighting is supplied by fluorescent tubes augmented by one or more incandescent light bulbs. The latter could be used, for instance, to highlight a few places in the tank and imitate sunlight, because fluorescent tubes produce a very uniform light that masks the ripple effect caused by the interplay of incoming light and the water movement at the surface.

What other factors influence and promote algae growth in the aquarium? We know from experience that green algae are among the most difficult species to cultivate in the marine aquarium, in contrast to the generally thriving growths of diatoms ("brown algae"), blue-green algae and a few species of red algae. The reasons for this have already been mentioned (page 43). Diatoms, blue-green algae and some red algae grow best in more or less polluted water. They absorb certain organic nitrogenous compounds and ammonia, which are available in larger quantities in contaminated water. If you doubt this, try suddenly doubling the population of a tank containing just a few fishes and a luxuriant growth of green algae. There is a very good chance that before long the green algae will start to die off, giving place to blue-green or red algae. If under these experimental conditions the amount of lighting is doubled, green algae might possibly survive, but their

French Angelfish, *Pomacanthus paru*, with Cleanerfish, *Labroides dimidiatus*.

growth would still be stunted. This shows that green algae cannot thrive in polluted water, and also that their requirements for light depend on the purity of the water. Relatively little light is required for non-polluted water; the more pollution, the more light that is required. This is why it is almost impossible to obtain a proper growth of algae in crowded tanks. Hückstedt (1963) states that phenol concentrations from 0.2 mg/liter upward impede the growth of green algae. The phenols themselves are not necessarily responsible, but the conditions which cause such a high concentration of phenols are a sign that there is excess organic matter in the water or, in other words, that the aquarium is fouled.

The following experiment also demonstrates the extent to which algae growth is more dependent on the purity of the water than on the lighting. Put a tank with non-polluted water and no fishes in a location with little daylight. Aerate the tank normally, but do not filter or light it. After a few weeks there will be a fair growth of algae. If you now place just one fluorescent tube over the tank, the growth of algae will be greatly accelerated.

The fewer fishes there are in an aquarium, the better the green algae will do. In a sparsely populated aquarium with pure salt water a light intensity of 100–200 lumens per 16 square inches of water surface will be adequate if the aquarium is not deeper than 18 inches. Crowded aquariums require more light to obtain the same results. The following table, giving some types of fluorescent tubes with their lumens, will enable the reader to work out the number of tubes he needs for the aquarium.

type	wattage	lumens	type	wattage	lumens
32	25	1130	33	25	1650
32	40	1880	33	40	2800
32	65	3000	33	65	4400

type	wattage	lumens	type	wattage	lumens
55	25	1250			
55	40	2120	F33	40	2460
55	65	3300	F33	65	4600

The best results are obtained by combining type 32 de luxe "warm white" with no. 33 white (also available with an internal reflector strip: F33) or with no. 55 daylight. Gro-lux® and Fluora® Fluorescent tubes, originally developed for the cultivation of terrestrial plants, have two maxima in their spectrum: one at the blue end and one at the red end. This kind of energy distribution forces the growth of green terrestrial plants and probably also of green algae, since these have the same pigments as the higher terrestrial plants (chlorophyll a and b, a and β carotene, lutein, etc.) and hence corresponding absorption spectra. Some people feel that the colors of the fishes are too garish under this type of lighting. A considerable optical change can be obtained by combining these lamps with a no. 32 tube. Not enough practical experience has been gained so far with this type of lighting to permit any definite conclusions. The concentration at the blue end might possibly have injurious side effects, as reported by Klee (1964), for eggs of freshwater species.

If the aquarist wishes to experiment with ultraviolet light for purposes other than sterilization, his best choice would be a blacklight tube, which produces a good deal of long-wave UV and little, if any, risk of overdosage.

It is difficult to discuss the possible usefulness of ultraviolet light to marine organisms with any degree of certainty, as we do not know its role in the lives of these animals in the wild, and what consequences its absence has in captivity. In view of the fact that long-wave ultraviolet light (3,200–3,400 angstroms) penetrates relatively far into clear ocean water, it is quite possible that it does have some effect on marine animals living in shallow water. At a depth of 40 feet, for instance, 50 per cent of the ultraviolet light measured at the surface is still present in clear water. In turbid inshore water, however, only 5 per cent penetrates to the same depth.

It can be concluded, from experiments conducted in recent years (Artis Aquarium, Amsterdam, and Seaquarium, Miami), that the effects of ultraviolet light may be favorable. It has been found, for instance, that some forms of exophthalmus (see page 174) can be cured by exposing the fishes to the light of a blacklight tube. Injuries to skin and fins will also heal quickly with this type of radiation. Then, too, there are indications suggesting that the mucoid skin of fishes grows better under ultraviolet lighting. This probably also explains why wild coral fishes, after a prolonged sunless spell, show a higher incidence of skin infections, which disappear after a few days of bright sunshine.

The results obtained in experiments with long-wave ultraviolet

Golden Blowfish, *Arothron citrinellus.*

light are still too limited to allow us to say what the correct dosage should be. This much is certain: after prolonged daily exposure (up to twelve hours a day) to black light, no visible harmful effects were observed in fishes, bacterial exophthalmus was prevented, and there were fewer instances of infections by skin parasites.

It is possible that long-wave ultraviolet light is also beneficial to those invertebrates that live in comparatively shallow water and are active by day, particularly such sessile species as sea anemones and corals. Experiments involving these animals would certainly be worthwhile, but care must be exercised in selecting UV lamps which will not produce unduly strong radiation.

The aquarium should be lighted from 12 to 16 hours a day to promote a flourishing algae culture. It would be wrong to have continuous lighting, since the fishes, and to a lesser extent the algae, require intervals of rest.

The amount of illumination which an aquarium requires depends partially on the depth of the water. Light intensities quickly decrease with increasing distance from the surface, because water absorbs different wave lengths at different rates.

The first to disappear are the red and infrared, while the greatest penetration is attained by green and blue light. To insure adequate lighting of the bottom, remember this: the deeper the tank, the more illumination required.

As we saw in the previous chapter, water movement is another important factor for algae culture, since it reduces the jacket of stagnant water surrounding each organism. This is one of the reasons that the "algae filter" should be constructed as shown in Figure 7 f. It is not only that the partitions guarantee a longer period of contact between water and algae, but also that the narrowed chamber will accelerate the flow of water, which in turn has a beneficial influence on the growth of the algae.

In addition to the complex of factors discussed so far—amount of illumination, purity of water, rate of flow—the growth of algae, like that of the fishes, is affected by such things as salinity fluctuations and nutrient availability. Trace elements in particular may play an important role, particularly in synthetic sea water, but as we said when we discussed the effect of water quality on fishes, it is too early to say anything definite about them.

Still another factor has been demonstrated by Pringsheim (1963): most algae require organic acids. These can be added to the aquarium water in the form of neutral salts. A hefty pinch of sodium acetate for each 25 gallons (100 liters) of water can do wonders for a feeble, sluggish culture.

Abrupt salinity fluctuations, which cause a sudden change in osmotic pressure, may damage certain species of algae so badly that they die. According to Fach (1965), *Caulerpa prolifera* (a Mediterranean algae) does not tolerate as little a change as 0.003 in the specific gravity of the water.

Finally, a great many coral fishes, including species that are not exclusively herbivorous, feed on algae. If there are too many algae eaters in an aquarium, the algae culture in the tank may never have an opportunity to grow properly.

The type of reflector hood used for the freshwater tank is also used in marine aquariums. If this is not placed on top of a cover glass to keep out condensation moisture, the light tubes must be mounted in waterproof polyethylene sockets with rubber seals, for copper oxides may fall into the water if the pins on the light tubes are allowed to corrode. Rather than use the fairly expensive waterproof sockets, the aquarist can make the standard terminal

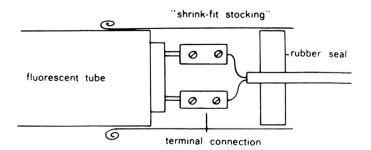

Figure 18. Standard terminal connection waterproofed by means of an insulating "shrink-fit stocking" and rubber seals.

connections waterproof himself by means of an insulating "shrink-fit stocking" and rubber seals (see Figure 18).

If the hood is placed on a glass cover, the air inside may become too hot for the tubes to produce the maximum light yield (which requires air temperatures between 68° and 86°F; 20° to 30°C), so the hood must be made self-ventilating (Figure 19). Ventilation will prevent the accumulation of carbon dioxide over the water. If a cover glass is used, it should not seal off the tank completely; the opening left may be used for siphon tubes, air releases, etc.

A few final words should be said about night lighting. In the wild, fishes seldom experience total darkness, except for those species that burrow into the sand or hide in deep coral clefts and caves for the night. In the upper water layers there will always be some residual light by which the fishes can orient themselves. In home aquariums, on the other hand, the animals are frequently left for the night with no light whatsoever. Loud noises penetrating from outside (such as slamming doors, backfiring cars, etc.) may provoke a sudden flight reaction in the fishes, causing them to bump into glass panes, stones or corals and injure themselves. The sudden shutting off of all lights simultaneously may provoke a similar response, and at the very least will deprive the fishes of an opportunity to seek a resting place for the night.

These risks will be greatly reduced if a few dimmed lights are left on all night. To enable the fishes to settle down in their regular resting places, either switch off one tube after another while the room lights are still on, or connect one or two light bulbs in the hood to a rheostat. With the normal lighting still on, switch these bulbs to full capacity. Next, switch off the tubes one after

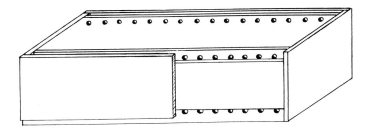

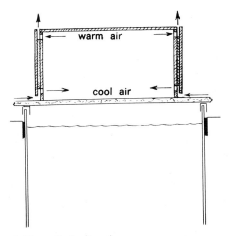

Figure 19.   Self-ventilating hood.

another and, finally, dim the bulbs slowly and leave them like that till morning.

Still another possibility is to keep some night light on in the room after slowly switching off the tank lighting.

Summary

In concluding this long and rather technical section, we shall summarize the minimum requirements for a marine home aquarium:
1.   A fair-sized, non-toxic tank which can not be corroded by salt water.
2.   A glass immersion heating unit with plastic casing.
3.   A thermostat which can be attached to the outside of the tank.

4. An easy-to-read, all-glass thermometer.
5. A hydrometer.
6. A protein skimmer.
7. A filter system of adequate capacity, equipped with such accessories as siphons, standpipes and airlifts and such media as sand, Dacron floss, and gravel.
8. A fairly powerful air pump with accessories (air tube, T-joints, control valves, thin celluloid tubing, air releases).
9. A hood with fluorescent tubes and light bulbs.
10. A pH indicator.

Green Damsel, *Chromis coeruleus.*

IV   Setting up the Aquarium

Because extreme cleanliness is so important, the first rule in setting up a marine aquarium is that all materials must be arranged so that uneaten food and dead animals can be readily seen and removed. Avoid inaccessible, though artistic, nooks and recesses; a simple setup is best.

All equipment and supplies to be used must be thoroughly cleaned and of materials that do not react to salt water. They must contain no dead organisms and, above all, should never have been previously treated with soap or detergents (see page 69 and next page).

The most important items are a bottom layer, a few decorative rocks and some pieces of coral to simulate the fishes' native habitat.

Bottom Layer

In a preceding chapter we saw that the material used to cover the bottom not only serves a decorative purpose but also provides a substratum for the bacteria that must decompose any organic matter not sucked into the filter (see page 78). If the filter system works properly, there will not be much detritus left in the tank, nor will there be a need to cover the bottom with a deep layer, which might promote anaerobic conditions. The best material is coarse-grained hard river sand (2–3 mm grains) or coarse quartz sand spread in a one-inch layer. Coral sand, which is crushed coral and consists almost entirely of calcium compounds, may also be used. However, with certain aquarium drugs it causes an adverse reaction. It is better to use this material in the filter, possibly combined with ground seashells, for automatic pH control. It can also be used effectively as a bottom cover for a tank populated mainly by invertebrates.

First wash the sand in tap water, stirring frequently until nothing but clear water runs off. (It is a good idea to buy a plastic bucket or basin exclusively for aquarium use; one which has been in contact with detergents is taboo for the aquarium.) Drain the sand thoroughly and put it into the tank after placing the other materials there. It must not get under corals or rocks, for anaerobic conditions may develop in sand packed to a dense mass by the weight of rocks and corals. In addition, it must be impossible for fishes to dig sand from under the rocks, causing them to tumble down. If a reversed undergravel filter is used, put it in first and cover it with a thin layer of Dacron floss.

Rocks

Rocks which contain soluble metals are not suitable for the aquarium. Lava rock, shale, sandstone and limestone are best. Although limestone slowly dissolves in sea water, it generally lasts a couple of years. Dolomite rocks, with their fantastic gnarled shapes, are excellent, but only the experienced aquarist should use them, as dirt collects very easily in the many holes and folds. Rocks must be cleaned thoroughly by boiling them for half an hour and then scrubbing and washing them vigorously under the tap.

Corals

Living corals are polyps or polyp colonies together with their membranes and skeletons. There are two types: the stony corals, consisting mainly of calcium compounds, and the branched forms of the order Gorgonaria, which have a hornlike skeleton. In the oceans corals have entirely different colors from those of the faded, petrified skeletons offered to the aquarist. Living corals are found in many soft pastel shades: green, yellow, orange, brown, pink and sometimes white. A few species are deep red. When the organisms that give it color die, the skeleton generally turns white, although the "organ pipe" coral has a red skeleton. The common practice of dyeing the white coral is really purposeless, because algae will soon cover the coral with varied patterns of brown, green and red hues if adequate illumination is provided. To keep its color, dyed coral would have to be cleaned regularly, and this would cause an undesirable upheaval.

Since coral is rather fragile (although fairly heavy), it must be shipped from the tropics in bulky breakproof packaging, which makes it quite expensive. For the aquarium, it is best to choose a few moderate-sized pieces rather than one or two huge formations.

Commercially available coral will, as a rule, have been cleaned only very superficially, dried in the tropical sun and bleached. Sometimes shippers use special bleaches to obtain maximum whiteness. If such pieces are placed in the aquarium without careful cleaning, the bleaches may poison the fishes, and the remains of dead organisms (polyps, sponges and other reef animals) would in no time turn the tank into a foul-smelling pool. The coral must therefore be leached out for 48 hours in a solution of ten ounces (300 cc) of 15 per cent potassium or sodium hydroxide (lye) for each $2\frac{1}{2}$ gallons (10 liters) of water. If the coral is very dirty, it should be left in longer, or the treatment repeated with chlorinated lime. (No metal basins or pails should be used unless they are enameled.) After this treatment the coral pieces are given a thorough scrubbing under the tap and then boiled for 30 minutes. Another thorough rinse under the tap will complete the cleaning job.

Setting Up the Décor

The décor of a saltwater aquarium is in many respects easier to arrange than that of a freshwater tank with its many plants. Good taste and an eye for the most effective grouping of stones and corals will go a long way, if the aquarist bears in mind that his miniature artificial reef should aim at resembling the real ocean reef. Underwater photographs of coral reefs found in many popular books about the oceans will give a fairly good idea of how to proceed. Resist the temptation to duplicate a reef section in its entirety—the result would be a warren of clefts and crevices that would produce dangerous pollution. To aid the beginning aquarist, a few sketches are given in Figure 20.

It is a good idea to conceal the corners either with slabs of shale that have one straight edge, or with sloping coral colonies. The impression of depth is improved if the back of the tank is not completely covered up. If there is a glass panel at the rear, paint it black or bluish green, or, to create a feeling of great depth, place behind it a box with a décor kit, as shown in Figure 21. The gentle slope of the aquarium sand continues into the box and then changes to a fairly steep incline. Rather than use a deep layer of sand, model a slope of fine-meshed wire netting, covered with a thin layer of wet cement sprinkled with quartz sand. This "backdrop" décor need not be more than six to twelve inches deep to suggest enormous depth and width. Paint the rear of the box black. If you aim the subdued light of a low-wattage tube over the box, but not toward the rear, you can obtain an even stronger impression of infinity.

In building a coral reef inside the tank, take good care to anchor all the elements firmly in place. A sudden fall may kill some valuable fish or even break a glass panel. In the literature it is frequently suggested that coral and other decorative materials be glued onto rocks or to a modelled slope but this does not work well in practice. From time to time the aquarium décor does need cleaning. Unwieldy conglomerations then prove to be liabilities, not least because delicate branch corals may snap. Of course, a coral stem that lacks a proper base can be cemented to a piece of

Figure 20.   Simple layouts of rocks and corals.

lava rock to keep it from toppling over. Only non-toxic glues that are inert in sea water (two-component epoxy or silicon-based cements) should be used. However, the aquarist should not create anything too large to be lifted easily from the tank. This is essential, should it later prove necessary to remove one or two fishes from the aquarium.

You have been distributing the rocks and corals in a natural-looking arrangement that combines plenty of swimming room with adequate hiding places—designed so that the fishes can always be kept under observation—and some open spaces on the bottom. Now complete the setup with a half-inch layer of sand in the bare areas and a few properly treated seashells. If the tank houses bottom dwellers (e.g., gobies, flatfishes) or species that bury themselves in the sand during the night (e.g., wrasses), cover the larger open spaces with an inch of relatively fine-grained sand. In all the other places use the coarser hard river sand, fine gravel or quartz sand. By mixing the various kinds of sand and gravel, you can obtain a more natural effect than with a uniform bottom cover. For invertebrate aquariums fine-grained sand is preferred.

If a sloping bottom is desired, model a clay relief with depressions for coral formations and terraces that can later be covered with sand. Dry the clay model thoroughly and then fire it in a kiln. Baked potter's clay has a neutral brown tint, which harmonizes well with the aquarium.

The siphons connecting the tank with the filter battery, the air releases, the filter return and other technical equipment are best hidden by corals or rocks. The thermometer and the heater (if not housed in the filter system) should likewise be given inconspicuous positions. It is a good idea to place an air release close to the heater to insure fast, even distribution of heat throughout the tank. The thermostat should be attached to the side panel farthest away from the heater.

After all these preparations have been completed, the tank can be filled with salt water. Place a large saucer on the bottom of the tank and pour the water carefully into this to avoid disturbing the setup. When the tank is three-quarters full, remove the saucer and finish filling. Then the technical apparatus can be put into operation.

If a milky mist clouds the water around a piece of coral, fungi start growing or the water begins to smell, immediately locate any pieces that have not been properly cleaned and repeat the curing procedure.

After the aquarium and filter battery have been allowed to mature for about two weeks, a few hardy fishes can be introduced. If after a few weeks there are still no untoward symptoms, the

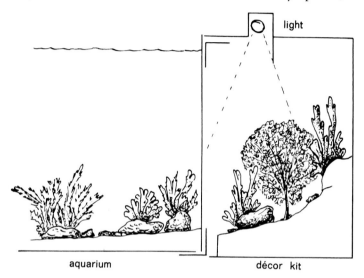

Figure 21. A décor kit placed behind the rear glass panel of the aquarium contributes to an impression of great depth.

population can slowly be augmented. An invertebrate aquarium needs more time to mature, and should not be stocked until a good growth of algae has developed. In Chapter VI we shall discuss how newly bought fishes should be treated.

V   Care of the Aquarium

If proper conditions are maintained in the aquarium, marine tropicals will live for years in captivity. We stress once more, however, that everything depends on the aquarist's willingness to utilize the techniques he has learned in the previous chapters.

There are a few practical rules to observe in all maintenance operations. Wash the hands thoroughly and, most important, rinse off all traces of soap. Any equipment—small nets, siphon tubes, sponges, algae scrapers, etc.—must be made of non-corrosive materials and never have been used for other than aquarium purposes. For safekeeping, store it under sanitary conditions where people cannot accidentally use it for unrelated purposes.

Unplug all electrical equipment—such as heaters, air pump, circulation pump, sterilizers, etc.—during maintenance operations. Water spilling on connections, plugs or sockets may blow a fuse or, worse, shock the aquarist or his fishes.

Another axiom is to limit severely maintenance operations in the aquarium. The less you interfere with the aquarium environment (provided it is healthy!) the better. Unnecessary cleaning every week, month or quarter may prevent the establishment of stable conditions. Above all, avoid constant tinkering with the aquarium—to improve a small detail here or there. Coral fishes need to feel safe in their own familiar, quiet nook. If the layout of the aquarium changes constantly, they will never settle down. Also avoid frequent tapping on the panes to startle out a fish reluctant to leave its hiding place. A newly stocked aquarium, or new specimens in particular, should be left alone as much as possible. Many coral fishes will become so tame that they take food from the owner's fingers, if only they are left in peace at the beginning.

Generally restrict daily maintenance to the removal of uneaten food particles and other detritus that has collected on the bottom. Use a siphon and sieve the water through a closely-woven cloth or a wad of Dacron floss inserted in a large funnel. Return the filtered water to the tank. This strict routine is indispensable in a newly stocked aquarium. Later, when the aquarium has become a well-regulated affair with flourishing algae growth, immediate removal of just a few uneaten food particles is no longer quite as urgent.

To avoid having a dead fish lie unobserved behind rocks or corals for days, check the entire population every day; this is not always easy to do, as certain species may hide for hours. We have previously recommended constructing the necessary hiding places in such a way that they are always open to inspection, but there will almost inevitably be a few places in the aquarium where fishes can hide. Therefore we must know the behavior of each

Harlequin Bass, *Serranus tigrinus*.

species. If it is a retiring one, there is no immediate reason for alarm even after a prolonged retreat. Wrasses and certain other species sometimes hide in the sand for over a week when newly introduced into the aquarium. If, on the other hand, an individual of an active species does not show up for a relatively long time, there is reason to assume that something unfortunate may have happened. The ensuing search operation must, of course, be conducted without frightening the other fishes too much. When a fish has not been seen for 24 hours, the most that can be done is to lift up stones and corals very gently. If the fish does not show up on the second day, watch the condition of the water closely. If there is a slightly milky clouding (caused by bacteria) or the water gives off an odor, the missing fish is probably dead and must be located at once, even if this means taking out half the decorative materials. Smelly water also indicates a need for partial water renewal. Feed very sparingly for a few days.

Besides counting the fishes, close daily observation of them is important; their appearance and behavior can tell much about the quality of the water and the possibly imminent outbreak of a disease. This subject will be discussed in the next chapter.

The daily inspection of our fish stock should be accompanied by a close check of the water's appearance and smell. If the water is a trifle opaque from suspended dirt, the filter system is not doing its job effectively: either its capacity is inadequate because of accumulated substances in one or more of the units, or it is running at too low a speed. If a white haze or clouding is observed in the water, a sudden abundance of organic matter has caused a bacterial population explosion. The cause of the trouble may be in the aquarium (e.g., a dead animal—see above—or a quantity of uneaten food) or in the filter (e.g., reduced capacity).

Several factors may be responsible for diminished filtration. The mechanical filter may have become so badly clogged with dirt that the water flow is impeded. Prevent this situation by cleaning the unit at least once a week. Second, the sand filter may have become densely packed with dirt, although this should not happen with a properly functioning mechanical filter. Try to make a densely packed sand filter permeable again by carefully raking over the surface with a twig or plastic backscratcher. If it is jammed again the next day, remove the top layer and wash it in salt water. Don't scrub it too vigorously, or the bacteria clustering around the sand grains may be lost. Once the aquarium is populated, it simply cannot afford the time needed for the sand filter to "mature" again after the loss of many bacteria. For the same reason never remove all the sand from the filter for washing. If an algae culture is growing on top of the sand filter, it may be necessary to thin out the algae to restore normal circulation.

On the other hand, the cause of the trouble may be in the airlifts; after some time a solid mass of salt and calcium compounds will be deposited on the surface of the connection between the air tube and the lift. Remove this blockage with the aid of a hard plastic rod; alternatively, rinse the airlift with warm water or, if the blockage proves refractory, bathe it in dilute hydrochloric acid.* Perhaps the siphons which carry the water from the tank to the filter battery have become choked with algae. If so, rinse them thoroughly under the tap. A round fiber brush of the type used for cleaning test tubes or teapot spouts is almost indispensable for the maintenance of siphons and airlifts.

If there is a foul odor or a smell of amines (see page 37), inspect the aquarium for dead animals, uneaten food, or, very important, dying algae colonies, and check the capacity of the filter system. If you can not locate the trouble in either place, these possibilities are left: the aquarium has become overcrowded,

---

*Concentrated hydrochloric acid is a very corrosive, very caustic liquid which must be handled with extreme caution. We do not recommend its use. What we are referring to in this book is *dilute* hydrochloric acid. This is a 5 per cent solution available commercially under that name.

and the filter battery can not cope with the organic wastes produced in the tank (check nitrite content!), or something has upset the population balance of the various species of bacteria living in the filter. The former possibility is a very real one. Most aquariums are stocked with young fishes whose total production of wastes is well within the existing filter capacity. As these juveniles grow up, however, their production of waste matter increases and may finally exceed the limits of what the filter system can cope with.

Another very real possibility is that the aquarist succumbs to the temptation of constantly adding more fishes to his thriving collection and thus oversteps the safety margin. If overcrowding is the cause of inadequate filtration, either the population must be cut back drastically or the filter capacity stepped up considerably. If neither is done, the only alternative is to renew the water very frequently. This makeshift procedure, however, will never result in a well-regulated aquarium with a thriving population. In fact, the only effective long-term solution is to cut down the number of animals.

If the water has turned slightly yellow or brownish yellow, replace the charcoal in the filter battery.

Of utmost importance are regular checks of the water's acidity to be sure that it remains between pH 7.8 and 8.5, optimally within the pH 8.0–8.3 range. In a newly set-up or freshly stocked aquarium daily acidity checks will suffice. The technique of pH correction has been described on page 99. If the pH needs correction more than once a month, something may have gone wrong. For example, inadequate aeration may be leaving too much carbon dioxide in the water. In this case, increase the pressure on the air release or add an additional air stone. The water returning to the aquarium from the filter may not be oxygenated sufficiently. Check the pH of the filter outflow—the filtered water may need additional aeration. Use a spray tube, return the water in a thin film over a sheet of glass, or use a special basin for vigorous aeration. The coral sand or ground seashell unit in the filter battery may not be functioning properly. Replace the materials or increase the capacity of the unit. If, after all of these measures, the pH still drops, either the aquarium is overcrowded or the water is due for renewal. But do not, under any circumstances, neglect this condition.

Salinity Checks

Periodic salinity checks are likewise essential. We have repeatedly pointed out the harmful consequences, particularly to algae and invertebrates, of abrupt salinity fluctuations. If the salinity has risen through evaporation, use chlorine-free tap water. If the salinity has dropped, partial water removal is indicated.

Temperature

Routine maintenance also includes temperature checks twice daily. Fluctuations within the range of temperatures suitable for the fishes and algae are harmless, provided they are gradual, but rapid drops are to be avoided. If for some reason (such as a malfunctioning heater) the water temperature has fallen below 68°F, raise the temperature quickly. In emergencies—that is, if the temperature has fallen below 64°F, which is the critical point for marine tropicals—heat some of the aquarium water in an enameled saucepan and pour it gently back into the tank to restore the normal temperature. Be sure that the heated water does not burn any of the inhabitants. If there is no emergency, readjust the heater or replace it promptly.

If a malfunctioning thermostat has raised the temperature to a point (usually above 95°F) at which the fishes are gasping for breath at the surface, or lying helplessly on the bottom, merely switch off the heater, take off the cover glass, and increase the aeration; in extreme cases, dip out a cupful of water and pour it back gently from a height of about twelve inches. Repeat until the temperature has returned to a tolerable level. The sudden drop in temperature that would result from adding cold water might be fatal, whereas slow cooling will generally prevent extensive harm.

Aeration

The air stones should be checked every day; if their output is falling off because the pores have become clogged or the material is disintegrating, then replace them. Boil congested air stones in fresh water or soak them in dilute hydrochloric acid (see footnote, page 119). Sometimes air releases do not work properly because the connection leading to the air pump is blocked by deposited salt and calcium compounds. If neither blockage nor bad air releases are to blame, the air pump may be at fault. The membranes in vibrator pumps eventually wear out and tend to crack, with the result that less air is pumped. It is usually easy to replace these.

If the algae suddenly start dying off, they must be removed as quickly as possible, and part of the water changed. However, things need not get this far out of hand. The fact is that algae, particularly the green variety (rather than the blue-green or the diatoms) give us an early warning that the quality of the water is deteriorating, at first by a diminished rate of growth and later by ceasing to grow altogether. Sometimes a pH correction will improve matters. Generally, however, the symptoms indicate an excess of organic substances in the water, caused by either an inadequate filter capacity (check nitrite content) or over-population. Water renewal may, in any case, be overdue. Too, stunted algae growth may point to a lack of certain trace elements or other essential nutrients; if such is the case, gradual partial water changes will no doubt put things right again. Thus, green algae are very useful in complementing pH checks as a means of assessing water quality.

Naturally, algae growths must be controlled. If they grow too luxuriantly, they may form such dense masses that the lower strata are liable to be smothered. Indeed, the entire culture may perish almost overnight, which in turn may give rise to pollution of the water and calamities among the fishes. Occasional "pruning" of an algae culture will keep the algae young and prevent untimely suffocation.

Cleaning

Regular aquarium chores include window cleaning. Just as in the freshwater aquarium, algae will attach themselves to the glass panes and in time interfere with the observer's enjoyment of the tank's inhabitants. Of course, any panes that we do not normally look through should not be cleaned. This gives the aquarium a more natural look and preserves valuable algae. If the outside of the rear pane has been painted or the décor kit used behind it, scrupulous cleaning of the rear pane is required so as not to spoil the effect. Use the same implements as in the freshwater aquarium, but scrapers made of brass or other corrosive metals are taboo. A razor blade in a plastic handle, handled inexpertly, is liable to cause scratches from which new algae growths can be removed only with great difficulty. Nylon or plastic sponges, the types used for cleaning, are very effective, particularly if the panes are cleaned regularly. If you have delayed so long that a thick coating of algae must be removed, take care to keep the algae from being scattered through the aquarium. Such relatively large amounts of dying organic matter thus introduced into the tank could easily upset the tricky balance of the water. A sponge passed along the pane with upward sweeping movements and squeezed out regularly into a bucket of water will do the job most effectively.

Corals that have become encrusted with dirt should be removed from the tank and cleaned one by one on successive days. Two pairs of hands are really needed for the job, one to lift the corals gently from the bottom and the other to siphon off the dirt that has collected around and under the base of the corals. Make this major cleaning operation coincide with water renewal. You can

Harlequin Sweetlips, *Plectorhynchus chaetodonoides.*

then wash the corals in the aquarium water that has been siphoned off, so that the algae and other organisms growing on the corals will not be killed.

If such cleaning jobs are spaced more or less evenly over the months, there will be no need for the rigorous yearly cleaning frequently recommended—much less monthly overhauls. A complete overhaul, which necessitates catching the fishes and other animals and involves a thorough washing of the stones, corals and bottom layer, is tantamount to setting up a new aquarium. The precarious balance of the aquarium will be completely upset and it will take a considerable time for stable conditions to resume. Regular cleaning on a limited scale will go a long way toward making the complete overhaul unnecessary. If the aquarium has become so fouled that piecemeal cleaning is no longer effective, proceed as follows. First, remove all the corals from the tank, and siphon off the water, together with as much dirt as possible, until four inches are left. Only then do you catch the fishes and other animals and transfer them to a temporary aquarium. Don't try to catch them in a fully set-up aquarium. As soon as they are frightened, fishes will almost invariably hide in the least accessible places. Then, too, the risk of harming the fishes would be very great. Another reason the water level in the tank must be lowered is that many species attempt to jump out of the water when chased. After you take the corals from the tank, check them very carefully, because frightened species often hide there and stay put even when the coral is removed from the water. If this should happen, gently rinse the piece of coral containing the fish in the tank water that is to be replaced and then place it in the temporary aquarium. As soon as the fish leaves its hiding place, remove the coral for cleaning.

Whether the overhaul merely consists of a proper washing of the corals and stones and other fixtures or whether it includes a really thorough scrubbing and disinfection with chlorine depends on your reason for taking apart the aquarium. If the only trouble is the fouling of the aquarium, the best procedure is merely to wash the materials carefully in the salt water which is to be replaced. You will thus preserve at least some part of the algae, microfauna and flora so badly needed in the aquarium. If, however, the entire aquarium needs cleaning because of a stubborn infectious disease, disinfect all the materials in a chlorinated lime

Koran Angelfish, *Pomacanthus semicirculatus*, juvenile form.

bath as described for newly bought corals (see page 112). You can also disinfect the tank itself by soaking it with fresh water to which chlorine bleach has been added.

Finally, aquarium maintenance includes the regular removal of salt deposits from the frame edges and cover glass by means of a sponge rinsed frequently in tap water. To remove streaks of salt left by sea water running down the outside of the panes, use a sponge and plenty of tap water.

Summary

A. Daily checks and maintenance
    1. Remove any dirt and uneaten food from the bottom.
    2. Count fishes and watch for unusual behavior.

3. Assess quality of water by checking for odors and cloudiness.
4. Clean mechanical filter, if necessary.
5. Check pH (in newly set-up or restocked aquarium).
6. Check the temperature twice daily.
7. Check air stones and airlifts.

B. Periodic checks and maintenance
1. Clean panes.
2. Clean dirt-encrusted corals.
3. Check pH (in well-regulated aquarium).
4. Check salinity and replace evaporated water.
5. Thin out dense algae growth.
6. Clean mechanical filter (at least once a week).
7. Check nitrite content.

C. Upsets (see also Chapter VI, page 175)
1. Water slightly opaque due to suspended dirt: check and improve filter capacity.
2. Water hazy or contains milky clouding caused by bacteria: check aquarium for the presence of excess amounts of dead organic matter or dying algae; check filter capacity; partial water renewal required.
3. Water has a rotten odor or smells of amines: partial water renewal required.
4. pH too low: check aeration and, if necessary, increase air flow through the air stones; renew ground shells or coral sand; pH correction possibly needed.
5. pH remains too low or drops too soon after correction: partial water change needed; renew ground shells or coral sand.
6. Green algae die off: check filter capacity; check aquarium for too much organic matter; partial water change possibly required.
7. Water foams a great deal; the froth bubbles do not burst quickly as under normal conditions; the foam is yellowish brown; when the bubbles burst, they leave a dirty brown coating on the panes above the water level: these symptoms are caused by excess concentrations of organic matter in the water or by a disruption of the decomposition process in the filter system. Check the aquarium for the presence of dead organic matter (e.g., uneaten

food, dead animals); check the filter; partial water change required.

Part B: Aquarium Inhabitants

VI Populating the Tank

General Behavior

We have already pointed out that marine tropicals are much more sensitive to change in their environment than are most freshwater fishes, and that it is these differences between the marine aquarium and ocean conditions that make it so much more difficult to keep marine fishes. We have repeatedly stressed that tropical marine fishes cannot tolerate low pH values, relatively low concentrations of ammonia and other inorganic and organic nitrogenous compounds, the clouding of the water and so on. Aquarium maintenance should therefore be aimed at preventing, or at least retarding, these changes as much as possible. Every once in a while irreversible changes in the composition of the water must be countered by a partial water change. The behavior of the fishes can serve as a warning that something is wrong with the aquarium environment; however, to be able to recognize abnormal behavior in fishes, the aquarist must first familiarize himself with their normal behavior.

As few actual behavior studies have been carried out in the fishes' natural habitat, what little we do know about their behavior stems mainly from aquarium observations. The aquarist can, by constant intensive observation of his own fishes, determine what their normal "aquarium behavior" is. In large public aquariums he can study the behavior of the fishes he will want to buy one day, or collect data for comparison with the behavior of his own animals. In general, we can say that most coral fishes, with the exception of the real predators and certain bottom dwellers, exhibit a behavioral pattern marked by great mobility. It is natural for periods of great activity to alternate with quiet spells. However, if normally mobile species become languid and apathetic, or hide too much, it may well be that faulty environmental factors are to blame. Fading colors, loss of appetite or accelerated respiration likewise indicate faulty environment, although these symptoms may equally be due to disease or to harassment by tank fellows.

Whenever the fishes show abnormal symptoms, first check the aquarium itself: water temperature, salinity, pH, odor, clarity and, of course, the filter system. If all environmental factors are normal and the animals show no actual disease symptoms, change part of the water. If no marked improvement is shown within 24 hours, the animals are probably sick, and other measures must be taken; these will be discussed later in this chapter (pages 160–180).

Aggressiveness and Territoriality

Most tropical marine fishes, and certainly the numerous true coral species, exhibit territorial behavior. This means that both in the wild and in the aquarium an individual claims a section of the habitat as its own, and defends this territory fiercely against other fishes, particularly those of the same species. The size of the territory varies but, generally speaking, small species maintain smaller territories and large species larger ones. Some species occupy a territory only during the spawning season, but most defend a small section of reef all year round. In the aquarium, territorial species must have ample room so that the territories of individuals do not overlap. If a fish fails to establish a territory, it may become very aggressive toward some or all of the aquarium inhabitants; on the other hand, it may pine away. If there is only enough room for one individual of a given species to establish a territory, it will forcibly chase away all its less fortunate fellows. This aggressiveness may lead to immediate casualties; alternatively, the continually harassed individuals may hide in obscure crevices where they can not get enough food, and eventually die anyway. Frequently, too, such a browbeaten individual can be seen hanging in a corner just below the surface, trying to prolong its miserable existence. In the wild, coral fishes are probably much less aggressive than in the close confines of the tank. On the reef the animals can take evasive action and need not come to blows; it is generally sufficient for the "landlord" of a territory to show itself to an intruder. The flashy colors of many species are important in this respect, since they advertise the presence of the "lord of the land." Animals of like species thus receive early warning and can avoid violent encounters.

Examples of intraspecific intimidation can often be seen in a large enough tank. An individual, after approaching to within six to eight inches of a territory holder, will abruptly turn tail. The stronger of the two will pursue the other briefly, but the further the pursuer gets from the center of its territory, the more rapidly its defensive and offensive urges will diminish, and it will give up the pursuit at the invisible edge of its territory. If the tank is too small for evasive tactics, the weaker animal will be set upon, and a violent fight is bound to ensue. It is frequently impossible to predict under what circumstances a certain species will become aggressive and which of the tank fellows will be the target. Individuals of the same species are the most likely victims, but often other species of the same genus, or even species in no way related to the aggressor, may be persecuted. A superficial resemblance between two individuals is often enough to arouse aggression. In Chapter VII we shall frequently give the degree of aggressiveness to be expected of a particular species, although of course there may be large individual variations.

Other factors, too, affect the behavior of the aquarium inhabitants. When the animals have had an abundant meal, they are less aggressive than when they are hungry. This leads to the hypothesis that food, no less than territoriality, is an important factor in arousing mutual aggressiveness. An aquarium population that is fed so well that the animals are hardly ever hungry will show little mutual aggressiveness. If, however, the fishes are fed so sparingly that they are hungry much or all of the time, there will be a commensurate increase in aggressiveness. At feeding time a species that is not normally belligerent may suddenly become aggressive. We shall return to this subject later.

The degree of aggressiveness is also affected by lighting conditions in the tank. As long as the aquarium is fully lighted, many species are not aggressive, or only to a small degree. As soon as the lights are dimmed, however, certain species suddenly become combative and start chasing other individuals away, no doubt to secure their hiding places for the night. This change in behavior can be experimentally induced at any moment of the day by

Koran Angelfish, *Pomacanthus semicirculatus*.

reducing the light above the tank. This proves that the behavior of these species is not governed by a fixed time rhythm (circadian rhythm), which in many species regulates the alternate periods of activity and rest; there are, however, species that do exhibit a recurrent 24-hour behavioral pattern, which reflects a "built-in biological clock." These are generally very active in the early hours of the morning and again in the late afternoon. Other species are active practically all day long or only at night. The predators, in general, hunt either in the early morning or in the afternoon or only at night. Most species are busy all day long getting food. When night falls, they cease their activities and return to their hiding places.

Mutual aggressiveness may cause great difficulties in the aquarium. It is a common occurrence for one or more individuals to become very aggressive suddenly in a tank in which the inhabitants have been housed together for a long time and in which the fishes seemed to have developed a mutual tolerance. Sometimes this combative behavior disappears quickly, sometimes it lasts longer, and in some cases this sudden intolerance may prove permanent. Such a flare-up may claim casualties, so the aquarist must always be on the alert.

It is often difficult to say what causes these outbreaks. Attainment of sexual maturity may be one cause; another, the fact that as the tank inhabitants grow, they attempt to expand their territories and, as the tank can't expand, they come into conflict with their neighbors who have the same intention.

Aggressiveness nearly always crops up when newcomers are introduced. The newcomers may be hounded so mercilessly that even if they are not killed outright, they may never get a chance to settle down. If they do succeed in escaping temporarily by hiding in dark corners, they are generally doomed anyway, since they are attacked when they emerge to eat. Even when a newcomer is tolerated and no longer automatically pursued whenever it shows itself, it may nevertheless be doomed to a slow starvation, for in its position at the very bottom of the established pecking order, it dare not assert itself in the general scramble for food. For such an individual, try to drop some food where it can reach it before being driven away, always remembering to avoid polluting the tank with uneaten excess. The situation described here is more likely to occur when young animals are introduced into an established community. However, it is difficult to make predictions. Sometimes a newcomer is left completely alone, while another of the same species is killed immediately.

Often a temporary glass partition through which the fish can see and thus become accustomed to each other helps to cushion the shock of the new introduction. Even a large jar can be floated in the tank as a means of segregating the established and new fishes. (Be sure to include an air stone.) Even those breeding traps sold for freshwater tanks may be used, but don't use one with metal hangers.

When large numbers of naturally aggressive species are crowded into a relatively small space, their behavior pattern is often disrupted to such an extent that their normal aggressiveness is temporarily suppressed. It is for this reason that overaggressiveness is rarely observed in the dealer's overcrowded tank. As a result, the hobbyist may buy an apparently unaggressive fish that turns out to be extremely intolerant when released in the home aquarium.

Populating the Aquarium

What should we look for when buying fishes? This question may seem superfluous, since it should be possible to rely on the dealer's experience and integrity. However, while many dealers do have enough professional knowledge to give their clients really good advice, the fact remains that aquarium keeping is as much an art as a science. Where one person with the knowledge and knack can keep certain fishes together with no difficulty at all, another may encounter only problems. Add to this the intraspecific variations in temperament and the different conditions found in the full-time professional tank as opposed to the amateur tank, and it soon becomes obvious that the hobbyist must educate himself to make his own decisions and rely on his dealer only for general guidance.

First, and most important, the hobbyist must make sure to select specimens strong enough to survive the shock of being transferred to the home aquarium. In assessing the health of a fish, the first thing to watch for is symptoms of malnutrition. The animal must have a well-filled body; its stomach must not be pinched or concave and certainly not have a depression just behind the top of the head. This symptom is most likely to be found in surgeon-, butterfly- and angelfishes. It means that the animal is completely off its food or has been on a faulty diet for a long time. Even experts usually can not save emaciated fishes. If the hobbyist buys fishes of species known to be finicky eaters, it is reasonable to ask the dealer to prove that the animals are eating.

Another indication of condition is the color of the fishes. Healthy specimens have bright colors and glossy skin. Specimens with skin injuries should only be bought with the condition that the wounds heal. Damaged fins are unimportant as long as there are only small bites on the fins and the edges of the wounds are not grayish white or bloodshot. This kind of fin damage is almost inevitable in overcrowded tanks, and it is surprising how quickly they heal if the animal is otherwise healthy.

Another important factor is the condition of the fish's eyes. Avoid specimens whose eyes are damaged or covered with a white film or protrude too far.

A fish's swimming pattern is also important. It is usually best to bypass abnormal swimmers, although sometimes the abnormal behavior is due to crowded conditions. If a fish has difficulty keeping its balance in the water (swims up and down jerkily, tends to topple over when resting, etc.), it is really sick and unfit to be sold. The same goes for fishes that remain in a corner near the surface or float listlesly about.

Finally, take a good look to make sure the animals do not have a skin disease, nor breathe too fast. In a later section we will discuss the symptoms of skin disease.

Naturally it is important to know whether the intended acquisition can be combined with the fishes already in the aquarium. Only too often aquarists buy young predatory specimens and later find them eating their smaller tankmates. Mishaps are also bound to occur if slow eaters, specialized feeders or timid, retiring species are put with active, gross-feeding species.

Finally, importers still bring in species that can not yet—or only under exceptional circumstances—be kept alive in captivity. It is best not to buy these species, but to leave them to the specialists until more is learned about their maintenance.

The number of fishes to be maintained in the marine aquarium depends on the size of the tank, the capacity of the biological filter and of the ozonizer, the presence of flourishing algae colonies, the feeding method and, of course, the particular species to be kept. With so many variable factors, it is difficult to lay down any hard and fast rules. To remain on the safe side, the aquarist should figure on six to eight fishes not bigger than three or four inches for every 27 gallons (100 liters) of water. The number of larger fishes should be reduced proportionally. The more fish that crowd the marine aquarium, the more frequent the need for water renewal and the greater the risk of sick fish. Keeping down the numbers, therefore, is just as essential as good filter equipment or regular water renewal. If young specimens are bought, take into account their size at maturity.

Lifespan is also important to consider when buying fish. Views differ widely about the longevity of marine tropicals in captivity. Many aquarists consider a species hardy and easy to keep if it stays alive in the aquarium a year or so; two years or more they consider exceptional.

In the author's opinion this is a mistake. If a fish whose natural longevity is approximately five, six or seven years can not be kept alive in the aquarium for more than ten or twelve months, either they should not be regarded as easy to keep, or there is something wrong with the treatment they are receiving. We will not be able

Lionfish, *Pterois volitans*.

to say that aquarium and fish-care techniques have been perfected until we are able to keep marine fishes alive for at least the better part of their natural lifespan. Unfortunately, few studies have been made of the lifespan of fishes in the wild. Generalizations have derived, however, from many years of practical experience with numerous species.

Small fishes—such as those belonging to the genera *Amphiprion*, *Dascyllus*, *Pomacentrus*, *Abudefduf* and *Anthias*—have a normal life expectancy in captivity of three to six years. Beyond five years they are apt to show old age symptoms. These may be due to captivity, or simply be an indication that in the wild their lifespan is not much more. Larger fishes—for instance, species of *Lutjanus*, *Diploprion*, *Maemulon*, triggerfishes, swellfishes and puffers—will live in captivity from five to eight years or more. Still larger fishes—such as *Platax*, *Epinephelus*, *Promicrops*, *Pterois* and *Carans* —may live ten years or more in captivity. Seahorses, pipefishes and shrimpfishes, in their natural surroundings, live from one to three years and, of course, have brief lifespans in captivity as well.

We do have, then, some information on lifespan. Thus, if butterflies or angelfishes or clownfishes can not be kept alive for more than a year or two, it would appear that proper environmental conditons are not being maintained. It is true that some species are imported which can live only under exceptional artificial conditions. These are best left to the specialist, however, who may be able to provide ways and means to sustain these forms of delicate fish life.

Finally, before purchasing new fishes, the reader should consult Chapter VII, which is devoted to the characteristics of the various species; it may prevent disappointment.

Quarantine

If you are populating a new aquarium for the first time, you can put the fishes right in. If, however, you are adding new animals to an already existing collection, you must first quarantine them in a separate aquarium (the quarantine tank) for some time before transferring them to the exhibition aquarium. This second, smaller tank may also prove useful as a hospital tank for sick fishes from the mixed aquarium and provide temporary accommodation if the main aquarium must be cleaned.

It is necessary to quarantine new fishes for several reasons. First, newly imported fishes are generally not in tiptop condition, due to the deleterious effects of capture, storage at the exporter's in the tropics and continual changes in the temperature, salinity and composition of the water. The poor health of such fishes sometimes results in the damage or inadequate secretion of their mucous skin coating. These fishes are in no condition to cope with infections by skin parasites and other parasitic forms (always present in the aquarium, albeit usually in small numbers). Nor are they in a condition fit to face the competition in an established aquarium. The quarantine period allows them time to build up their health.

Second, recently imported fishes may be latent or overt carriers of parasites, which are liable to spread to the aquarium population. Even fishes that have been at the dealer's for a long time may be infected, though they show no visible symptoms. The conditions under which dealers keep their fish can hardly ever be ideal. (This is in no way intended to disparage the bona fide dealer. It merely points up what difficulties he faces in maintaining his usually large supplies.) The constant influx of newly imported fishes greatly enhances the risk of repeated infection to fishes he has had for quite some time. It is the buyer's own fault if a fish introduced straight from the dealer's infects the rest of the aquarium or, at best, dies prematurely. Even fishes acquired from a fellow aquarist ought to be quarantined. Any change of environment, combined with the rigors of transpor-tation, may cause a latent disease to break out. Many a marine aquarist who has failed to quarantine has found to his dismay that a single diseased fish can even kill off a whole aquarium population. Quarantining reduces such a risk by as much as 90 per cent.

Third, newly bought animals must be given time to become acclimated to the water composition in the aquarium. The better their condition—improved by quarantining—the more quickly and easily they will adapt.

Some aquarists, on the basis of their experience with the fresh-water aquarium, reject quarantine as superflous. These must be reminded of a basic difference in the origins of marine and fresh-water species. The marine fishes have, without exception, been caught in their native habitat, while the numerous strains of freshwater fishes have been tank-bred for thousands of gener-ations.* These "domesticated" creatures are much hardier than those fishes caught in the wild. (Actually, quarantine for even the freshwater aquarium could prevent many casualties, particularly for those fishes just imported from their native habitat.)

The Quarantine Tank

Actually, a quarantine tank is nothing but a second, smaller marine tank made of materials inert in sea water, as we have described earlier. It requires the same handling as the normal marine aquarium, but need not be as expensive or intricate, especially if only a few specimens are quarantined from time to time.

Water movement is just as important in the quantine tank as in the display aquarium. The air pump in the main aquarium must therefore have sufficient reserve capacity, or a smaller air pump be bought for the quarantine tank alone.

Filtration presents a less serious problem in the quarantine tank than in the main aquarium. The water gets less clouded, for it

---

*While spawning, particularly in large public aquariums, is not unusual, saltwater fry continue to prove extremely difficult to rear. There is no doubt, however, that before too long the secret will be learned, and saltwater fishes will become as commonplace as tank-raised freshwater fishes.

contains only a few animals for relatively short periods of time; thus a simple inside filter or a simplified outside filter (Figures 5 and 11, pages 74 and 84) will suffice. An immersible heater unit (with a thermostat) and a thermometer are indispensable. The size of the tank will depend on the species to be quarantined; a 15-gallon tank of 24 × 12 × 12 inches will probably be adequate for most.

There are two ways to set up a quarantine tank. The first is the "natural" method, in which the natural environment is duplicated as closely as possible. The quarantine tank in this case is a normal aquarium, in operation all the time even when there are no animals to be quarantined. Algae colonies are required, as are plenty of hiding places; intensive filtration is also needed. Now and again it may be necessary to place an animal in the tank for a time.

The advantage here is mainly "psychological": algae provide food; the fishes settle down more quickly because they have hiding places; the water attains a normal balance and there is a filter system. But there are serious disadvantages, too: it is impossible to watch the fishes closely because there are many obstructions; because other fishes have been kept in it, the water is not sterile, so parasites may be present at the initiation of the quarantine period; and medication is difficult because it may kill off the algae and other microorganisms and cause accumulations of dead organic matter. For these reasons the "natural" method is severely limited. It may have uses if there are very young fishes that can not yet be put into the mixed tank and must be kept on their own until they have grown quite a bit, or if a species must be allowed to "graze" on algae before it can be induced to accept other food as well. In that case, however, it is preferable to isolate the animals in a bare "hygienic" tank for several days and administer prophylactic drugs before putting them into the "natural" quarantine tank.

The "hygienic" method involves keeping the tank as bare as possible, without even a bottom cover unless this happens to be necessary for a particular species. There must be no algae, and the hiding places must be few and open to inspection so that the fishes can be observed easily. Fill the hygienic quarantine tank with fresh salt water each time it is to be used. It is best to get it ready only a few days before the new animals arrive. For hiding places, use flower pots turned upside down with holes knocked out of their sides, pieces of shale slanting against the tank walls, short lengths of plastic pipe or bricks piled on top of each other, depending on the needs of the animals.

These materials have certain advantages: they are easy to clean and disinfect, and the fishes can be readily observed inside them and, if need be, removed. The inside or outside filter is filled with activated charcoal, Dacron floss and ground seashells or coral sand. The filter requires scrupulous attention and should be cleaned as soon as even a little dirt accumulates there. If drugs must be administered in the quarantine aquarium, use only Dacron floss and coarse gravel in the filter.

The "hygienic" method is preferable to the "natural." The composition of the water is known; the water is not infected with parasites at the start of quarantine; the animals can be observed at all times; preventive medication is possible without killing off algae; treatment of diseases is possible; the filter can be cleaned easily and the medium renewed whenever necessary. The only

Long-Nosed Butterflyfish, *Chelmon rostratus*, with Cleaner Shrimp, *Hippolysmata grabhami*.

disadvantage is that a bare tank without algae growths may possibly be "psychologically" unacceptable to the fishes. Practical experience, however, shows this disadvantage to be negligible. All the same, if the aquarium proves too bare for a certain species, put in a few additional pieces of upright slate.

After the quarantine aquarium has been set up and the air stones and filter have been in operation for a few days, purchase the new specimens. The first concern is acclimating them slowly to the water of the quarantine tank. Check the salinity of the water in which the dealer sent them home so that the salinity of the quarantine tank can be adapted to it. See also that the water temperature is the same or a bit higher. Then remove about half the water from the plastic container bag and put an air stone in it. Gradually fill the bag with water from the quarantine tank. Make a siphon from a plastic air line, using a spring clothespin to pinch the tube and slow the flow of water. This process should take about 15 to 30 minutes. To transfer the animals to the quarantine tank, close the top of the plastic bag and put it upside down under the water surface. Then open the bag slowly and squeeze the other end gently, to release the water and animals without commotion.

It might be argued that this process incurs a risk of introducing infected water into the quarantine tank. However, if the transport water is infected, the fishes that are in it are already infected, so it really makes no difference.

Now that the animals are in quarantine, it is absolutely necessary to inspect closely for skin parasites twice daily. If no parasites are visible after a week, slowly raise the water temperature to between 82° and 86°F. At this higher temperature, skin parasites will become visible more quickly, as their metabolic and reproductive rate will speed up. After a week the temperature can be lowered to normal. Even if there are still no signs of disease, take the precaution of adding a non-specific prophylactic, such as copper or zinc sulfate, to destroy any possible parasites. (See Diseases, page 160.)

Feeding techniques during the quarantine period are, of course, very important. If the animals accept normal food immediately, feed them as much as they will eat. If not, try to find out what they want by offering them a variety of foods. Once the hobbyist has discovered a food they like, he should stick to it for about two weeks, and then gradually induce them to take other things.

After three weeks of quarantine—preferably four—healthy animals can be put into the mixed aquarium. (Haste makes waste, especially for aquarists.) If the fishes remain skinny or show poor appetite, however, it is best to continue the quarantine until they are in perfect condition.

The first step in transferring fishes from the quarantine to the display tank is to insure that the water in the quarantine tank is the same as that in the aquarium. Replace some of the quarantine water with water from the aquarium and repeat this at intervals until the water quality of the two tanks is as alike as possible.

Since newcomers to an established aquarium community are often attacked, take measures to prevent casualties. The only safe method is one by which the older inhabitants can get used to the newcomers without being able to get at them. Put the newcomers in a perforated glass or plastic container inside the tank, as described earlier. When the older inhabitants find their initial aggression thwarted by the transparent container, they will soon learn to accept the newcomers' presence. After about a week, release them, and they will probably be left in peace. To prevent further aggressiveness, feed the others just before letting the newcomers go.

The only other safe method, certainly not preferable to the first, is to empty the whole aquarium, set it up afresh and put in all the original fishes and the newcomers. Such a rigorous method is justified only if the aquarium requires a thorough cleaning anyway.

Metabolism and Nutrition

Metabolism is the sum of the processes whereby body tissues are built up and broken down. The chemical changes that occur provide energy for life functions and enable the organism to transform nourishment into new body tissue. Limitations of space prevent us from discussing these processses in great detail. However, the following general discussion of metabolism and nutrition in fishes should suffice for our purposes.

Fishes, like all other living creatures, require the proper foods in order to carry out metabolic functions. Carbohydrates, proteins and fats, as well as minerals and vitamins, must be present and in the correct proportion in the diet if metabolism is to proceed properly.

Unfortunately, little as yet is known about aquarium fish nutrition; this is because investigation thus far has been limited largely to fishes raised for human consumption. Yet proper nutrition is essential if our fishes are to develop to their full potential.

Fats

The energy potential of a food is measured in calories and, weight for weight, fats are twice as rich in calories as are carbohydrates and proteins. Fats are broken down in the intestines into mono-glycerides, diglycerides and fatty acids. Their final destination is the liver, where they are stored until needed for energy.

The tissue of the natural prey of wild fishes contains only one to two per cent fat. A fish in captivity should not be fed a diet containing more than five per cent fat, or it will suffer such ill effects as fatty liver degeneration, decreased egg production, reduced chances of successful hatchings and accumulations of fat around the internal organs. Also the aquarist should be aware that fats in prepared foods can turn rancid and cause serious metabolic disorders.

Carbohydrates

Fishes obtain carbohydrates—sugars and starches—by eating vegetable foods, as well as animal prey that has fed on vegetable foods. (The animal body cannot manufacture carbohydrates.) After carbohydrates are ingested, the body converts them to fats and to glycogen, a starch-like substance stored in the liver and muscles. Glycogen is converted to sugar by the body and then used as fuel for physical activities.

Although carbohydrates are an essential part of nutrition, a diet too rich in carbohydrates proves harmful. The fishes that are not vegetable eaters should not be fed more than about six grams of carbohydrates per kilogram of body weight a day.

Research conducted in American fisheries has indicated that trout can not cope with a diet containing more than nine to twelve per cent carbohydrates. Sardines fed mainly on carbo-

Marginate Damselfish, *Dascyllus marginatus*.

hydrates were shown to suffer from fat accumulation around the organs; those fed on proteins grew better and did not gain excess weight.

Proteins

Protein is composed of amino acids, necessary to build, maintain and replace body tissue. Certain amino acids can be synthesized by the body. Those that can not—approximately ten of them—must be ingested in the diet. Protein containing all ten of these "essential" amino acids is called "complete" protein. Certain body functions may be seriously impaired if one or more of these amino acids is missing. Incomplete proteins—those not containing all the essential amino acids—can be combined in the diet in order to supply all the essentials.

Experiments have demonstrated that trout require about twenty-eight per cent pure protein to insure health and normal growth. Furthermore, animal proteins are more nutritious than vegetable proteins. In fact, prolonged feeding on vegetable proteins has led to metabolic disorders, sometimes accompanied by blindness and anemia.

Enzymes

Without enzymes (also called biocatalysts) the body can not digest food. Enzymes, which the body itself produces, break down the raw materials of ingested food into components that can pass through the intestinal wall into the blood. To better understand their function, let us look at the digestive tract of the fish.

Unlike most other vertebrates, the fish has no enzyme-producing glands in its mouth. With mouth and esophagus it processes the food mechanically, cutting it up and mixing it by chewing. The digestive process starts in the stomach, where hydrochloric acid and *pepsinogen* are produced. The hydrochloric acid maintains a pH in most fishes' stomachs between 4.0 and 7.0, breaking down all calcium-containing substances in the food (such as bones and other skeletal parts of animal prey) and inhibiting bacteria growth that might otherwise take place in the stomach.

Measurements have shown that the surface layer of a fish swallowed by a predator is much more acidic (pH 1.2–3.0) than the predator's stomach itself. A few millimeters inside the prey, however, the pH is 3.4–5.0. Because the hydrochloric acid infiltrates the prey quite gradually, the rate of digestion is correspondingly slow; this partially explains why a predator (a pike, for instance) takes large prey only once every three to five days.

Hydrochloric acid is also needed to activate *pepsinogen*, which it changes into the enzyme *pepsin*. Pepsin partly breaks down proteins into peptones and enhances the action of the enzyme *trypsin* (which also acts on proteins). It enters the intestines via the pancreatic duct as *trypsinogen*, where it is changed and activated by *enterokinase*, an enzyme secreted in the intestine.

The enzyme *amylase* reduces carbohydrates to simple sugars, such as glucose. These pass through the intestinal wall and into the blood. Surplus sugar is stored in the liver as glycogen. The liver itself continuously produces bile salts and stores them in the gall bladder. These salts act on the fats as an emulsifier, breaking them down into smaller particles in much the same manner as soap breaks down oil or grease. (In experiments on fishes in which the bile ducts were severed, more than fifty per cent of the fats left the body undigested.) These globules are digested by the enzyme *lipase*, which breaks them down into simple fatty acids, such as glycerol.

It appears that in some fishes the cells of the stomach wall itself absorb and further break down a certain proportion of partially digested proteins and fats. This is called intracellular digestion.

The acid environment of the stomach is separated from the alkaline environment of the intestine by the pylorus or pyloric valve. When this sphincter relaxes, a portion of chyme (semi-digested food mixed with hydrochloric acid) enters the intestine. The pylorus closes while the acid reacts with prosecretin, the inactive form of a hormone produced in the intestinal wall. (Hormones are substances which relay chemical "messages" via the bloodstream.) The reaction changes prosecretin to secretin, the active form, which is then absorbed into the blood, reaching the pancreatic organ in a few seconds and stimulating the secretion of its enzymes into the digestive tract. These enzymes contain sodium bicarbonate, which neutralizes the hydrochloric acid in the intestine—whereupon the pylorus opens again and the process is repeated.

The pancreatic organ lies near the pylorus and produces

Moorish Idol, *Zanclus cornutus.*

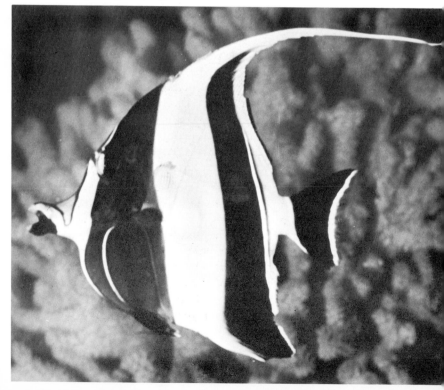

enzymes in a manner comparable to the pancreas of mammals. In fishes, however, the gland is "diffuse"; a part of it may penetrate into the liver and gall bladder. For this reason it need not necessarily be regarded as a separate organ.

Curiously, several species return part of the food that has already passed the pylorus back into the stomach. This might be regarded as a kind of rumination' and is reminiscent of another curious aspect of the digestion of herbivorous fishes. In the intestines of herbivorous mammals, such as cows and deer, there are extensive bacterial fauna that play an important part in the digestion of certain parts of vegetable food (cellulose, lignin) that cannot be broken down by the animals' own enzymes. When, antibiotics are administered to herbivores, their digestion is often badly upset because the antibiotic destroys some or all of the intestinal bacteria.

Remarkably, neither herbivorous nor carnivorous fishes possess such characteristic bacteria. Some bacteria may be found in the intestine, it is true, but the assortment of species depends entirely on the food intake and the water. They are all species that have nothing to do with digestion but are simply taken up from the environment. Examination of a fish that has gone without food for several weeks will show that its intestinal tract contains practically no bacteria. Therefore, fishes apparently digest a very large proportion of their vegetable food without help from other organisms.

Certain enzymes found in many invertebrates (mainly marine animals that live on vegetable matter such as algae) specifically aid the digestion of this kind of food. These invertebrates have no symbiotic bacteria either; the enzymes themselves enable them to digest the food. It would seem that herbivorous fishes manufacture at least three enzymes—*lichenase*, *salicinase* and *amygdalase*—which apparently facilitate this task. Herbivorous fishes are the only vertebrates possessing these enzymes, none of which have ever been found in mammals.

It is also interesting to note that the passage of food through the intestine of a fish is probably the slowest in the whole animal kingdom. As in other poikilothermic animals, the rate of digestion is influenced by the temperature of the environment. A rise of 18°F (10°C) speeds up digestion two to four times; a drop of 18°F (10°C) reduces the rate two to four times. The aquarist will therefore want to keep his fishes at a low temperature when food is scarce—when he is on vacation, for instance.

Vitamins

After this brief survey of the digestive process, we come to a discussion of the additional substances required for anabolism, the manufacturing or build-up part of metabolism. A fish fed only carbohydrates, proteins and fats would sicken after a while because of a vitamin deficiency.

We know very little about the part that vitamins play in the body—even in mammals, whose needs have been the object of much study. As far as we can tell, vitamins (like enzymes) have a kind of catalytic effect essential to the various body processes. Therefore, most animals, including fishes, require certain vitamins in minute quantities. Some vitamins can be synthesized by the body (different animals manufacture different ones), while others must be ingested. These statements are based on experiments in which one vitamin or another was excluded from the fish's diet; if deficiency symptoms occurred, it was assumed that the absence of the vitamin was the cause. On the other hand, an overdose of vitamins, particularly the fat soluble ones, may also be harmful to the organism and cause specific disease phenomena.

Ocellated Puffer, *Canthigaster margaritatus.*

The vitamins can be divided into two large groups: fat-soluble vitamins (A, D, E and K) and water-soluble vitamins (B-complex and C).

Vitamin A. In fishes this vitamin is found in the liver and the eyes. It is also found in the eggs of various species. Both vitamins A_1 and A_2 are found in the liver. A_2 is present in the eyes of freshwater fish, and probably only A_1 in the eyes of marine fish; both A vitamins occur in the eyes of species that regularly migrate from the sea to fresh water and vice versa (euryhaline fishes).

Vitamin A is formed by animals from carotene, which is found in algae, higher plants and minute crustaceans (including *Daphnia* and *Cyclops*) that feed on plankton algae. Carotene is probably converted into vitamin A in the intestinal mucous membrane of fishes. Carotene deficiency can cause fatty liver degeneration and endanger protein metabolism. Vitamin A probably also plays a part in the formation of the mucous membranes and the skin of fishes, just as with warm-blooded animals, but this has not yet been proved. If true, vitamin A deficiency could cause an increased susceptibility to infectious skin diseases. It is also possible, but not an established fact, that vitamin A deficiency causes eye conditions in fishes as it does in mammals.

Vitamin B. This vitamin actually consists of a large complex of different vitamins, all of which are found in green plants. In fishes, too, many B vitamins have been found—vitamins B_1 and B_2, for example, in the muscles and particularly the heart. B_1 (thiamine) is primarily responsible for proper carbohydrate metabolism, and a deficiency will cause enteritis and other disorders of the digestive tract. Trout need a daily intake of 0.15—0.18 mg per kilogram of body weight.

Vitamin B_2 (riboflavin) has been found indispensable for the growth of young trout; it is important in fat and protein metabolism, as well as in vision processes. Pantothenic acid, niacin, B_6 (pyridoxine), biotin (which used to be called vitamin H) and vitamin B_{12} have all been found in fish. The latter—abundantly present in phytoplankton—is indispensable for the formation of red blood corpuscles. If the diet of a trout is lacking in vitamin B_6, the same symptoms occur as when vitamin B_2 (riboflavin) is absent. Even blindness may result. A deficiency of biotin and

Orbiculate Batfish, *Platax orbicularis*.

pantothenic acid will cause a loss of appetite, which (in trout, at least) will be followed by a skin ailment called "blue shine disease." The required daily intake of biotin is 0.02—0.04 mg per kilogram of body weight—a tiny amount, but essential for well-being.

Vitamin C. Little is known about the vitamin C requirements of fish. In adult fishes relatively high concentrations have been found in eggs as well as in the ductless glands. It is therefore undoubtedly important to their health. The natural sources for vitamin C are tuberous plants like potatoes, nearly all fresh vegetables, many fruits, germinated seeds, alfalfa leaf meal, green algae and water plants. In animal organs it is found mainly in the liver, spleen, kidneys, adrenal glands and eye lens. In mammals vitamin C plays a part in the formation of antibodies as well as in mineral metabolism.

It has been demonstrated that excessive doses may be very harmful to young fishes. Young trout have been killed by an excess of vitamin C in their diet.

Vitamin D. This vitamin is not a single substance, but comprises ten or eleven sterols (a type of alcohol, e.g., cholesterol) that are involved in the prevention and treatment of rickets. Two of these, D_2 and D_3, are found in fishes. D_3 occurs mainly in the liver of bony fishes. In mammals it is produced in the skin by the action of the ultraviolet rays in sunlight on the provitamin 7-dehydro-cholesterol. (A provitamin is a precursor that can be converted into a vitamin by the body.) We don't know whether fishes produce it the same way. It seems unlikely, since ultraviolet light can not penetate very far into water. For fishes living at great depths, it is out of the question. Still debatable is whether fishes can synthesize vitamin D themselves or must obtain it from their diet. Possibly they do both.

Plankton contains small amounts of vitamin D itself. Larger amounts of the provitamins are found in plankton, and also in worms (including *Tubifex*), snails, rotifers and algae and, of course, in the internal organs (especially the liver) of fishes that are eaten. Vitamin D does not occur in plants, although its provitamins do.

Vitamin D deficiency is thought to cause weak and improper bone formation in fishes, just as in other cold- and warm-blooded animals, because of the vitamin's ability to regulate calcium and phosphorus metabolism. Since vitamin D is fat-soluble, it is stored in the body.

Vitamin E. This vitamin, which has also been found in fishes, is any or all of a group of compounds called tocopherols. In warm-blooded animals it plays a part in reproduction, growth, heart activity, muscular coordination and functioning of the pituitary gland. In addition, it acts as a fat preservative, protecting vitamin A and carotene (provitamin A) in the intestinal tract against rancid fatty acids. We know next to nothing of how this vitamin affects fish metabolism, however. We do know that doses of vitamin E may cure fishes suffering from fatty liver degeneration. Water fleas do not mature sexually if their diet lacks vitamin E; we do not know whether this is also true of fishes.

Vitamin E is found primarily in water plants and algae, so fishes may directly or indirectly (via animal prey) satisfy their requirements of this vitamin.

Vitamin K. In mammals this fat-soluble vitamin, found in certain green vegetables, is associated with blood clothing. Its function in fishes, however, is not yet known.

The Use of Vitamins

In summary, little is known of the part that vitamins play in the metabolism and other bodily processes of fishes. From dietary experiments on freshwater fishes it has become clear that they do need vitamins; however, which ones and how much of each must still be determined.

The necessary vitamins are probably supplied in sufficient amounts when fish are given a varied diet, so vitamin supplements are usually unnecessary. There are, nevertheless, situations when doses of vitamins in empirical quantities do seem justified—when certain species do not deposit fertilized eggs, for instance, or in periods of food scarcity when the animals can not be given a varied diet. In such cases a multivitamin preparation can be added to the food in very small quantities. The correct dosage depends on size and species. If certain fish species prove difficult to maintain in captivity because of susceptibility to skin infections, a relatively high dose of vitamin A can be given. There may be other situations in which the use of vitamins appears justified, but for a normal community aquarium fed a varied diet, extra doses of vitamins seem superfluous and inadvisable.

The following table shows which vitamins or their precursors occur in the foods suitable for our marine fishes.

> *Vitamin A and carotene:* beef and fish livers, crustaceans, arthropods, egg yolk, algae, lettuce, spinach, water plants.
> *Vitamins B_2 and B_6:* crustaceans, beef, beef liver, fish, mussels, chicken eggs, spinach, lettuce, yeast.
> *Pantothenic acid, niacin and vitamin B_{12}:* green, brown and red algaes; lettuce; yeast; beef; beef liver; egg yolk; mussels.
> *Biotin:* yeast, beef liver, egg yolk, wheat germ oil.
> *Vitamin C:* green algae, water plants, lettuce, spinach, beef liver, fish eggs.
> *Vitamin D:* earthworms, mealworms, *Tubifex*, egg yolk, snails, fish liver, water fleas, shrimps.

Vitamin E: green algae, lettuce, spinach, egg yolk, wheat germ oil.

Vitamin K: beef liver, lettuce, spinach, water fleas.

Minerals

Minerals that play a part in metabolic processes are calcium, sodium, potassium, magnesium, chlorine, iron, copper, manganese, sulphur and phosphorus. It would take us too far afield to discuss extensively the role of these elements in the fish's body, so we shall make only a few remarks on the subject.

Sodium and potassium control muscular function, regulate body fluids and are involved in the conduction of nerve impulses. Calcium not only constitutes the most important element of the skeleton, but is also important in many bodily processes such as reproduction, and muscle, nerve and heart function. Magnesium is necessary for bone building, nerve and blood function, growth, and also active in several enzyme systems. Phosphorous, too, is involved in the formation of the skeleton and regulation of body fluids and active during the digestion of carbohydrates and in fat and protein metabolism. Chlorine is a component of gastric

Pakistani Butterfly, *Chaetodon collaris.*

juices and urine, and regulates blood and cell fluids. Sulphur is important as a component of several essential amino acids.

In addition to these minerals, which the body needs in fairly large amounts, several so-called trace elements are necessary. Hardly anything is known about their role in the lives of fishes, but we do know that a few are indispensable. Among these are iron, iodine, copper, manganese and cobalt.

Iron is a component of red blood corpuscles and is important for oxygen transport. It is found in the thyroid gland, where it is essential for thyroid health—the thyroid regulates metabolism—and for normal growth. Minute quantities of copper are involved in the manufacture of blood and some enzymes. Manganese, like magnesium, is probably an activator of certain enzymes. Finally, cobalt is a component of vitamin B_{12} and, thus, involved in blood production. Other trace elements have been demonstrated in the bodies of marine fishes, but we know nothing yet of their possible functions.

To conclude, certain mineral elements are indispensable for growth and skeleton formation. They also serve as building blocks for the blood, enzymes and hormones and play a role in such physiological processes as digestion and respiration. As dissolved salts in the body fluids, for instance, they determine the osmotic pressure and pH of blood and the contents of body cells. If the diet is lacking in these mineral elements, deficiency symptoms, and in many cases death, will result. Several minerals can be assimilated directly from the water through the gills, so the fishes are not completely dependent on their food.

Chances are that a varied diet will prevent any mineral deficiencies. It is inadvisable, therefore, to experiment with these substances. In small quantities, the trace elements are indispensable but in larger concentrations many of them, such as copper, are highly toxic.

Feeding

It should be clear by now that proper diet and correct feeding techniques are just as important as control of the water quality.

In the wild, the diets of many species of coral fishes are so specialized that even closely related species can live side by side on the reef without fighting over food. Even specialists, however, will snap up other tidbits that come their way. A few species refuse to touch more than one type of food; naturally, these will give the aquarist the most trouble. Seahorses, for example, eat only small mobile prey (tiny crustaceans and fish larvae), and some butterflyfishes and filefishes eat only coral polyps. Between the strict specialists and the omnivores are numerous species that, with a little effort, may be taught to accept various kinds of food.

Among the omnivores are the crownfishes, damsels, snappers, gobies and triggerfishes. The seahorses, pipefishes, shrimpfishes and some butterflyfishes and filefishes are strict specialists. The intermediate group includes primarily the long-nosed butterfly-fishes (such as *Chelmon rostratus* and *Forcipiger longirostris*), wrasses of the genus *Comphosus*, *Heniochus* species and the Emperorfish, *Pygoplites diacanthus*.

The predators are the least difficult to feed, although scorpion-fishes and anglerfishes can be reluctant. Give them fish meat, pieces of beef heart, mussels and shrimp. Feeding them live fishes is risky, as these may carry diseases. Even freshwater fishes may pass on a particular diease (*Ichthyosporidium hoferi*) to marine fishes. It is therefore safest to feed frozen fish, which must, of course, first be warmed to aquarium temperature and cut up into manageable pieces.

Some predators can not be persuaded to eat dead food at first; their reflexes respond only to mobile prey and never to food lying on the bottom. To start with, therefore, drop a little food close to the fish, which may snap at it as it sinks. Sometimes it may be necessary to thread a piece of fish or other food loosely and move it through the tank to make the fish react. When the fish takes the food, the thread can be pulled through. Turning up the air supply creates water motion that can cause the food to swirl about as though alive. Another trick is to toss the food bit by bit diagonally into the water, somewhat like "skipping" a stone. With practice you can give it a very lifelike motion. It is necessary to feed very heavily during the breaking-in period, but be sure to clean up all of the excess promptly.

Other fishes can also be fed pieces of fish meat, scraped beef heart and mussels and a large number of other foods to vary the menu. These include shrimps, prawns, crabmeat or small beach crabs, lugworms, earthworms (chopped), snails (land as well as water), water fleas, *Cyclops*, mosquito larvae (red, black and

Pearl-Scale Butterfly, *Chaetodon chrysurus.*

white), mealworms (chopped), *Tubifex,* white worms (*Enchytraeus*), grindal worms, water insects and their larvae, all stages of *Artemia salina* (brine shrimp), ant pupae, beef and fish liver, egg yolk, fish eggs and minute crustacea such as *Mysis,* amphipods (marine as well as freshwater) and marine isopods. Vegetable eaters or partly herbivorous species can also be fed lettuce, spinach, soft water plants, oatmeal soaked in water, marine and freshwater algae and yeast. Favorites among water plants are water thyme, *Synnema triflorum* and *Riccia fluitans.* In captivity, most of the true herbivores will also accept animal food or cooked oatmeal. Add algae meal to the porridge while it is cooking, and upon cooling it will set into a rather firm rubbery semi-solid that can be cut into portions. Agar-agar or a cellulose thickener may be used in place of the algae meal. Canned foods, such as crab-meat, fish roe and shrimp, can be offered after the food has been rinsed thoroughly in tap water to remove any preservatives.

The aquarist will do well to offer all these different kinds of food from time to time to prevent habit-forming. When food is scarce, as it is in winter, he can make use of high-quality dried foods sold in pet stores. Deep-frozen *Mysis* and *Artemia salina* are available all year round. Feed live food regularly if at all possible, because hunting prey will keep the fishes in better condition.

One of the dangers threatening aquarium fishes is overeating, which can cause malfunction of the organs. Death due to fatty degeneration, especially of the liver, is a frequent occurrence. The following precautions should therefore be observed. First, the diet should be low in fat, so feed lean beef and fish meat or scraped beef heart; for the same reason *Enchytraeus* and mealworms must be fed sparingly. Second, the carbohydrate content must be low. Third, overfeeding any type of food must be avoided. As this is not always possible with quick eaters in a mixed community, it is advisable to institute one or more fast days a week, except for young specimens, which must never go hungry.

To aid digestion and prevent constipation or colitis, feed plenty of "ballast" food or roughage. Its harder consistency will stimulate the peristaltic movements of the intestinal wall, thereby promoting digestion of the rest of the food. Excellent roughage is provided by the chitin, the hard material that forms the outer surface of crustaceans, such as shrimp, prawns, *Mysis* and water fleas. Crustaceans are also important because they make up a large part of the natural diet. *Mysis* or live shrimp can help nearly all recently imported fishes through their difficult period of adjustment. Since *Mysis* live only in brackish water and can not be caught inland, they must be obtained from the pet store.

Water fleas, on the other hand, can be caught almost anywhere and are eagerly accepted by most fishes. The one snag is that they stay alive in salt water for only about ten minutes, so do not feed more than can be eaten at once. *Cyclops* will stay alive in sea water for nearly two hours but are not attractive to larger fishes. White mosquito larvae (*Corethra*) stay alive in sea water somewhat longer than the red larvae. They are eaten eagerly by many fish species and are an excellent food.

Tubifex are found in polluted water (e.g., near sewage treatment plants), and the intestine may contain all kinds of pathogenic bacteria. Newly collected *Tubifex* may therefore cause intestinal trouble in susceptible species like the butterfly- and angelfishes and for this reason should be kept in running water for at least twenty-four hours to allow the worms to void their intestines. After flushing they make an excellent food.

Nearly all coral fishes eagerly accept mussels. To prevent water clouding, cook the mussels for a short time and chop them up after cooling. Feed *only* good-quality mussel meat; spoiled mussels may cause digestive disorders and intestinal infections.

If there is not enough algae available, algae eaters may be offered lettuce, soft water plants, spinach and rolled oats. The water plants can simply be floated in the water, where the fishes will quickly recognize them as edible. It may, however, take some time for the fishes to get used to lettuce. They will nibble more readily at a leaf that is anchored underwater with a small stone. Once they have learned that lettuce can be eaten, float it in the water. It is advisable to rinse lettuce or spinach thoroughly to get rid of any insecticides.

Rolled oats are also an excellent food for partial or total vegetarians. To keep the flakes from swelling in the intestinal tract, soak them beforehand. The fish must learn to accept this food. Sometimes it is necessary to feed small quantities for many days in a row before the oats are recognized as food and eaten.

We have learned from experience that marine fishes in captivity succumb fairly quickly to deficiencies of vitamins A and B_{12}. Pieces of fresh liver once a week will prevent this.

Brine Shrimp

In conclusion we must say a few words about the cultivation of *Artemia salina* nauplii. This crustacean lives in salt lakes that have a much higher salinity than ordinary sea water. *Artemia* lays eggs that can endure a long period of dryness. It is these eggs that we buy in aquarium departments.

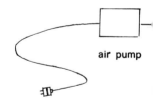

air pump

Figure 22. How to set up brine shrimp hatcheries.

Placed in sea water, they hatch at a temperature of 75°F (24°C) in about twenty-four hours. A simple method for hatching the eggs is illustrated in Figure 22. Two half-gallon bottles are half-filled with natural or artificial sea water (1½ ounces of cooking salt per quart of water may also be used) and ¼ teaspoon of the eggs put in. After thorough shaking, the bottles are closed with rubber stoppers, in which two holes have been drilled, and connected to the air system of the aquarium, as shown in the illustration.

The water must be thoroughly aerated for successful hatching. If the results are bad, either aeration is not strong enough, the temperature is too low or the eggs are too old. The yield of good eggs should be close to one hundred per cent. Sometimes results can be improved by increasing or decreasing the salinity.

As soon as the nauplii are hatched, they can be fed to small species or to very young fishes. To release the nauplii from the culture bottles, disconnect the air system and let the bottles stand for some time. Generally, the empty eggshells will float to the water surface, while the nauplii cluster near the bottom. You can now suck the nauplii out with a small siphon without bringing up a great many empty eggshells, which may cause constipation if eaten in large numbers by small fishes.

If there are empty eggshells both at the surface and on the bottom, it is still possible to collect the nauplii. Wrap a piece of dark paper or cardboard around the bottle. Midway between the water surface and the bottom make a fairly small hole in the paper cylinder and direct a strong light beam onto this spot. The

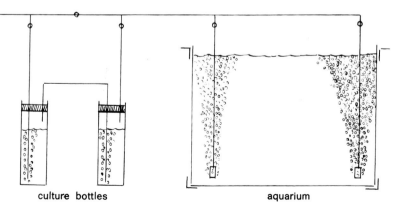

culture bottles   aquarium

nauplii will collect in the light beam, and can easily be siphoned up.

If the aquarist wants to feed his fishes larger nauplii, or raise brine shrimp to adulthood, he can add small amounts of yeast or farina to the water. This should be done with caution. The nauplii do not eat much, and the hatchery could easily turn into a smelly bacteria culture if too much food is given. To raise *Artemia* to maturity, larger containers, such as all-glass aquariums, preserving jars or small asbestos cement tanks, are needed. Good results will be obtained using a light strong enough to stimulate a flourishing algae colony. Some aeration is necessary, but filtration is not. The water temperature should be between 71° and 79°F (22°–26°C).

Feeding Techniques

If the species in the tank have the same feeding habits, there will be no problem. A given amount of food, distributed evenly over the water surface, will reach all the inhabitants.

It is harder to feed an aquarium population of varying feeding habits. Some species get very excited at feeding time and snap madly about in order to devour as much food as quickly as they can. Other species take their time, and still others carefully examine each and every morsel before they swallow it. Some retire into their hiding places during the mad scramble for food and reappear only when peace and quiet have returned, by which time the food has disappeared completely. There are also species that feed only from the bottom, and others that snap up food only while it is dropping down through the water.

The fast eaters will, of course, always get enough, but if the aquarist is not careful, there will be too little left for the slow eaters, the timid breeds and the bottom feeders. On the other hand, there is a danger of the fast eaters' overeating if the aquarist puts enough food into the tank for the slower species to eat their fill. Ideally, therefore, an aquarium should combine only those species with more or less the same eating habits. If fast and slow eaters are kept together, the only solution is to satisfy the gluttons first and then feed the slow eaters.

During the quarantine period the hobbyist may have difficulty feeding a newly imported animal. If the refusal to eat is not due to fear or sickness, a temporary increase in the water temperature may help. A frightened fish will sometimes start eating if a few

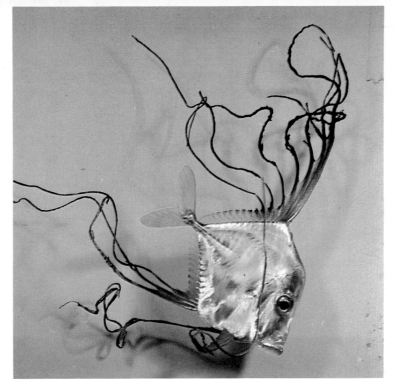

Pennant Trevally, *Alectis crinitus*.

good hiding places are provided and the aquarist stays out of sight for a while. Coral fishes can die of starvation very quickly if they can not be persuaded to eat, do not eat enough or do not get the right kind of food. It sometimes helps to place a poor eater in with a happy glutton. On the principle of "if you can have it, I can have it," the reluctant feeder may find itself competing with the other fish for the formerly despised morsels.

If during quarantine a fish can not be tempted even with *Artemia*, *Mysis*, young guppies or any other food, try the following method: smear a mixture of crushed mussels and small bits of lettuce or algae meal on a dry slab of shale or slate. After the mixture has set, slant the piece of shale against the inside of the tank. In many cases the starving fish will inspect the slab and start browsing on it. Of course this method can only be used for fishes that also graze on rocks and corals in their natural surroundings—fishes like the butterflies and angels, surgeons and many wrasses.

Whether the fishes are fed once, twice or more times a day depends on the amount of time the aquarist has available. Since

159

wild coral fishes—aside from predators—are busy practically all day or night finding enough to eat, it is better to feed small amounts several times a day than a large amount once daily.

Diseases

Far less is known about the diseases of marine fishes than about those of most freshwater fishes. What little we do know we owe primarily to the existence of the large public aquariums, whose keepers ponder this problem constantly to keep their expensive collections alive and in the best possible health.

In all likelihood the marine aquarist will find himself with sick charges on his hands more often than the freshwater hobbyist. The causes of the diseases to which our marine fishes are subject can be divided into the following categories: bacteria, flagellates, ciliates, crustaceans, worms, sporozoa, fungi, viruses and, finally, faulty or toxic environmental factors.

Before we concern ourselves with the different diseases and their cures, we must say something about the technique of treating sick fishes. If the new purchases show no disease symptoms after a few days in the quarantine tank, a broad-spectrum prophylactic such as copper sulfate, or the less effective zinc sulfate, can be administered as a precaution. A single dose in the quarantine tank is enough.

If sickness strikes the aquarium, the aquarist will generally have to treat all the inhabitants. If he is quite sure, however, that the disease will remain limited to one specimen, he should transfer the fish to a quarantine tank for treatment. For some guidance on judging whether to treat the whole aquarium or merely a single individual, see pages 166–177, where treatments are discussed.

It is, of course, important to adhere strictly to the prescribed doses, as many drugs are very toxic in higher concentrations. Copper and zinc sulfate are extremely dangerous. A dose suitable for fish is generally lethal for most invertebrates and algae—one of the reasons it is difficult to keep fishes and invertebrates together.

If you must treat the aquarium with copper or zinc sulfate, first remove the invertebrates and most of the algae. If the fish are treated outside the exhibition aquarium, use a bare tank without sand, corals or algae. During medication, filter only mechanically, over Dacron floss, to maintain an effective concentration of the

Picasso Trigger, *Rhinecanthus aculeatus.*

drug as long as possible. A single dose is often insufficient, so repeated treatment will be necessary, especially in the exhibition aquarium, where algae, dissolved organic substances, and so on, will rapidly decrease the concentration of the drug.

While copper sulfate is a nearly universal remedy against infections by flagellates, ciliates, and many bacteria and skin fungi, it is not easy to apply. Copper can not stay in solution in sea water for long. It precipitates, mainly as copper carbonate, and may form a temporary chemical bond with protein colloids. It will also weaken rapidly in the presence of calcium, corals, shell grit, coral sand, etc., but will remain in solution somewhat longer if citric acid is added to the stock copper sulfate solution. A booster dose will therefore be necessary in most cases. From many measurements carried out at the Artis Aquarium in tanks ranging from completely bare to full décor, we have worked out a rule-of-thumb index for booster doses, which is given in the list of drugs.

In determining a drug dosage, calculate the water volume of the aquarium carefully. While too much of the drug may be

Pink Skunk Clown, *Amphiprion perideraion*, in symbiotic association with sea anemone, *Radianthus* sp.

harmful, too little will be ineffective. The space taken up by the bottom cover, stones, corals, and so, must, of course, be subtracted from the water volume.

Drugs should never be combined unless this is specifically stated in the instructions. Some combinations are more toxic than the same doses of the separate substances; zinc and copper sulfate, for example, must never be combined.

Most drugs will degrade if allowed to remain in the aquarium, so it is not necessary, unless specified, to change the water after the recommended treatment has been administered. Of course, if the fishes are treated in a hospital tank, then the medicated water can be discarded afterwards. Where a dip is indicated—that is, when the fishes are kept in the medication for only a short period of time—the medication should be discarded and a fresh solution made up each time.

The primary indication of sickness is abnormal behavior of the fishes. although this can also be due to water pollution (see page 175). If colors fade and the fishes become languid, breathe heavily, hang at the water surface or swim abnormally, they are either ill or suffering from toxic water conditions. Other symptoms are scraping the bottom and rubbing against stones and corals. Close inspection of the skin is required in these cases to find out whether skin parasites are present.

Disease Symptoms	Diagnosis
Skin Conditions:	
Small, white to yellowish dots on the skin, especially on the fins	Coral fish disease (*Oodinium* infection)
Coarse white to grayish white dots on the skin, especially on the fins	White Spot disease
White to grayish white blotches on the skin	White Blotch disease (Bacterial infection)
Scattered skin hemorrhages, producing a mottled effect	*Vibrio* infection
Whitening and deterioration of the fin tissues	Fin rot (Bacterial infection)
White to bluish white clouding of the skin. Later pinpoint hemorrhages and small crater-like holes in the mucous skin surface	*Trichodina* infection
Milky-white clouding of the skin mucus, sometimes combined with pinpoint hemorrhages	low pH
Puckering and slow disappearance of the epidermis	Bacterial infection
Patches of erect, bristly scales	Bacterial scale infection
Open sores	Bacterial skin infection, *Ichthyosporidium* infection

White subcutaneous splotches or white glazy patches on the skin of seahorses	*Hippocampus* disease (*Glugea* infection)
Immobile or mobile skin parasites, visible to the naked eye—usually oblong	Skin infection by parasitic crustaceans or worms
Growths like absorbent cotton on skin or skin wounds	Fungus skin infections
Small, cauliflower-like white tubercles on fin edges or skin	Lymphocystic infection (virus infection)

Eye Conditions:

Bulging eye(s), gas in the eye	Exophthalmus (tuberculosis), *Ichthyosporidium*, bacterial eye infection or damage
Cloudy eyes	*Vibrio* infection, *Cryptocaryon* infection, White Spot disease, coral fish disease, bacterial eye infection
White spot in the middle of the eye	Bacterial eye infection

General Abnormalities:

Fading colors	Fright, tuberculosis, poisoning, fatty degeneration, old age
Diminishing appetite	Tuberculosis, slow poisoning, low pH
Gradual emaciation	Tuberculosis, intestinal worms, faulty diet
Swollen posterior, red anus, abnormal feces	Intestinal infection
Swollen posterior, no feces	Constipation, caused primarily by unvaried diet

Scraping the bottom, corals and stones; fin contraction; shaky body movements	Skin parasites, poisoning
Abnormal swimming behavior	Usually poisoning
Hopping swimming movements; fish tends to sink to the bottom	Swim bladder infection (bacterial infection)
Constantly heavy respiration	Coral fish disease (*Oodinium* infection), *Cryptocaryon* infection, *Trichodina* infection, *Dactylogyrus* infection of the gills, lack of oxygen, excess of carbon dioxide in the water
Sudden darting swimming movements, combined with heavy respiration; fishes try to jump out of the aquarium	Ammonia poisoning, pH too low
See-sawing swimming movements with snout at the water surface, combined with labored respiration	Abrupt change in salinity from low to high
Fishes lie on the bottom, breathing heavily, after transfer to a new tank; can rise only temporarily and with difficulty	Abrupt change in salinity from high to low
Symptoms of shock after transfer	Too sudden change in water composition
Progressive swelling in the throat region; mouth wide open all the time	Goiter (iodine deficiency)
Heavy, irregular respiration	Ammonia poisoning, carbon dioxide poisoning, lack of oxygen, metal poisoning
Swollen belly, often combined with erect scales	Bacterial (*Pseudomonas*) infection

Diseases Caused by Bacteria

Fin Rot. Caused by a bacterium that has been isolated but not yet identified. It is not highly contagious.

Symptoms: The fin edges turn white and cloudy. In the later stages the fin tissue dies off and the fins become ragged, torn and gradually shorter. Still later, the skin mucus is also affected, showing bloodshot patches that originate in the epidermis. If the disease is not checked, the mucus begins to come off in patches, and deep bloody wounds develop in the skin. Sometimes the disease progresses so rapidly that the fins rot completely off within twenty-four hours.

Treatment: The disease can seldom, if ever, be cured in the acute state, but in the earliest stage can be cured with copper or zinc sulfate. If it progresses slowly, a cure can be effected fairly easily by treating the fish with acriflavine, streptomycin or a combination of streptomycin and penicillin.

Vibrio Infection. Caused by *Vibrio anguillarum.*

Symptoms: Hemorrhages occur in the skin, first in dispersed blotches and later in larger patches. The fin edges and the anal area are inflamed and bloody. At a still later stage the eyes also become inflamed. The disease is fairly contagious, but fortunately rarely occurs in warm-water aquariums.

Treatment: In its earliest stage the disease can be treated with copper or zinc sulfate, later stages with antibiotics (aureomycin, streptomycin or sulfanilamide). The sick animals should be given food soaked in aureomycin.

White Blotch Disease. Cause unknown, probably a bacterium.

Symptoms: Small grayish white blotches develop on the skin and spread slowly. The blotches are larger than those seen in White Spot disease, and the outlines are not so clearly defined. In the earliest stage, the edges of fin tissues in particular are affected. Later the disease spreads to the interior surfaces, which take on a cloudy and "coarse" appearance and disintegrate. Tissue mortification occurs in the fins. Normally, the disease develops slowly. Much later the eyes are also affected and become bleary. The disease is fairly contagious.

Treatment: As for *Vibrio* infection (see above). Alternatively,

Porkfish, *Anisotremus virginicus*.

a cure may be effected by treatment with quinine hydrochloride, combined with copper or zinc sulfate. Other possibilities are acriflavine, methylene blue and streptomycin.

Tuberculosis. Caused by *Mycobacterium* species.

Symptoms: Tuberculosis is a slow, insidious disease. The earliest symptoms are diminishing appetite, fading colors, gradual emaciation and listless behavior. In a later stage the mucus coating degenerates, opening the door to secondary infections by other bacteria and ciliates. The disease is only mildly contagious but an animal suspected of having tuberculosis must be removed from the aquarium as soon as possible. Healthy fishes are seldom if ever affected. Dissection of fishes that have died of tuberculosis reveals small, grayish, knob-like excrescences in and on the interior organs (especially the liver, intestines and spleen). If tuberculosis bacteria infest the eye sockets, the eyes may protrude.

Treatment: Unfortunately, the early symptoms are difficult to discern, but if they are spotted, a cure may be effected by keeping the fishes in a streptomycin bath for a week or more. Once there are unmistakable symptoms of tuberculosis, the sick fish can not be saved and had best be destroyed.

Enteritis. Causes unknown.

Symptoms: The posterior is swollen; the feces are excreted as a white pasty mass or in thin white strands. Later they are mixed with, and the anal area becomes suffused with, blood. Enteritis is usually due to a restricted diet of soft food without enough roughage, or to spoiled food (*Tubifex* that has not been properly cleansed, spoiled mussel meat, etc.). It is not contagious.

Treatment: Sick animals should be fasted for two or three days and then fed a diet containing plenty of roughage such as *Mysis*, shrimp or water fleas. In addition, the fishes should be given *Tubifex* or mussel meat soaked in terramycin or chloramphenicol solution. During treatment the water temperature should be raised to about 82°F (28°C).

Skin Swellings and Sores. Cause(s) unknown.

Symptoms: Skin swellings occur in marine fishes in a variety of forms, so there are probably different causes. Sometimes they are small subcutaneous boils that come to a head and rupture, leaving small pits in the skin that close slowly. Another type of swelling is larger and covered over with a thick layer of mucus. If the swellings rupture (which is not always the case), deep crater-like wounds, slow to heal, are left. At times death occurs quickly but in other cases the swellings are chronic. Secondary infections, mainly fungal, are liable to occur in open abscesses. (See also *Ichthyosporidium* infection, page 174.) Although most bacterial infections causing swellings are not very contagious, it is advisable to isolate sick fishes for treatment.

Treatment: The disease can often be cured at an early stage with copper or zinc sulfate. If the swellings do not respond to treatment, they may be a sign of a generalized infection of the body. The copper or zinc sulfate treatment should then be reinforced by daily feedings of some soft food soaked in aureomycin, terramycin, streptomycin or chloramphenicol.

Loss of Epidermis. Cause unknown (perhaps not bacterial).

Symptoms: Fish that suffer from this disease lose increasingly large portions of the epidermis, which is apparently rolled up before it drops off. Loss of the epidermis generally starts on the head, especially around the mouth and nostrils, but spreads to the entire body. The infection may become fatal very quickly, or it may be of a lingering character. It is contagious, especially for animals in poor condition. There is some evidence that it occurs mainly in aquariums where water changes are neglected.

Treatment: Unknown (to the author at any rate, who has had no personal experiences with the disease). Copper or zinc sulfate, antibiotics or sulfathiazole sodium should be tried.

Scale Hispidity. Cause not yet described; probably *Pseudomonas* species.

Symptoms: The scales are locally erect and the skin of the affected areas may bleed superficially. The infection often starts near the caudal peduncle. Generally, it spreads rapidly all over the body, causing increasingly larger hemorrhages. It is often accompanied by a pronounced swelling of the belly. The syndrome is reminiscent of certain forms of abdominal dropsy in freshwater fish. The infection may quickly terminate in death, sometimes within twenty-four hours. If at all contagious, it is barely so. Nevertheless, it is advisable to isolate infected animals.

Treatment: Immediate treatment with copper sulfate may be effective, if the disease is discovered early. Treatment with streptomycin is probably preferable.

Swim Bladder Inflammation. Cause not yet isolated.

Symptoms: Improper functioning of the swim bladder causing abnormal swimming behavior. The animal has difficulty in keeping its balance in the water and can barely remain afloat. The hopping swimming movements of the fish are characteristic; affected animals tend to sink to the bottom and at a later stage may remain lying there. Swim bladder inflammations are not contagious.

Note: in many bottom-dwelling species the swim bladder is absent or non-functional. Abrupt salinity changes may cause temporary abnormal swimming movements, though these are of short duration.

Treatment: Since swim bladder inflammations may develop as a result of low temperatures (e.g., during transport), the sick animal should be isolated in a warm aquarium of about 82°–86°F (28°–30°C). Food soaked in antibiotics, particularly aureomycin, will assist the cure.

Queen Angelfish, *Angelichthys* (*Holacanthus*) *ciliaris*, juvenile form.

Diseases Caused by Flagellates (parasites with whiplike tails or flagella)

Coral Fish Disease. Caused by *Oodinium ocellatum*, a dinoflagellate.
Symptoms: As the parasite often settles on the gill branchiae first, the earliest sign of an *Oodinium* infection is accelerated respiration. Very small white or yellowish dots appear on the skin, sometimes immediately, sometimes later; these are clearly visible, particularly on the fins. During this primary stage, when there are few such visible symptoms, the fish rubs against stones, corals and other materials. At a later stage the fish appears to be completely covered with powdered sugar. If the disease is not checked, the eyes also become affected, and the mucous skin gets a coarse and cloudy appearance and comes off in patches. Respiration becomes more and more labored, and the sick fish hangs about at the water surface or lies on the bottom breathing heavily. *Oodinium* infections are very contagious.

Oodinium ocellatum infests not only the epidermis and gill filaments, where it is highly visible, but sometimes the mouth and the intestine of its host as well. When it is full-grown, it leaves the host and sinks to the bottom, where it forms a sporocyst (a type of sac). In this it divides into two daughter cells, which in turn divide, and so on. When the divisions number 32 or 64 cells, the sac ruptures and the spores that are now ciliated and free-swimming emerge and seek a host. This stage is called Dinospore. On finding a fish, a spore bores its way through the mucus and lodges in the epidermis, where it drops its flagella and exists as a parasite. At a temperature of $75°-78°F (24°-26°C)$, the whole life cycle from spore to mature parasite takes about ten days.

The time to complete the cycle is dependent on the temperature and degree of illumination. The lower the temperature and the dimmer the light, the slower the cycle. In a brightly lit tank at $75°F (24°C)$, for example, the lapse between the time of sporocyst formation and the emergence of the last free-swimming Dinospore takes fifty to seventy hours; at $59°-63°F (15°-17°C)$, the cycle may take as long as eleven days. The free-swimming Dinospores themselves may live as long as twelve to twenty-four hours at $75°F (24°C)$. At this temperature the parasite stage is three to four days from first attachment to dropping off.

Oodinium ocellatum, one of the most common parasites of marine tropicals, is highly contagious. Imported fishes, especially those shipped via Singapore, are very often infected. A major breakthrough will be achieved when all tropical exporters can be persuaded to treat their fishes prophylactically against *Oodinium ocellatum* before shipping. Before World War II this notorious disease made it almost impossible to keep marine tropicals in captivity for any length of time. After the war, effective treatments were developed independently at the Steinhart Aquarium in San Francisco and the Artis Aquarium in Amsterdam.

Treatment: The disease can be cured readily, particularly in the primary stage, with copper sulfate, zinc sulfate, acriflavine or quinine hydrochloride. The latter two, although less effective, may be used for species sensitive to copper and zinc. Since parasites in the intestine can not be destroyed by these two drugs, reinfection from the intestine may occur, so the cured animals must stay in quarantine for at least ten days after the skin eruptions have healed.

Diseases Caused by Ciliates

White Spot Disease. Caused by *Cryptocaryon irritans.*

Symptoms: The same as in White Spot disease in freshwater fish. The surface of the fish is covered with fairly large white to off-white or gray spots. When the parasite spreads over the body, the mucous skin coarsens and sheds in patches. The epidermis becomes inflamed; the eyes may turn cloudy. At an early stage of the infection the fish frequently rubs against stones and corals and along the bottom. If the parasite also infects the gill branchiae (filaments), the respiration of the fish becomes increasingly labored and accelerated. In the later stages other ciliates, bacteria or fungi, even those that may not normally be pathogenic, often settle on and infect the damaged areas. *Cryptocaryon* infections are very contagious.

The life cycle of the parasite is similar to that of *Ichthyophthirius multifiliis* in fresh water. In fact, at one time *Cryptocaryon irritans* was mistaken for a marine form of *Ichthyophthirius*.

Treatment: In the primary stage, treatment with quinine hydrochloride is effective. For stubborn infections combine this with copper or zinc sulfate. Responses have also been obtained with acriflavine, sulfathiazole sodium, methylene blue, aureomycin and terramycin.

Cloudy Skin. Caused by *Trichodina* species.

Symptoms: Milky-white or grayish clouding of the skin mucus, later accompanied by pinpoint hemorrhages in the skin. Sometimes craterlike patches appear in the swollen skin mucus. Clouding of the lenses may also occur.

Treatment: The same as for *Cryptocaryon* infections.

Diseases Caused by Crustaceans

Infections by Parasitic Copepods.

Symptoms: Parasites, visible to the naked eye, are attached to the skin or move across it. They are sometimes concentrated near the eyes, sometimes on the gills. These parasites generally can not reproduce in the aquarium, so most infections die of their own accord. Thus the disease is usually not contagious.

Treatment: If necessary, use a formalin bath (for 15 minutes at most) composed of sea water to which 1 cc of 35 per cent formalin per liter has been added. Aerate well during treatment.

Diseases Caused by Worms

Skin and Gill Parasites. Chiefly monogenetic trematodes of the genera *Gyrodactylus* and *Benedenia* (formerly *Epibdella*).

Symptoms: Grayish white skin parasites up to 1½ mm long are sometimes visible to the naked eye. They often occur only on the gill branchiae. Badly infected fishes breathe heavily and their mouths can not close completely. The eyes may become cloudy and inflamed. Infected fishes rub against stones or corals, shake their heads or bodies now and then and hover in the water with clamped fins. Very contagious!

Treatment: As prescribed for infections from parasitic crustaceans, or treat with copper or zinc sulfate.

Intestinal Worms. Nematodes and tapeworms.

Symptoms: Gradual emaciation without loss of appetite (unlike tuberculosis infections); sometimes bloody feces. It is uncertain whether these infections are contagious.

Treatment: Unknown; thiabendazole mixed with the food may prove effective.

Diseases Caused by Sporozoa

Hippocampus Disease. Caused by *Glugea* species.

Symptoms: In the primary stage, small white subcutaneous spots appear, which later extend to form large glossy patches. Sporozoa most frequently infest muscular tissue. The infection is specific to seahorses.

Treatment: As yet unknown.

Diseases Caused by Fungi

External Skin Parasites. Pathogens of unknown identity.

Symptoms: Varying from short velvet-like strands to tufts an inch or two in length, cotton wool-like growths appear on the skin or eyes. Skin fungi do not infect healthy or uninjured animals, but rather those with mucous injuries or skin wounds. Faulty environmental conditions, such as too much dissolved organic matter (a fouled aquarium), accumulations of inorganic substances, or a low pH indirectly favor the occurrence of parasitic skin fungi. Fungal infections occur less frequently in marine aquariums than in freshwater tanks and are hardly, if ever, contagious.

Treatment: The infection can be treated very effectively in its earliest stage with copper or zinc sulfate. Sometimes water changes alone will effect a cure. In serious cases, griseofulvin, freshwater baths or potassium permanganate baths may destroy the parasites.

Internal Parasites. Ichthyosporidium hoferi (formerly called *Ichthyophonus hoferi*).

Symptoms: Since this parasitic fungus infests the vital organs, the infection may not be discovered until it is too late. Chiefly infected are the liver and the kidneys, but the fungus occurs in all other vital organs as well. Once external symptoms appear, the affected animal usually can not be saved. Bulging eyes (exophthalmus) may be symptomatic, especially if accompanied by poorly healing skin infections. Other symptoms include gradual or sudden emaciation, decay of fin tissue, abnormal swimming movements, blackish discoloration of the skin, and swelling of the body cavity.

The disease is widespread and occurs frequently in the wild and among freshwater fishes as well. It is not very contagious in a healthy aquarium population, although individual fishes not in top condition may easily become infected. Healthy fishes often survive by encapsulating the parasite in connective tissue. Live fishes offered as food may transmit the disease, so frozen fish should be given whenever possible.

Treatment: Since no effective cure is known, the only solution is to raise the water temperature to 82°–86°F (28°–30°C) and feed liver (vitamins A and B$_{12}$) and food soaked in phenoxyethanol or para–chloro–phenoxetol. Even if the parasites have been encapsulated, the disease may break out again if the host's physical condition weakens.

Diseases Caused by Viruses

Lymphocystis infection.

Symptoms: Dead-looking, cauliflower-shaped growths appear

on the fins, then spread to the skin. The infection, only slightly contagious, is most likely to appear in midsummer and disappear in late autumn or winter.

Treatment: The disease often disappears with good food and proper care. The growths should be treated regularly with mercurochrome or tincture of iodine. Sometimes results can be obtained with extended copper sulfate baths or the addition of potassium iodide to the water. If none of these methods is effective, the morbid growths should be cut from the fins with sharp scissors. Fins normally grow back again quickly.

Diseases Caused by Faulty Environmental Factors

Water poisoning from metal-water contact produces symptoms similar to those caused by various parasites, so it is often hard to tell whether a fish is ill or poisoned. Fishes react to high concentrations of toxic metals (copper, zinc, aluminum) with accelerated respiration, because the metals coagulate the slime on the gill

Queen Triggerfish, *Balistes vetula*.

filaments, thus interfering with efficient gaseous exchange. The thin skin of the fins is also readily affected by excessively high concentrations of toxic metals, and dies off. The mucus on the body may coagulate and appear cloudy and swollen.

Ammonia poisoning produces somewhat different symptoms. Respiration is usually accelerated and irregular, though it can also be normal. Periods of abnormally increased activity (rapid swimming) alternate with periods during which the fishes are abnormally quiet, even apathetic. If the ammonia concentration remains too high, they will show symptoms of increased excitability. A tap against the aquarium may make them jump out of the water or dash into panes or stones. Sometimes even without outside stimuli, they shoot wildly through the water, only to lapse into a shock-like state, with rigidly extended fins and wide-open mouths.

The reaction to phenol poisoning is probably similar. In fact, these sudden fast and uncoordinated bursts of swimming are the only specific symptoms of ammonia or phenol poisoning. If they occur, change a large part of the water as quickly as possible or transfer the animals temporarily to another tank. To prevent a recurrence, you must trace the source of the increased concentrations and eliminate it.

Other symptoms of toxicity can also occur. For example, fishes often rub over the sand or against stones and coral as they do when suffering from skin parasites. Fading colors, loss of appetite and decreased activity may likewise result, as well as skin fungi, which attack a mucous weakened by faulty environmental conditions. A low pH may result in labored respiration, or it may make the fishes lose appetite and mobility, causing a milky-white clouding of the mucus—a condition often accompanied by pin-point hemorrhages.

If the fishes recover perceptibly soon after a partial water change, and if in a few hours their behavior returns to normal, the problem was water poisoning. If, however, they do not respond fairly soon, the animals are sick and must be treated accordingly.

After transfer from one tank to another, or after a substantial water change, the fishes may show symptoms similar to those of certain diseases. If we transfer them too abruptly to a differing salinity, they may react either by lying on the bottom, breathing

Red Soldierfish, *Myripristis murdjan.*

heavily, or by swimming jerkily near the water surface in a slanted or vertical position. If the change has been very abrupt, they show shock symptoms and sink to the bottom with fully extended fins and the opercula wide open. Shock symptoms may also occur when they are transferred from relatively fresh to very old sea water or vice versa, even though the salinities are about the same.

Should this occur, we must give the equivalent of artificial respiration. Catch them in a net and move them back and forth through the water. Larger fishes must be grasped underwater and the gills moved by pressing them with thumb and forefinger until the fishes start breathing again.

List of Drugs

Drug	Dose and duration of bath
Acriflavine	Dose: 1 gram per 25 gallons of water, to be added a few drops at a time over a period of 24 hours. The water will turn fluorescent-green. After three-four days, filter the

	water over charcoal until all traces of the color are gone. Repeat if necessary.
Aureomycin	15–20 mg per quart of water. Repeat as often as necessary. Before each new dose, change a substantial portion of the water or filter over charcoal.
Chloramphenicol	20 mg per quart of water. Maximum duration of bath: six hours. Repeat daily if necessary.
Copper sulfate	Stock solution: dissolve four grams of copper sulfate ($CuSO_4.5H_2O$) plus 0.25 grams of crystalline citric acid per liter of distilled water. Dose: one cc per gallon of water. Booster doses for specific aquarium type: 1) Decorated tanks with filter and coral sand: daily booster dose of one cc per five quarts of water. If the fish seem adversely affected, change part of the water and use a smaller dose next time. 2) Decorated tanks with filter but without sand: booster dose of 0.5 cc per gallon after 24 hours; 0.25 cc per gallon after 48 hours; 0.25 cc per gallon after 72 hours, etc. (dose constant, time-gap lengthened) till full recovery. 3) Bare quarantine tanks: booster dose 0.5 cc per gallon after 48 hours; 0.25 cc per gallon after 96 hours. Thereafter, should a further dose be necessary, change the water completely and repeat the schedule.
Formalin	Standard solution: 35 per cent. Dose: one cc per quart of bath water for 15 minutes at most. Ten-minute

	dip for small fish.
Griseofulvin	25 mg per liter of water.
Hydrogen peroxide	Standard solution three per cent. Dose: 0.5 cc per quart of water.
Iodine	See potassium iodide.
Mercurochrome	Standard solution: two per cent for touching up skin wounds.
Methylene blue	Stock solution: one per cent (ten grams per 1,000 ml) in water. Dose: three cc per ten quarts of water.
Para-chlorophenoxetol, (2-*para*-chlorophenoxy-ethanol)	Make up one per cent solution for soaking food.
Penicillin	10,000–30,000 International Units per liter of water. Repeat every two days. Generally used in combination with streptomycin.
Phenoxethol, (2-phenoxyethanol)	One per cent stock solution for soaking food.
Potassium iodide	Stock solution: one gram of iodine plus 100 grams of potassium iodide in one quart of distilled water. Dose: one cc per gallon of water. Repeat once every ten days. If fish

Redheaded Butterflyfish, *Chaetodon larvatus*.

	show adverse effects, stop treatment and change part of the water. Filter normally during treatment. Turn TUV lamps off.
Potassium permanganate	One gram per 25 gallons of sea water. Bathe for 30 minutes maximum. One gram per 25 gallons of fresh water. Dip the fish at most three minutes.
Quinine hydrochloride	1–1.5 grams per 25 gallons of sea water. Dip the fish at most three minutes. After three days, filter for 24 hours through charcoal. Repeat, using one gram per 25 gallons, as often as necessary.
Streptomycin	20 mg per quart of water. Repeat if necessary after two days, but only after changing at least one-third of the water. Within about twenty-four hours the water may emit a smell of onions or carbide (caused by amines). This is normal, probably due to certain bacteria dying off.
Sulfanilamide	100–250 mg per quart of water. Repeat every three days after partial water change.
Sulfathiazole sodium	ten grams per 25 gallons of water.
Terramycin	10–15 mg per liter. After two-three days, filter over charcoal for 24 hours and repeat dosage, if necessary.
Trypaflavin	See Acriflavine.
Zinc sulfate	Stock solution: four grams of zinc sulfate per quart of distilled water. Dose: one cc for each two-four quarts of sea water. A booster dose may be given after four days, but at least half the water must be changed beforehand.

VII Fish Catalog

It is impossible within the scope of this book to give exhaustive descriptions of the many hundreds of tropical marine species imported at one time or another. The chief criterion for inclusion has been suitability for the home aquarium. Other species of interest are mentioned, but not discussed in detail. For each species the most frequently occurring "popular" name is given first, followed by the alternate "popular" name(s), where extant, and then the Latin name in italics. The length given for a species is the maximum size in which it has been known to occur. To locate a particular species, consult the index.

Sharks

Sharks are unsuitable for the living room aquarium, since all species grow too big even for fair-sized tanks. Some species are imported when young and small, but with proper care grow so fast that the owner's pleasure is short-lived. Furthermore, they eat smaller fishes. All species imported to date are bottom-dwellers. It is possible to keep the open water species only in aquariums specially made and fitted out for them.

Some of the species imported are the **NURSE SHARKS,** *Ginglymostoma cirratum* and *G. brevis*; the **CATSHARK,** *Chiloscyllium indicum*; and the **CARPET SHARK** (Spotted Wobbegong), *Orectolobus maculatus*. Bottom-dwelling sharks are not difficult to keep. They soon adjust to eating pieces of meat, fish and bivalves. Lugworms (sandworms), too, are very suitable food.

Rays

Rays also will grow much too big for a living room aquarium. An exceptionally beautiful and slow-growing species from the

Pacific and Indian Oceans is the **BLUE-SPOTTED RAY,** *Taenioura lymma*, of which small specimens are sometimes imported. In the aquarium they need plenty of swimming room and a bottom where they can hide.

Rays feed almost exclusively from the bottom. In a tank with many corals and stones they may get stuck occasionally and will die if not freed quickly. Because they are slow feeders they often suffer in competition for food. Pieces of fish and sandworms are excellent food for them; they regard small fish, too, as welcome prey. Rays cannot be kept with triggerfishes, which often attack a ray's eyes and long tail.

Besides *Taenioura lymma*, **ELECTRIC RAYS** or Crampfish (Torpedinidae) are sometimes imported. Their powerful electric organs, used to numb their prey, make them extremely dangerous to life in a mixed aquarium. They feed mainly on crustaceans and fish. Unless they are kept with live prey, it is difficult to induce them to feed.

Catfishes

Compared with fresh water, the oceans have few representatives of the sub-order Siluroidei. These are seldom imported, because they are not colorful, but nearly all black or grey. The one exception is the striped species, *Plotosus lineatus*, which is imported fairly often in rather large numbers. Although commonly kept in aquariums, this catfish is extremely dangerous to handle as the pectoral fins carry poisonous spines. Even slight contact with one can cause severe pain.

Plotosus lineatus, while young, flock together in schools near the coasts of the Pacific and Indian Oceans. When danger confronts them, they quickly group into a kind of ball with their heads turned outward. This behavior is reminiscent of a swarm of starlings when attacked by a predatory bird. Mature specimens, however, probably do not school, having defenses adequate to insure survival. The coloring of this species ranges from brown to black, with two white or yellow longitudinal stripes. They have four pairs of mouth barbels they use to search along the bottom.

Young catfishes need very finely chopped food such as small

Red-Spotted Hawkfish, *Amblycirrhites pinos*.

pieces of cooked mussels, *Tubifex*, white worms, dried shrimp and small crustaceans. Avoid imported specimens which arrive in emaciated condition. If properly cared for, healthy catfishes grow fast and attain a length of ten inches. Younger specimens should be segregated from larger, faster eating fishes, as they are not equal to the competition for food. They appreciate hiding places.

Moray Eels

Numerous species of these eel-like fishes occur in the tropics. They are active at dusk and during the night. During the day they hide or leave just their heads sticking out of holes and crevices on the ocean floor. Species such as **SNAKE EELS** (Ophichthyidae) burrow into the bottom, letting only their heads protrude. All species grow too big for the small display-aquarium. Only large fishes should be kept with morays as small ones will be eaten. Specimens recently imported, especially the Snake Eels, sometimes prove difficult feeders. This problem can be solved by waving a small fish, held in a pair of tweezers, before the moray until it rises to the bait. Once moray eels can be persuaded to eat, they may be kept for years in captivity. Here are a few species:

WHITE-EYED MORAY (Mottled Moray), *Gymnothorax undulatus*. Its basic coloring is brownish yellow with a pattern of small white lines, a pattern which may vary considerably, ranging from dark spotted to marbled. Its eyes are white-rimmed. Maximum length: 60 inches.

BLACK-SPOTTED MORAY (Leopard Moray, Tesselated Reef Eel), *Gymnothorax tesselata* (*favagineus*). A beautiful black and white spotted eel. Easy to keep; takes food readily. Very aggressive, even when young. Maximum length: 60 inches. (See photograph, page 23.)

DIAMONDBACK MORAY (Starry, Snowflake or Cloudy Moray), *Echidna nebulosa*. A smaller, 30-inch species, which may be kept together with rather small fishes because it is not very aggressive.

ZEBRA MORAY, *Echidna zebra*. A beautiful moray with many transverse white rings against a dark-brown or black body. Rather aggressive and not very suitable for a mixed aquarium. Maximum length: 48 inches.

STRIPED MORAY (Harlequin Snake-Eel), *Myrichthys colubrinus*. It is often very difficult to persuade this unusual, very slender, black-and-white-ringed moray to eat in captivity. It is, therefore, more difficult to keep than the above. In the daytime it burrows in the sand. Be sure that food reaches it.

Seahorses

There are more than twenty-five species of seahorses. These occur in temperate as well as subtropical seas. Seahorses swim in an erect posture, moving only the dorsal and pectoral fins; the anal fin has almost disappeared. The tail—a very mobile, prehensile organ—is anchored during rest to sea grasses, corals and rocks. Good decorative materials are therefore of utmost importance.

Males have a fold of skin across the abdomen. This forms a brood pouch into which the female deposits her eggs. The young remain in the pouch until they have developed into tiny replicas of their parents, able to fend for themselves upon expulsion into the sea. Imported males with full pouches often release their young prematurely, and these young usually die. Parents and other adults will eat the young, so separate them quickly. Seahorses have, nonetheless, been bred successfully in captivity.

They are indifferent to the quality of water, and would therefore not cause the aquarist much trouble, were it not for their need for live food, and a good deal of it. To make sure they thrive, it is preferable to feed them several times a day. Because of their feeding habits, they suffer immensely when competing for food with faster-eating fish. They are, for this reason, quite unsuitable for a mixed aquarium, but as they do not need much room, they may be kept by themselves in a small tank.

Living *Mysis* and the somewhat bigger brine shrimp (e.g., *Artemia*) are the best food. You may also feed seahorses white mosquito larvae, baby guppies, black mosquito larvae and water fleas. Smaller species will also eat the *Artemia* nauplii and *Cyclops*. Although most authorities recommend feeding newly hatched brine shrimp to the young seahorses, Dr Wilfred Neugebauer's observations at the aquarium in Stuttgart dispute this practice. Apparently the nauplii are indigestible. Some of them even pass through the alimentary tract to emerge alive from the droppings. Dr Neugebauer suggests first feeding *Euplotes*, a saltwater ciliate available at biological supply houses. After a week of this food, the young should have developed to the point where they can safely eat the newly hatched brine shrimp. However, the Dwarf Seahorse (*Hippocampus zosterae*) gives birth to few but, oddly enough, relatively large young, already capable at birth of digesting newly hatched brine shrimp.

During the winter, when small, live crustaceans are not available, the aquarist must fall back on frozen *Mysis* or *Artemia*. Seahorses will recognize the dead animals as prey, especially if they float through the water. For this reason the air stones must operate with more pressure than usual. Small dead shrimp will also be recognized as food. The better fed the seahorses, the less likely they are to swim actively after their prey.

Seahorses are very susceptible to gas embolisms caused by oversaturation of the water with oxygen and other gases. They sometimes eat small air bubbles as well, which may stick in the alimentary canal, causing the fish to lose balance. Sometimes small air bubbles from the air stones find their way into the brood

Rock Beauty, *Holacanthus tricolor.*

pouches of the males, forcing the latter to float on the water surface. Gas formation in the brood pouch may also occur when eggs or young die off. If this should happen, suck the gas out of the brood pouch with a pipette tapered off to a thin, smooth point. Gas bubbles under the skin may be punctured carefully. Here are some imported species:

MEDITERRANEAN SEAHORSE, *Hippocampus guttulatus,* and **SHORT-SNOUTED SEAHORSE ,** *Hippocampus brevirostris.* Found in the Mediterranean and the Atlantic and ranging into the subtropics. They may be kept at temperatures as low as 68°F (20°C), although it is better to keep them at room temperature.

YELLOW SEAHORSE (Oceanic Seahorse, Spotted Seahorse), *H. kuda* (see photograph, page 273), and **CRESTED SEAHORSE** (Spiny Seahorse), *H. hystrix.* These tropical species are native to the Pacific and Indian Oceans. The former are generally black when imported but assume the normal yellow if conditions are favorable.

DWARF SEAHORSE (Pygmy Seahorse), *H. zosterae*, and the **ATLANTIC SEAHORSE** (Common Atlantic or Northern Seahorse), *H. hudsonius*. Natural to Florida and the Caribbean. The Dwarf Seahorse does not grow bigger than two inches and may be fed *Artemia* nauplii, water fleas and *Cyclops*. This species breeds very readily in captivity, the incubation lasting less than ten days. The young grow quickly if enough food is available, and mature sexually within a few months. Their normal longevity is over one year. Other species live two to three years. The Atlantic Seahorse occurs variously as black, brownish black, white, orange-yellow and red. Incubation is about six weeks. By the time they are released from the pouch, the young are two-thirds of an inch long. Large, fully grown specimens (eight inches) are known to eat even grown male guppies.

GHOST PIPEFISH, *Solenostomus.* An apparent transition between the seahorses and the pipefishes, these fish are rarely imported from their Pacific and Indian Ocean habitats. They have greatly extended, relatively wide, tube-like mouths. The female of this unusual species has the brood pouch. Specimens have never been kept successfully in captivity.

Pipefishes

Numerous species occur in all the oceans, with the greatest variety in the tropics. A few species are imported. The pipefish is closely related to the seahorse, which it somewhat resembles. Lacking its bulbous mid-section, it is long and slim with a flat back formed to the flat sides at almost an acute angle. Where the seahorse maintains a vertical posture, the pipefish swims in the horizontal attitude of most fish. It demands the same habitat and food. Like the seahorse, the male pipefish has a brood pouch, which in some species is closed. In species where the pouch is open, the eggs are fastened to the abdominal skin.

MESSMATE PIPEFISH (Waite's Pipefish), *Corytoichthys intentinalis*. Native to the Pacific and Indian Oceans, and the most frequently imported species. It is a small, mobile fish that readily takes to *Artemia* nauplii, water fleas and *Cyclops*.

Trumpetfishes and Cornetfishes

Though closely related to seahorses and pipefishes, these form a sub-order of their own, Aulostomoidei. It includes a large number of very bizarre fishes, all more or less difficult to keep. They have pointed, generally thin, tube-like, extended mouths, so that they can manage only very small live prey.

The **CORNETFISH**, *Fistularia tabaccaria*, and related species have the largest mouths, relatively speaking, and resemble pipefish. They do nicely on guppies, brine shrimp and shrimp. The following three species are sometimes imported: *Aulostomus valentini*, native to the Indian Ocean, and *A. maculatus* and *Fistularia tabaccaria*, from tropical parts of the Atlantic Ocean and the Caribbean. The latter, often called the **CIGARFISH,** is said to reach a length of five feet. The other species are much smaller.

Shrimpfishes (Razorfishes)

The Centriscidae are remarkable and desirable aquarium fish, with razor-thin, almost transparent bodies. They swim vertically, head pointed downward. Their thin, tube-like mouths make it difficult for them to eat anything larger than *Artemia* nauplii, *Cyclops* and water fleas. Even adult brine shrimp are generally too big for them. If they are fed suitable small food more than once a day, they keep easily in an aquarium. They will even eat dead *Cyclops* lying on the bottom. If they are very hungry, they may nibble brine shrimp, but never swallow them whole. Shrimp-fishes, like seahorses and pipefishes, should either be kept separately from other fishes or placed in an aquarium without other fishes that live on small prey. More than other fishes, they are sensitive to copper, so proper care must be taken with the use of copper sulfate to fight certain diseases. Imported species:

STRIPED SHRIMPFISH (Striped Razorfish), *Aeoliscus strigatus*. Marked by a black longitudinal band from the mouth to the dorsal fin, this species is found, safe from possible enemies, among the spines of certain sea urchins (*Diadema* species).

RAZORFISH, *A. punctulatus*. From the Pacific and Indian

Oceans, this fish lacks the band but has black spots all over a shorter and stockier body.

Tigerfishes

Theraponidae are predatory, moderate-sized fishes from the Pacific and Indian Oceans. Often found in brackish coastal waters, they can adjust to fresh water fairly quickly. Adults grow to twelve inches. Because of their size and aggressiveness, they are not suitable for an aquarium with coral fishes. They do very well, however, in a brackish-water aquarium together with, for example, Scats (*Scatophagus argus*) and Monodactylids (*Monodactylus argenteus*). Imported species are:

The **TIGER** (Crescent Perch, Pest of St Lucia), *Therapon jarbua*, and the **GRUNTER** (Banded Grunter), *Therapon (Ecterapon) theraps*. In captivity both species are content with all sorts of animal food.

Squirrelfishes (Soldierfishes)

Holocentridae, comprised of many different species, occur in all tropical seas. In the wild, most species are active only after dusk. In the daytime—alone, paired or in groups—they hide in crevices on the reefs. Their predominant color is red. All species, especially the Soldierfishes, have large eyes. When caught in a net, they can easily damage their eyes, which then become liable to infection. Avoid nets, therefore, whenever possible.

These fishes do well in captivity if amply provided with hiding places. They eat all sorts of animal food and quickly get used to eating in the daytime. They are fast eaters, pouncing from their hiding places upon the food. Sometimes newly imported specimens refuse dead food. In that case, start them on live fish. Nearly all specimens are suitable only for the larger aquarium and can not be kept together with small fish. Imported species:

The **COMMON SQUIRRELFISH** (Red Squirrelfish, Red Soldierfish), *Holocentrus rubrum*, is the most frequently imported species, attaining a length of up to eleven inches. The **RED SQUIRRELFISH** (Spiny Squirrelfish), *H. spinifer*, is red without any stripes and attains a length of about 15 inches. The **ALAIKI KAKALOA** (Crowned Soldierfish), *H. diadema*, whose main characteristic is a black dorsal fin and a white front, is—like the foregoing and other, rarely imported species—native to the Pacific and Indian Oceans.

The **LONGJAW SQUIRRELFISH**, *H. ascensionis*, originates in the Caribbean. Its length does not exceed 20 inches. The **RED SOLDIERFISH** (Blotcheye, Crimson or Big Squirrelfish), *M. murdjan* , is the most commonly imported of the genus *Myripristis*. It is a very beautiful red fish with enormous eyes marked with a black stripe. It has a maximum length of about one foot but in captivity usually remains much smaller, a characteristic shared by its cousins.

The **BLUE SQUIRRELFISH,** *M. adustus*, a rarer species from the Pacific and Indian Oceans, generally resembles the Red Soldierfish. It is differentiated only by a stockier build and purple-red coloring. (See photograph, page 32.)

The **CARIBBEAN SOLDIERFISH,** *M. jacobus*, frequently imported from the Caribbean, is a smaller species and therefore recommended for smaller aquariums.

M. murdjan (see photograph, page 177) and *M. adustus* have spawned in the Artis Aquarium. Their eggs are free-floating. While courting, the male and the female revolve rapidly in ever-diminishing circles at a short distance from the bottom of the tank. At a given moment both fish, still circling each other, move up toward the water surface, where they mate. After the release of eggs and sperm the fish part with a final sweep of their tails, scattering the eggs. Similar mating behavior among *H. rubrum* has also been observed at Artis Aquarium.

Snappers

The Lutjanidae, comprising many different species, inhabit tropical seas. They are coastal fishes, often found on the coral reefs. Nearly all species live in shoals and grow to a respectable length (30–40 inches). They thrive in captivity if provided with

Royal Empress Angelfish, *Pygoplites diacanthus.*

hiding places and a lot of swimming room. Snappers are fast swimmers and voracious eaters, and therefore not suitable for small tanks, nor can they be kept together with small fishes, which they quickly convert to snacks. They accept all sorts of live animal food. When fully grown, they sometimes become aggressive towards their tankfellows.

The most commonly imported species, all from the Pacific or Indian Oceans, are: The **CHECKERED SNAPPER**, *Lutjanus deussatus*; the **BLUE-BANDED HUSSAR** (Yellow-and-Blue Sea Perch, Blue-Striped Snapper, Kasmira Snapper), *L. kasmira*; the **BLUE-BANDED SEA PERCH** (Red Emperor, Government Bream), *L. sebae*, which grows to three feet or more (see photograph, page 35); the **RED SNAPPER** (Saddle-Tailed Sea Perch, Blood-Red Snapper), *L. sanguineus*; and the **SCHOOL-MASTER PERCH** (Black-Spot Sea Perch), *L. fulviflamma.* Another Schoolmaster, *L. apodus*, is the only significant species imported from the Caribbean.

Grunts

The Haemulidae, from the Caribbean Sea and western Atlantic Ocean, are closely related to the snappers. They have teeth in their throats (the pharynx) which produce a remarkable sound intensified by the resonance afforded by the swim bladder. There are some beautifully colored species that adapt themselves easily to tank life. All species live on animal food.

Suitable for the aquarist are the **PORKFISH,** *Anisotremus virginicus,* yellow with blue stripes on the hindquarter and two black diagonal bands across the head; and the **FRENCH GRUNT,** *Haemulon flavolineatum,* blue with irregular yellow, longitudinal stripes. Young grunts clean other fishes. For this behavior trait, see Cleanerfishes, *Labroides.* (See photograph of Porkfish, page 167.)

Sweetlips

This family (Plectorhynchidae), which occurs in the Pacific and Indian Oceans, and the Haemulidae are sometimes classified nowadays as one family, called Pomadasyidae. Nearly all Plectorhynchids live together in schools of varying sizes, although old specimens are sometimes solitary. The coloration of the young differs greatly from that of adults. All species are omnivorous.

Not all, though, are as easy to keep as **YELLOW SWEET-LIPS,** *Plectorhynchus albovittatus* (see photograph, page 244), and **PAINTED SWEETLIPS,** *P. (Spilotichthys) pictus.* The competition for food, though, affects even these, when young, since they are relatively slow eaters.

YELLOW-BANDED SWEETLIPS, *Plectorhynchus lineatus,* and **YELLOW-FINNED SWEETLIPS,** *P. gaterinus,* are more difficult to keep. Neither should be kept with fast eaters. Furthermore, a varied diet is absolutely necessary for them. Like all Plectorhynchidae they are fond of taking mouthfuls of bottom material, which they then sieve out of the mouth.

Still more difficult to keep are **ORIENTAL SWEETLIPS,** *P. orientalis,* and **HARLEQUIN SWEETLIPS** (Clown

Sweetlips), *P. chaetodonoides* (see photograph, page 123.) These can probably be kept alive only if they are fed exclusively on live food, particularly small crustaceans.

Past experience with these fishes has not proven hopeful. Despite good appetites, they often lose weight. A condition that does not stem from infections by intestinal worms or parasites, we attribute the weight loss to inadequate diet. Information about their feeding habits in the wild is unfortunately not yet available.

Sea Basses and Groupers

A large family, the Serranidae comprise about four hundred species of mainly big, predatory fishes native to all tropical and subtropical seas. (Some authorities classify certain genera in a separate family, Grammistidae). Without exception they keep well in captivity, but their size and aggressive nature make most species unsuitable for the living room aquarium. Therefore we shall not consider any species of the genera *Epinephelus, Cephalopholis, Promicrops, Enneacentrus,* and *Variola.* Suitable for the larger aquarium are species of the genera *Grammistes, Chromileptis, Diplectrum* and *Hypoplectrus.*

GOLDEN-STRIPED GROUPER (White- and Black-Striped Sea Bass), *Grammistes sexlineatus.* Grows to a maximum length of ten inches but usually remains much smaller in the aquarium. This beautiful fish will do nicely in captivity if the aquarist keeps it with fish its own size. There is only one objection to this animal: when frightened—by the aggressive behavior of tankfellow or an unusual commotion—it is capable of secreting a substance extremely poisonous to other fishes. It may also release this substance when dying. Range: Pacific and Indian Oceans.

LEOPARDFISH (Polkadot Grouper, Barramundi Cod, Hump-Backed Rock Cod), *Chromileptis altivelis.* A splendid fish, not very predatory or aggressive as long as it is with fishes of the same size. In the wild it attains a length of about 20 inches, but in captivity will not exceed one foot. It swims by paddling its great pectoral fins and, like all sea basses, needs not only plenty of swimming room, but also good hiding places. Range: Pacific and Indian Oceans.

BUTTER HAMLET, *Hypoplectrus unicolor,* and **SAND PERCH,** *Diplectrum formosus.* One foot in length, but usually smaller in captivity. Both species are native to the western Atlantic Ocean and the Caribbean. Desirable and fairly easy to keep.

The family of sea basses also contains smaller species eminently suitable for the living room aquarium. These belong to the genera *Anthias, Serranus, Serranellus* and *Liopropoma.*

ORANGE SEA PERCH (Lyre-Tail Coralfish), *Anthias squamipinnis.* Beautiful, small sea basses, sometimes classified with related species in a separate family, Anthiidae. In the wild they are found in big schools on the coral reefs at depths ranging from 10–250 yards. Red and orange-red specimens are common, and there are many closely related, brilliantly colored species as well. The fins of males are much larger than those of females. These fish are extremely suitable for the living room aquarium, though too difficult for beginning aquarists. As solitary specimens they quickly pine away so they should be kept in groups of at least four. They will give more trouble than other sea basses, because they are fastidious eaters. Their diet should be varied, and all food chopped fine. Optimally, they should be fed small crustaceans exclusively. They require a good deal of swimming room as well as perpendicular hiding places. Maximum length in captivity: about five inches. Range: Indo-Pacific.

HARLEQUIN BASS, *Serranus tigrinus* (formerly *Prionodes tigrinus*). Caribbean native. Easy to keep, making no special demands on the habitat. Not very active. Provided with adequate hiding places, it is content. Maximum length in captivity: five to six inches. (See photograph, page 118.)

BELTED SANDFISH, *Serranellus subligarius.* A Caribbean native sometimes classed within the genus *Serranus.* The members of this species do not grow much beyond six inches. The body is olive-green, the back reddish, the belly silver-white. Like some other species, this fish is hermaphroditic. The male and female reproductive organs are sexually mature when the animals are one inch long. In the spawning period they have ripe sperm as well as eggs. Normally, they spawn in groups, although isolated individuals have been known to fertilize their own eggs.

CANDY BASSLET, *Liopropoma carmabi*. One of the most beautiful of saltwater fishes but unfortunately very rare, it lives at relatively great depths in the Caribbean. First described by Randall in 1963, it has been kept in captivity only once—in the Artis Aquarium, where it survived two years. There its behavior strongly resembled that of *Serranus tigrinus*. The animal hid away in small crevices most of the time, and when swimming about, did not leave the protection of the coral formations. It was observed to be more active at night.

YELLOW EMPEROR (Two-Banded Perch), *Diploprion bifasciatum*. Sometimes placed in its own family, Diploprionidae. Maximum length: ten inches. Range: Indian Ocean and Indonesian Archipelago. The body is yellow with two broad black transverse bars, the upper running over the head through the eye. As they are predatory animals (even the young eat prey as big as themselves), they cannot be kept together with smaller fishes. If frightened or excited (e.g. when moved from container to tank), they secrete a fluid that can be fatal to their tankfellows.

Basslets (Grammidae)

The extremely beautiful **ROYAL GRAMMA** (Fairy Basslet), *Gramma loreto* (formerly *G. hemichrysos*), has been imported regularly. These fish dwell in caves in the Caribbean at relatively great depths. They always swim with their undersides turned towards a solid surface, so when they are at the roofs of their caves, they will turn their backs downward as they propel themselves forward. This behavior may also be observed in the aquarium. The color of the anterior or forward part of the body ranges from violet-blue to purple; the posterior parts are yellow. Adults are probably solitary in nature and become aggressive to individuals of the same species. In the aquarium they may start building nests of algae and nylon floss. This behavior is probably related to reproduction, but no studies are available. Royal Grammas are proficient jumpers, so it is a good idea to cover the tank carefully. They are not very particular about their food, but in view of their secretive habits, it is better to keep them apart from very active fishes that may frighten them away from their hiding places before they have eaten enough. Juveniles, especially, have been observed to clean other fishes. For this behavior trait, see Cleanerfish, *Labroides dimidiatus*. (See photograph of Royal Gramma, page 198 and Cleanerfish, pages 103 and 227.)

Bigeyes (Catalufas, Bulleyes)

Priacanthidae can be recognized by their red bodies and large eyes. They occur at fairly great depths, are active only at night and do not readily become accustomed to eating in the daytime. These factors, plus their inability to compete for food, make them very difficult to keep. A few individuals of the genus *Priacanthus* are sometimes imported, but they are not recommended for the mixed aquarium.

Cardinalfishes (Soldierfishes, Siphonfishes)

Apogonidae occur over a wide range, especially in the tropics. They are attractive little fishes, often beautifully marked. Their large eyes indicate they are nocturnal; particularly the red ones are active only at night. Most species live in schools, but there are a few exceptions. It is believed all species are mouthbrooders (i.e., they incubate their eggs in their mouths). A few days before spawning, the male fertilizes the female's eggs internally. The eggs, when laid, are then carried in his mouth until they hatch.

Not all cardinalfishes are easy to keep. They demand a high quality of water, suffer from competition for food and become nervous among fast-moving fish. Although they accept only live food at first, they quickly get used to eating anything.

The species most suitable for the aquarium are **CARDINAL-FISH,** *Apogon nematopterus* and *A. novemfasciatus*, and **NINE-BANDED SOLDIERFISH,** *Lovamia novemfasciatus*. (See photograph of Cardinalfish, page 40.)

Jacks and Pompanos

Occurring mainly in the open oceans, this family (Carangidae) is represented mostly by species which grow to a respectable size. The most commonly imported jacks are juveniles of the **GOLDEN JACK** (Golden Trevally), *Caranx (Gnathanodon) speciosus*. Though attractively colored and marked, they are not suitable for the amateur, since under good conditions they quickly outgrow the confines of the small home aquarium. Maximum length: about three feet.

Two interesting and bizarre species of Pompano are **DIAMOND TREVALLY** (Threadfin, Diamondfish, Mirrorfish or Moonfish), *Alectis indica*, and the **PENNANT TREVALLY** (Threadfin), *Alectis crinitus*, commonly called Threadfishes. When young, these deep-bodied, laterally compressed fishes possess long, thread-like streamers extending from the first rays of the dorsal and anal fins. These streamers can be many times longer than the body itself, but gradually disappear as the fishes mature. Threadfishes are difficult to keep as they are very sensitive. They need a good deal of swimming room and should be kept in a separate tank, for other fishes sometimes consider their streamers edible. Young specimens need live food (small crustaceans). Later on they accept all sorts of dead animal food. The *crinitus* grows to 15 inches, but in Hawaii the *indica* has been recorded as two feet and in Indian waters is said to reach five feet. (See photograph of Pennant Trevally, page 159.)

Croakers (Drums)

These fishes (the Sciaenidae) are found in all subtropical and tropical seas. The first dorsal fin is narrow and usually greatly elongated; the second is long and low. In most species the snout is rounded. The majority of species produce a loud sound, using the muscles attached to the sides of the air bladder. Only the Ribbonfishes of the Caribbean qualify for the tropical saltwater aquarium, but often do not thrive. Attractive, quiet animals, they usually do not give any trouble during the first few months

Royal Gramma, *Gramma loreto*.

in a tank, then suddenly show a heightened susceptibility to skin infections, refuse food or die without any visible cause. Relatively slow eaters, they can not 'be kept together with fast-moving, voracious fishes. They are best fed on crustaceans or crab meat. All need a great deal of swimming room. Adult specimens are quarrelsome among themselves. The least difficult species, *Equetus acuminatus*, commonly called **CUBBYU** (High-Hat), has spawned in the aquarium. Next comes the **STRIPED DRUM** (Striped Ribbonfish), *Equetus pulcher*, and the most delicate of all is the beautiful **JACKKNIFEFISH** (Ribbonfish), *Equetus lanceolatus*.

Goatfishes (Mullidae)

Active, bottom-dwelling animals, these fishes range widely through the tropics, living inshore in schools. Observers of limited experience maintain that goatfishes are "easy to keep." (Whenever we use that term in this book, we mean a species can live for years in captivity—provided, of course, their normal life expectancy is that long. Unfortunately, many authors apply the term as soon as the fish has been kept for one year or less.) In point of fact, goatfishes show up well in an aquarium but have not been kept successfully so far, not even in the big public aquariums. The trouble may stem from the fact that they are usually imported in small numbers, so that they can not school.

Goatfishes are quickly recognized by the two long barbels on the lower lip, with which they feel the bottom for food—mainly worms, crustaceans and snails. Like all bottom-haunters, they suffer severely from food competition. In captivity they usually accept all kinds of food, but after a few months start losing weight and die six to nine months later.

The most commonly imported species are the **INDIAN GOATFISH** (Yellow-Spot Goatfish), *Parupeneus indicus*, and the **BAR-TAILED GOATFISH** (Mottled Goatfish), *Upeneus tragula*—both native to the Indo-Pacific.

Fingerfishes (Silver Batfishes)

Monodactylidae will be familiar to the freshwater aquarist. All species can be maintained in fresh water, though they do better in brackish, where they breed, particularly in the estuaries of large rivers and in mangrove swamps. The older they get, the closer they move to the sea, ultimately to dwell in shallow inshore waters. The most frequently imported species, the **SINGAPORE ANGEL** (Diamondfishes, Mono or Common Fingerfishes), *Monodactylus argenteus*, found in the Indo-Pacific, will probably die if kept in fresh water too long. It is nonetheless ideal for the beginning saltwater aquarist. Monodactylidae accept all sorts of animal food. As they are a schooling species, it is advisable to keep them in groups of at least four. Isolated specimens become nervous, and more aggressive fishes may mistreat them. Maximum length: eight inches.

The **MOONFISH** (West African Mono), *Monodactylus sebae*, occurs along the West Coast of Africa. It is the most beautiful species, having elongated dorsal and anal fins. The **CAPE LADY,** *M. falciformis*, found along the Red Sea coast and throughout the Indo-Pacific, is rather plain and therefore seldom imported.

Archerfishes (Riflefishes)

Toxotidae inhabit mangrove swamps and the brackish water of estuaries. They should not be kept in a saltwater aquarium, but will do nicely in a brackish-water tank.

Butterfishes (Scats)

Some ichthyologists consider Scatophagidae a subfamily of Chaetodontidae. Like the fingerfishes, the scats also inhabit mangrove swamps, estuaries and, when adult, shallow inshore waters, but seldom coral reefs. They will give little trouble in a saltwater or brackish-water aquarium. They are omnivorous and require vegetable matter (algae, lettuce or aquatic plants) in addition to animal food.

The species most commonly imported is the **SPOTTED SCAT,** *Scatophagus argus*, which occurs in two color variations: one basically green, and the other mostly red, concentrated on the top of the head and back. Red individuals can be found among the green ones; thus there is no reason to consider them a separate subspecies (*S. a. rubrifrons*), although this is sometimes done.

AFRICAN SCAT, *Scatophagus tetracanthus*, ranges throughout the coasts of South and Southeast Africa. It differs from the Spotted Scat in that it has four brown-black vertical bars across its body.

The **FALSE SCAT** (Many-Banded Scat, Striped Butterfish),

Scatophagus multifasciata, is marked by transverse dark bands, and often considered under another genus (*Selenotoca*).

Batfishes

Platacidae are a small family of deep-bodied fishes, whose elongated and enlarged dorsal fins are especially evident in youth. Resembling leaves, young specimens will drift through the water without any discernible movement of the fins. Although this might seem a strange form of camouflage, it is in fact very effective, because young batfishes usually inhabit mangrove swamps, estuaries and large brackish lagoons along Indo-Pacific coasts, where there is an abundance of floating and submerged leaves.

In captivity they are usually easy to care for. Though occasionally some individuals cause great difficulties, usually these are sick upon arrival. Normal, healthy specimens readily accept all types of animal food in large quantities. They grow exceptionally fast, and may outgrow a small tank within a year, most species attaining a length of 20 inches or more. They are rather quarrelsome and, if transported in groups, not a single specimen will arrive with undamaged fins. Batfishes may be kept together in an aquarium if there are at least four the same size. If not, aggressiveness may develop, resulting in the death of one or more fishes. Although most ichthyologists distinguish different species, there is reason to believe that there is only one wide-ranging species.

ORBICULATE BATFISH (Narrow-Banded Batfish), *Platax orbicularis*, is the most commonly imported species. The coloration of juveniles varies widely; some are light brown, others orange-brown with black or white spots. Older specimens, usually uniformly brown, have three dark vertical stripes, black pectorals and much shorter fins than young specimens. The profile of all stages, from young to adult, is markedly aquiline. (See photograph, page 148.)

SEA BAT (Long-Finned Batfish), *P. pinnatus*. This species is immediately recognizable by the red to orange-yellow band

Sea Bat, *Platax pinnatus.*

running from the snout over the head to the base of the dorsal fin. The same colors may appear on the edges of the anal and dorsal fins. In older individuals the red coloration slowly disappears. (See photograph above.)

The **ROUND-FACED BATFISH,** *P. teira,* closely resembles *orbicularis,* but may be distinguished by its longer dorsal, anal, and pectoral fins and its straight profile.

Butterflyfishes

The family Chaetodontidae consists of two sub-families—both entirely tropical: the butterflyfishes (Chaetodontinae) and the angelfishes (Pomacanthinae) discussed below. Typical coral fishes, they may also occasionally be found near rocky coasts and ship-wrecks. Almost all the butterflies and angels are so compressed laterally that they can slip easily into reef clefts and crevices.

Nearly all have brilliant color patterns. Unfortunately, they are the most sensitive of creatures, so, in spite of their alluring appearance, the beginning aquarist should hesitate to keep them. Like all true reef fishes, most species, especially the angelfishes, are territorial and aggressive towards their own kind. If hiding places are generously provided, they will swim freely through the tank in the daytime; otherwise they will remain shy and accept food only hesitatingly.

In the wild butterflyfishes constantly hunt for small prey on the coral reefs or among the algae fields. Many eat algae: some species probably specialize in feeding on coral polyps. They can not be kept together with small sea anemones, living coral or tubeworms as they nibble or devour these invertebrates. In captivity, their diet should be as varied as possible, with small crustaceans an absolute must, and vegetable matter, algae, aquatic plants, lettuce and oatmeal, in addition. Algae meal is probably very good for them. Butterflyfishes often lose weight in captivity even if they eat well. Emaciation can first be observed in the area just behind the head and is probably due to an inadequate diet. Never keep them with fast eaters, as they suffer from competition. They can swallow only relatively small morsels, and let themselves be chased away from food by cocky tankmates. Most are aggressive towards their own species, so best keep only one of a kind. Other species they will sometimes tolerate, sometimes not. The availability of ample room for evasive tactics and the absence of any superficial resemblance among the individuals favorably affects the compatibility of tankfellows.

Wimplefishes (genus *Heniochus*) school in the open water of the coral reefs. The least demanding of the butterflyfishes, they are less specialized eaters and will not, as a rule, present any great problem. They are, however, nearly as sensitive as the "true" butterflyfishes to the quality of the water. The most commonly imported species is the **FEATHER-FIN BULLFISH** (Wimple-fish, Pennant Coralfish, Poor Man's Moorish Idol), *H. acuminatus*, the members of which grow to eight inches in the wild as well as in large tanks. Other imported species are the **HUMPHEAD BANNERFISH**, *H. varius*, the **HORNED PENNANT,** *H.*

monceros, and the **BROWN WIMPLEFISH**, *H. singularis*. Young *Heniochus* act as cleanerfishes.

The **LONG-NOSED BUTTERFLYFISH** (Copperbranded Butterflyfish, Beaked Coralfish), *Chelmon rostratus*, has a long, pointed snout to catch small organisms living among the corals. In captivity, it is a touchy eater. If the composition of the water changes, it generally reacts by fasting; if this happens, try a pH correction and tempt it with brine shrimp and *Tubifex*. Do this immediately, because a Longnose loses weight rapidly and, once emaciated, is even more difficult to persuade to eat.

You need a very large tank if you want to keep more than one specimen, as Longnoses are very aggressive towards their own kind. Range: Indo-Pacific. Maximum size: six inches. (See photograph, page 138.)

The **FORCEPSFISH** (Long-Snouted Coralfish, Long Bill), *Forcipiger longirostris*, is almost the same shape as the Longnose, but differently colored. The upper side of the head is brown, the lower side yellowish white, and the body yellow. It requires the same treatment as the Longnose and has similar sensitivities to the environment. Maximum length: eight inches. Range: Indo-Pacific, particularly around the Philippines. (See photograph, page 64.)

The "true" butterflyfishes (genera *Chaetodon*, *Parachaetodon*) include numerous species, all brilliantly colored, most of which occur in the tropical Indo-Pacific and the Red Sea. Far fewer species are found in the tropical parts of the Atlantic and the Caribbean. Many species have already been imported, and new ones are frequently offered. The following list makes no pretense of being complete. Included, however, are the most commonly imported, with descriptions of those which, with a reasonable amount of care, can be kept in captivity:

THREADFIN BUTTERFLY, *Chaetodon* (*Anisochaetodon*) *auriga*. Frequently imported and fairly easy to keep. The adults have a large, dark spot on the dorsal fin, which is elongated into a filament extending beyond the tail. Maximum length: $7\frac{1}{2}$ inches. Range: Red Sea, Indo-Pacific. (See photograph, page 227.)

FOUR-EYE BUTTERFLY, *Chaetodon capistratus*. Fairly easy to keep, these have a large, white-ringed dark spot near the base of the tail. Maximum length: six inches. Range: the tropical parts of the Atlantic and the Caribbean. (See photograph, page 65.)

PEARL-SCALE BUTTERFLY, *C. chrysurus.* Seldom imported. Body color yellow-white with small black spots marking the flanks. The backs of the dorsal, anal and tail fins are red-brown. Maximum size: six inches. Range: Red Sea, Indo-Pacific. (See photograph, page 154.)

SPECKLED BUTTERFLY (Citron Coralfish), *C. citrinellus.* A small species, with a maximum length of 3½ inches. The body is yellowish white, marked on the sides with diagonal rows of dark spots. Range: Indo-Pacific.

PAKISTANI BUTTERFLY, *C. collaris.* Frequently imported and fairly easy to keep. A dark bar runs through the eye with white bands on either side. The dorsal and anal fins have red edges at the back. Maximum length: six inches. Range: Indo-Pacific. (See photograph, page 151.)

SADDLED CORALFISH (Saddleback or Black-Blotched Butterfly), *C. ephippium.* This fish is easily identified by the large black marking on the back. The lower part of the head is yellow, and the dorsal fin elongated into a long filament. Maximum length: eight inches. Range: Philippines and Hawaii.

SADDLED BUTTERFLY (Pig-Faced Butterfly), *C. falcula.* Recognizable by its yellow dorsal, anal and caudal fins, the black band running through the eye and the two large, wedge-shaped dark patches on the back. Maximum length: eight inches. Range: Red Sea, Indo-Pacific.

BLUE-STRIPED BUTTERFLY, *C. frembli.* Pale yellow with oblique blue stripes across the flanks. Maximum length: eight inches. Range: Red Sea, Indo-Pacific.

KLEIN'S CORALFISH (White-Spotted Butterfly), *C. (Anisochaetodon) kleini.* Relatively easy to keep, this species has a yellow body with rows of black dots on the flanks. Maximum length: 4½ inches. Range: Indo-Pacific.

REDHEADED BUTTERFLYFISH, *C. larvatus.* A beautiful species, with a red to reddish brown head, a blue body with diagonal yellow stripes, a black tail, and orange pectoral fins. It is one of the few butterflies found in small schools. Difficult to keep and often temperamental about its food, it is best started on the nauplii of *Artemia* and *Tubifex.* Size: about three inches. Range: Red Sea. (See photograph, page 179.)

RED-STRIPED BUTTERFLY, *C. lunula.* Relatively easy to keep, this species is identified by a yellow to yellowish green body and a sickle-shaped shoulder patch separated by a broad white band from the dark bar running through the eye. Maximum size: eight inches. Range: Red Sea, Indo-Pacific.

C. meyeri. Body color blue with diagonal black stripes. The belly is orange. Very difficult to keep. Maximum length: ten inches. Range: Indo-Pacific.

SPOTFIN BUTTERFLY, *C. ocellatus.* Known to clean other fishes, this species has a yellow body with a black, vertical band running through the eye and a large black spot on the base of the second dorsal fin. Maximum length: six inches. Range: the tropical parts of the Atlantic Ocean and the Caribbean.

EIGHT-BANDED BUTTERFLY, *C. octofasciatus.* Recognizable by seven black transverse bars across the body and one across the head. Fairly easy to keep. Maximum length: eight inches. Range: Red Sea, Indo-Pacific. (See photograph, page 52.)

C. pictus. Whitish with a black, transverse bar passing through the eye and a black bar at the rear of the body covering the whole back part of the dorsal fin. Fairly easy to keep. Many authorities consider *pictus* a color variant of *C. vagabundus* (see below) and the latter the correct name. Maximum length: eight inches. Range: Red Sea, Indian Ocean (especially around Ceylon).

C. semilarvatus. Yellow body marked with thin, vertical, orange lines. The eye is in a black patch extending backwards to the gill covers. This species adapts readily to living in an aquarium. Size: about six inches. Range: Red Sea.

BANDED BUTTERFLY, *C. striatus.* White with two broad, dark bars on the flanks and a narrow, black band passing through the eye. Fairly easy to keep. Size: eight inches. Range: tropical parts of the Atlantic Ocean, along West Africa, and the Caribbean.

REDFIN BUTTERFLY (Lineated Butterfly, Three-Banded Butterfly), *C. trifasciatus.* One of the most beautiful butterflyfishes. The body is pale yellow, the anal fin red or orange-red with two black longitudinal stripes, and the dorsal fin yellow or orange. Probably a specialized eater limited to coral polyps, this fish will seldom eat in captivity. Maximum length: five inches. Range: Red Sea and Indo-Pacific.

VAGABOND BUTTERFLY (Vagabond Coralfish, Criss-Cross Butterfly), *C. vagabundus.* Resembles *C. pictus* (see above), except for a partially black dorsal fin and a yellow rear part. This species does quite well in captivity. Maximum length: eight inches. Range: Indo-Pacific, Red Sea.

ONE-SPOT BUTTERFLY, *C.* (*Anisochaetodon*) *unimaculatus.* The body ranges from pale yellow to yellow, while the dorsal, anal and caudal fins are always yellow. A large dark spot edged with white appears just above the center of the body. A dark bar runs through the eye and another one through the posterior parts of the dorsal fin, the tail base and the anal fin. Fairly easy to keep. Maximum size: 4½ inches. Range: Indo-Pacific.

YELLOWHEAD BUTTERFLY, *C. xanthocephalus.* An orange yellow head, and a whitish blue body marked with angular transverse stripes. Fairly easy to keep. Size: eight inches. Range: Indo-Pacific.

Skunk-Striped Anemone Fish, *Amphiprion akallopisus.*

Angelfishes

Pomacanthinae are distinguished from the butterflyfishes by thicker bodies, laterally, and the presence of a sharp spine on each gill cover. The variation in color pattern of juvenile and adult is so considerable, that they used to be described as separate species. The conversion in marking usually occurs when the fish reaches $3\frac{1}{2}$-$4\frac{1}{2}$ inches, but may take place later.

Angelfishes are territorial and extremely intolerant of their own kind, so don't keep two individuals of the same species in one tank, or the young specimens of different species, since they resemble each other. Those that do not resemble each other, however, may be kept together.

Angelfishes, particularly the larger species, accept only relatively small pieces of food and are fastidious feeders. Fast-swimming, quick-eating fishes often snatch food away from them. In the wild they eat, among other things, sponges and scrape small animals and algae from rocks and dead corals. In captivity they regard pieces of lettuce, algae and aquatic plants as tasty additions to their diet, so vegetable food appears to be indispensable for their successful maintenance. Easier to keep than butterflyfishes, angelfishes are of a retiring nature, and should be generously provided with hiding places.

EMPEROR ANGELFISH (Imperial Angelfish), *Pomacanthus imperator*. Young specimens are blue with angular, ringlike, white stripes and a closed white ring just before the base of the tail. The front of the head is marked with white transverse lines. Adults are blue to blue-green with 20 somewhat oblique yellow lines. The head is also yellow with a black bar through the eye and one behind the gill plate. Maximum length: 16 inches. Range: Red Sea and Indo-Pacific. (See photograph, page 56.)

KORAN ANGELFISH (Semicircle or Zebra Angelfish), *P. semicirculatus*. The young are blue with white, slightly curved, transverse bands, and white, longitudinal striping on the front of the head. Adults have a greenish yellow body with anterior black spots, a black posterior and elongated dorsal and anal fins. Maximum length: 16 inches. Range: Red Sea, Indo-Pacific. (See photographs, pages 125 and 130.)

BLUE KING ANGELFISH (Blue-Ring Angel, Circled

Angelfish), *P. annularis*. Juveniles are blue with almost straight white transverse bands. White longitudinal stripes mark the front of the head. The tail fin is nearly colorless, unlike the half blue-white one of the young Koran Angels. Adults have a brown body, and oblique stripes of blue occur on the flanks. The tail fin is yellow. Maximum size: 16 inches. Range: Red Sea, Indo-Pacific. (See photograph, page 29.)

SEABRIDE (Purple Moon Angelfish), *P. maculosus*. A blue body with a yellow patch across the flanks. Maximum length: 16 inches. Range: Red Sea.

BLUE SEABRIDE (Purple Crescent Angelfish), *P. asfur*. Resembles the preceding species closely, but the yellow band across the flanks starts just before the base of the anal fin. Unlike *P. maculosus*, the anal fin is as greatly elongated as the dorsal fin. The tail fin is yellow, the body itself dark blue. Fairly easy to keep, but very aggressive towards individuals of the same species. Size: six inches. Range: Red Sea.

FRENCH ANGELFISH, *P. paru*. The young are black with four yellow transverse bands, and a tail fin with a small rear yellow band and a wide, curved front yellow band. The adults are black with yellow-edged scales. Maximum length: one foot. Range: tropical parts of the Atlantic Ocean and the Caribbean. (See photograph, page 103.)

BLACK ANGELFISH (Gray Angelfish), *P. arcuatus*. The juveniles are black with four transverse yellow bars. They are distinguished from the French Angelfish by the coloring of the tail fin, which has a nearly straight, anterior, yellow stripe, separated from the nearly colorless rear edge by a straight, black band. The third yellow bar in the body is shorter and does not extend to the top of the dorsal fin. Adults are gray-black with a black dot on each scale. Maximum length: two feet. Range: the tropical parts of the Atlantic Ocean and the Caribbean. (See photographs, pages 8 and 9.)

ROCK BEAUTY, *Holacanthus tricolor*. The young specimen, predominantly yellow, has a large, black spot, ringed with blue, on the back. As the fish grows, it turns yellow-orange, and the black spot spreads until it covers the greater part of the body. The dorsal and anal fins have red edges. The Rock Beauty is rather difficult to keep. In captivity it is very susceptible to all types of skin infections, as well as infection by *Ichthyosporidium hoferi*. It needs vegetable matter in addition to its animal diet. Size: almost two feet. Range: the tropical parts of the Atlantic Ocean and the Caribbean. (See photograph, page 186.)

ROYAL EMPRESS ANGELFISH (Regal Angel, Blue-Banded Angelfish), *Pygoplites diacanthus.* An extremely beautiful species, which up to now has not been kept successfully, because almost all specimens refuse to eat. They are sometimes interested in the food offered and even swallow it, later spitting it out again. We know no reason for this behavior; perhaps this species has a specialized diet of which we are unaware. Size: ten inches. Range: Red Sea and Indo-Pacific. (See photograph, page 191.)

BLUE ANGEL, *Angelichthys* (*Holacanthus*) *isabelita.* Very rarely imported and difficult to keep, these fishes make great demands upon the water quality and are very fastidious eaters. The coloration of the young differs greatly from that of adults. Size: 18 inches. Range: the tropical parts of the Atlantic Ocean and the Caribbean.

QUEEN ANGELFISH (Queen Angel), *Angelichthys* (*Holacanthus*) *ciliaris.* Rarely imported and as difficult to keep as the Blue Angelfish, it is very particular about food and the quality of water. Both species must be treated with utmost care and should be kept in tanks specially fitted out for them. **TOWNSEND'S ANGELFISH,** *A. townsendi,* is believed to be a hybrid of the Blue and Queen Angels.) Size: two feet. Range: the tropical parts of the Atlantic and the Caribbean. (See photograph of Queen Angelfish, page 170.)

CHERUBFISH (Pygmy Angelfish), *Centropyge argi.* Easy to keep, but must struggle in competition for food. Maximum length: $2\frac{1}{2}$ inches. Range: the tropical parts of the Atlantic and the Caribbean. (See photograph, page 45.)

TWO-COLORED ANGELFISH (Oriole Angel, Black and Gold Angelfish, Yellow and Black Angelfish), *C. bicolor.* This species is seldom imported, and little is known about its adaptability to aquarium life. Maximum length: five inches. Range: Indo-Pacific.

FISHER'S ANGELFISH, *C. fisheri.* A rare species. Basically orange with flanks shading to gray and ventral fins crested in blue. Size: three to five inches. Range: Indo-Pacific.

DUSKY ANGELFISH, *C. bispinosus.* This species is fairly easy to keep. Maximum length: five inches. Range: Indo-Pacific.

YELLOW-FACED ANGELFISH, *Euxiphipops xantho-metopon,* and **BLUE-GIRDLED ANGELFISH,** *E. navarchus.* Fishes of this genus are strikingly beautiful, but very expensive. These two species, the more splendid of the genus, attain a respectable length and require the same treatment as other angelfishes. Somewhat more frequently imported is the **SIX-BANDED ANGELFISH,** *Euxiphipops sexstriatus.*

Damselfishes (Demoiselles, Coralfishes)

The numerous coral reef fishes that comprise this family (Poma-centridae) are, for the most part, small and very hardy. They are considered among the "easier" fishes for the beginning aquarist. Many species have hatched fertilized eggs in captivity, but up till now it has been impossible to feed the fry adequately. Though every possible substitution for their natural plankton diet has been tried, the fry have always refused to eat and died of starvation after a few days. However, tests by Dr Wilfred Neugebauer of Stuttgart indicate *Euplotes* may be used successfully as food, as in the case of young seahorses.

Some authorities group the damselfishes as various families within the order Amphiprioniformes. Thus, the Clownfishes (genus *Amphiprion*) would be in the family Amphiprionidae, the genus *Chromis* in the family Chromidae, and so on. However, this has not been generally adopted, so we will retain the classification of the family Pomacentridae, divided into various genera.

No survey of the many species of damselfishes has ever been completed. In fact, so many species have already been imported that it would be impractical to describe them all here, and unnecessary as well, since all require more or less the same treatment. We will mention only the main representatives of the principal genera.

In general, so far as we know, all damselfishes guard their eggs until they hatch, just like the freshwater cichlids, to which they are related. Unlike the cichlids, their care does not extend to the young fry.

All species of damselfishes that live on the reefs—rather than in schools in the open water above the reefs—are territorial and, in the tank, extremely aggressive, especially to individuals of the same species.

Clownfishes (Anemone Fishes). The members of the genus *Amphiprion* live symbiotically with the giant sea anemones of the genera *Discosoma*, *Radianthus* and *Stoichactus*. These sea anemones are dangerous to all other fishes because their tentacles are covered with stinging cells (nematocysts), some of which upon contact discharge small darts of poison into the body of their prey. Other nematocysts on the tentacles eject sticky threads, which hold the prey until it is swept into the mouth of the sea anemone. The Clownfish is protected from the sea anemones by a substance in the mucus of the outer membrane which inhibits the sea anemone from discharging its stinging cells. A piece of sponge that has been rubbed over the skin of a Clownfish will not be stung and grasped by a sea anemone, whereas an untreated bit of sponge will trigger off the stinging-grasping mechanism. If a Clownfish is deprived of its mucous membrane, it will fall prey to the sea anemone. Thus, a sick Clownfish will leave the sea anemone, because its infected membrane apparently does not produce enough mucus.

Although the association between sea anemones and Clown-fishes is called *symbiosis*, it is not symbiosis in the strictest sense, as this term presumes a relationship that is advantageous to both animals. The advantage to the Clownfish is evident: nestled among the tentacles of the sea anemones he is safe from enemies. But the advantage to the sea anemone remains obscure. It was once thought that the fishes purposely provided the anemones with food or even lured other fishes towards the tentacles. Probably neither belief is correct. It is true that in captivity Clownfishes sometimes do take large chunks of food to the anemones, but not in order to feed them. They put the food among the tentacles, close to the edge of the disk, but as soon as the tentacles take hold, the Clownfish starts to tear away at the chunk and eat pieces of it at the same time the anemone is trying to carry the food to its mouth. Just as the food is about to reach the mouth, the Clownfish removes the chunk, putting it between tentacles farther from the anemone's mouth. Taking chunks of food to a sea anemone, thus, appears to be nothing but a device to enable the Clownfish to tear its prey more easily. The sea anemone does not profit at all. For that matter, it can hardly be a common occurrence in the wild for a Clownfish to capture a large chunk of food, so the behavior described above is relatively rare. Clownfishes feed mostly on small, free-swimming crustaceans, which they devour in one gulp. Adding to this the fact that in captivity sea anemones are healthier and remain alive longer if there are no Clownfishes living in the tank, it seems safe to assume that the association of sea anemones and Clownfishes is profitable only to the fishes. It would, therefore, be better to use the term *commensalism*, where only one partner benefits while the other remains generally unharmed.

Almost all Clownfishes are easy to keep in captivity. Their requirements as to quality of water and diet are not rigid. Properly cared for, they will spawn regularly. One pair can be very prolific. At the Artis Aquarium, *Amphiprion percula* and *Amphiprion xanthurus* spawned between one hundred and four hundred eggs regularly every two weeks over a period of two and four years, respectively. Furthermore, the eggs yielded viable fry. The fishes prefer to deposit their eggs at the base of a sea anemone, but once the site is selected, they continue to use it even if the sea anemone is moved away. Clownfishes can be kept quite well even when deprived of sea anemones, but they will not spawn as easily and as regularly. Experiments have shown that in captivity species will accept as hosts even sea anemones from the Mediterranean. In the wild, however, each species has its own commensal sea anemone.

When a Clownfish becomes sexually mature, it defends a territory of at least two or three feet around an anemone. Fishes of the same species are not tolerated in another's territory. Clownfishes occur throughout the Indo-Pacific, and some species are found in the Red Sea as well.

CLOWNFISH (Clown Anemone Fish, Orange Anemone Fish), *Amphiprion percula*. More sensitive than most Clownfishes, this is, however, the most commonly imported and least expensive species. The body is orange with three white transverse bands. Several pairs can live together in one large sea anemone, but not in a small one. Size: four inches. (See photograph, page 48.)

PINK SKUNK CLOWN (False Skunk-Striped Anemone Fish), *A. perideraion*. Flesh-colored with one white band along the back and a vertical one over the head. More sensitive than the common Clownfish. Maximum length: three inches. (See photograph, page 162.)

SKUNK-STRIPED ANEMONE FISH (Yellow Skunk Clown, White-Backed Anemone Fish), *A. akallopisus*. Easy to keep, this species resembles the preceding, but does not have the band over the head. Size: 2½–3 inches. Occurs mostly in the Pacific Ocean. (See photograph, page 207.)

TOMATO CLOWN (Fire Clown, Saddle Anemone Fish, Black-Backed Anemone Fish), *A. ephippium*. Not easy to identify, for coloration and markings vary widely, depending on origin. The body is bright or brownish red. On the back there may or may not be a large saddle-shaped black patch, which occasionally covers both flanks entirely. Sometimes a white stripe runs over the head. This hardy species is ideal for the beginner. Size: 4½–5 inches. (See photograph, page 234.)

YELLOW-TAILED ANEMONE FISH (Black Clown Fish), *A. xanthurus*. Very often imported and easy to keep. Three vertical white bands run over a dark-brown to black body. In juveniles the middle bar goes through to the top of the dorsal fin, but in adults does not extend so far. Fin color differs from one specimen to the next. Sometimes they are partly black and partly yellow; sometimes only the pectoral and tail fins are yellow, while the other fins are black. Size: four inches.

BANDED CLOWN (Two-Banded Anemone Fish), *A. bicinctus*. The body color ranges from orange to orange-brown, with two white vertical bands tapering into points. Juveniles have a third white band near the tail. The belly, as well as half the tail base, is orange-yellow. Easy to keep. Size: six inches.

WHITE-TIPPED ANEMONE FISH (Saddle-Back Clown, Yellow-Finned Anemone Fish, Black Clown), *A. polymnus*. Often confused with another species, *A. sebae*. The mature fishes have a brown to black body marked with two vertical bands, of which the second is oblique and curves into the dorsal fin. The belly and part of the tail base are yellow. The fins are black or partly black. Size: 4½–5 inches.

SADDLE-BACK CLOWN, *A. laticlavius*. Readily identified by a large, white, saddle-shaped patch on the back. It probably occurs only in the Indo-Pacific. In captivity it grows poorly and loses some of its brightness—almost certainly due to an inadequate diet. Maximum length: 4½ inches.

Spanish Hogfish, *Bodianus rufus*.

BLACK CLOWN, *A. sebae*. The body is black or dark brown. Juvenile forms have three white bands across the body, the second of which extends into the dorsal fin. The third band fades and disappears from back to front as the fish matures. The tail and pectoral fins are yellow, the others black. This species was at one time confused with *A. polymnus*. Easy to keep. Maximum length: five inches. (See photograph, page 13.)

DUSKY ANEMONE FISH (Black Anemone Fish), *A. melanopus*. Resembles *A. perideraion* but lacks the band across the back and has a darker body. Easy to keep. Maximum length: 2½ inches.

SPINE-CHEEKED ANEMONE FISH (Tomato Clownfish), *Premnas biaculeatus*. Distinguished from the species of the above genus by a spike below the eyes. Some authorities even place it in its own family, Premnidae. The body, which varies from brown to red, is marked with three white transverse bands. It probably has a symbiotic relationship with only one species of sea anemone. Sometimes its aggressive nature creates difficulties in the tank. Maximum length: six inches. Range: Indonesian Archipelago. (See cover photograph.)

YELLOW-TAIL DAMSELFISH, *Microspathodon chrysurus*.

Spiny Boxfish, *Chilomycterus schoepfi*.

A small, easy-to-keep damselfish. Young specimens are dark blue with small bright blue spots. It can be very aggressive, even towards fishes other than its own species, but less so when kept in a medium to large tank with plenty of hiding places. It requires a mixed diet, that is, food of both animal and vegetable origin. Maximum length: six inches. Range: tropical western Atlantic Ocean and Caribbean.

Dascyllus. The species of the genus *Dascyllus* are among the easiest marine fish to keep in captivity. In the wild they live in schools around isolated coralheads. When some danger threatens, the members of the school dive in unison into the interstices of the coral. The juveniles in particular, like the Clownfishes, can live among the giant sea anemones. Adults never do this, at least not in captivity.

Mature specimens become aggressive, especially in the breeding season. Spawning is initiated by the male cleaning branches or flat stones where the eggs are to be deposited. He then tries to lure the female by swimming quickly up and down in the vicinity of the nest, and guards the eggs until they hatch. In captivity damselfishes have spawned quite readily, including the following in the Artis Aquarium: *Dascyllus carneus*, *D. trimaculatus*, *D. reticulatus*, *D. aruanus*, and *D. marginatus*.

The Clownfishes and the *Dascyllus* species produce a clearly audible clicking noise. In the wild they live on plankton; therefore, finely chopped food is best. Small crustaceans and pieces of mussels and fishmeat are ideal.

CLOUDY DAMSEL, *D. carneus*. Imported in large numbers from Ceylon. The large round white spot on the back disappears when the fish is sick. The tail is white. Maximum length: 3½ inches. Range: Indo-Pacific.

WHITE-TAILED DAMSELFISH (Banded Humbug, Humbug Damsel, White-Tailed Footballer), *D. aruanus*. The white body is marked with three black bars, the first two of which are oblique. The tail fin is white. The female, which is smaller, has a white spot on the front of the head. Maximum length: 3½ inches. Range: Indo-Pacific.

BLACK-TAILED HUMBUG (Black-Tailed Footballer), *D. melanurus*. Looks very much like the preceding species, but with vertical instead of oblique bars, and a black tailfin, except for a thin white edge. Maximum length: 2½–3 inches. Range: Pacific Ocean. (See photograph, page 25.)

DOMINO DAMSEL (Three-Spot Humbug, White-Spot Puller), *D. trimaculatus*. Most frequently imported of all species. Its body is velvety black with three white spots. The brighter these spots, the more at home the fish feels. Older fishes may lose their spots altogether. Size: four to five inches. Range: Red Sea, Indo-Pacific.

RETICULATED DAMSELFISH (Reticulated Puller), *D. reticulatus*. The body has a yellowish brown tone, the darker edges of its scales giving it a reticulated appearance. A dark band runs from the base of the dorsal fin to the base of the ventral fin. Maximum length: four inches. Range: Indo-Pacific.

MARGINATE DAMSELFISH (Marginate Puller), *D. marginatus*. Closely related to *D. reticulatus*. The head and part of the lower body is gray or gray-brown, the rest yellow-white with blue margined scales. The upper border of the dorsal fin is blue or black. Maximum length: four inches. Range: Red Sea and possibly the Persian Gulf. (See photograph, page 142.)

BLUE DEMOISELLE (Yellowtail), *Chromis xanthurus.* Often imported from Ceylon and Singapore. Juveniles are bright blue with a yellow tail base and tail fin. Adult specimens turn dark blue or brownish and the yellow of the tail fades. The young are easy to keep, especially in small schools in spacious tanks. The mature fishes can be very aggressive, particularly toward individuals of the same species. They accept all types of animal food and spawn fairly readily. Maximum length: four inches. Range: Indo-Pacific.

BICOLOR CHROMIS (Half-and-Half Puller), *C. dimidiatus.* Quite similar to the preceding species but distinguished by a sharply defined yellow patch on the hindquarters. Easy to keep. Maximum length: six inches. Range: Indo-Pacific.

BLUE DEVIL (Electric Blue Damsel), *Pomacentrus coeruleus.* With coloration much like that of *C. xanthurus*, it has a more slender, yellower tail and a more pointed head. Easy to keep. Maximum length: four inches. Range: Indo-Pacific. (See photograph, page 29.)

GREEN DAMSEL (Blue-Green Chromis, Blue-Green Puller, Blue Puller), *Chromis coeruleus.* The body color ranges from blue-green to sea-green. Because these fishes live in large schools and feed on plankton, they are not as easy to maintain as other damselfishes. In addition, they are susceptible to bacterial infections of the skin. Size: three inches. Range: Red Sea, Indo-Pacific. (See photograph, page 110.)

THE REEF FISH, *Chromis cyanea.* Easily identified by a blue body and deeply forked tail. Living on the outer fringes of the coral reefs, it is accustomed to turbulent water and therefore needs plenty of aeration. Other damselfishes snap at its long fins. Fairly sensitive in captivity. Maximum length: seven inches. Range: tropical parts of the Atlantic Ocean and the Caribbean.

BEAU GREGORY, *Eupomacentrus leucostictus.* The upper half of the body and the head are blue, the belly and the tail are yellow and there are blue spots on the gill plates. Bright blue in the wild, the fishes raised in captivity will turn dark blue. Mature specimens in particular can be exceptionally aggressive, especially toward newcomers in the tank. The young tolerate each other if put in the tank at the same time, but may become temperamental as they age. Aside from this, they are very easy to keep if their diet contains both animal and vegetable matter. Size: six inches. Range: Caribbean.

Abudefduf. The damselfishes of this genus occur in numerous species, particularly in the Indo-Pacific. They usually have brilliant colors and are easy to keep except for their aggressiveness. In the wild, young animals live mostly in schools, while the adults are solitary or live in pairs. In the aquarium they usually take food readily.

SERGEANT MAJOR (Five-Banded Damselfish, Coralfish, Five-Banded Sergeant Major), *A. saxatilis.* The upper half of the body is golden yellow, the belly white. The fish is marked with five vertical, black or green-black bars. This schooling species is very lively, but older specimens may suddenly turn aggressive.

Splendid Rainbowfish, *Halichoerus marginatus.*

Size: seven inches. Range: Indo-Pacific and the tropical parts of the Atlantic.

BLUE-BANDED DAMSELFISH (Ocellated Sergeant Major), *A. biocellatus*. This species occurs in many color variations. Usually the back is blue and the rest of the body yellowish, but sometimes the whole body is uniformly blue. Thin, blue lines mark the head. The dorsal fin usually has two eye spots—though sometimes only one. It is a lively fish, but mature specimens become aggressive. They are easy to keep, especially in a fair-sized tank. Maximum length: four inches. Range: Red Sea, Indo-Pacific.

BLUE VELVET DAMSEL, *A. oxyodon*. Bluish black with an indistinct yellowish white, vertical bar behind the head. Fluorescent blue stripes cross the head and body. This species sometimes does not adapt very well to captivity, but specimens perfectly healthy when imported will not cause any great difficulty. These fish, probably solitary, are very aggressive toward individuals of their own kind. Maximum length: 4½ inches. Range: Indo-Pacific.

YELLOWTAIL SERGEANT MAJOR, *A. annulatus*. The body, light in color, is marked with five vertical black bars. The back is yellow between the bars, as are the tailfin and the outer edges of the dorsal and anal fins. The ventral fins are black. This species, usually imported from East Africa, is more sensitive in captivity than other damselfishes. Size: three inches. Range: Indo-Pacific.

YELLOW-BACKED DAMSELFISH, *A. melanopus*. The back is yellow from the eye till the insertion of the first soft dorsal rays. The dorsal fin is yellow except for the hind part which is blue like the rest of the body. The caudal fin has a yellow border on the upper and lower lobes. The species is, like most damselfishes, aggressive toward its own kind and other small species. Easy to keep in not too small tanks with plenty of hiding places. Maximum length: about three inches. Range: Indo-Pacific.

Wrasses

Labridae occur in all the oceans, but the majority of species are found in tropical seas. Most are beautiful and easy to keep. All need sand in the tank. Some bury themselves in it at night or when they are frightened, while others rest on their sides on the bottom. If wrasses are transferred from one tank to another, they usually remain invisible for a few days, hiding in the sand or behind or under stones. Sand is also necessary in the quarantine tank, where it can be put in a plastic box or a flat dish. This way the aquarist can lift it out of the tank for cleaning and find the fishes for inspection. In the first few days of captivity wrasses, especially the big species, can be very nervous and, if startled, may dash into the sides of the tank with fatal results.

Most species are not very particular about their food, though some are limited in the variety they will accept. They like to feed from the bottom, stirring up the sand and turning over shells in their hunt, but quickly learn to eat food floating through the water.

In many species the males build nests of algae or sand which they guard until the eggs are hatched. During this time they are aggressive.

To swim, wrasses move only their pectoral fins; the tailfin is exclusively for steering. The numerous species vary widely in build, but a slender, torpedo-like shape is most common. The color pattern of most species changes greatly at maturity and the differences between adult males and females can also be considerable.

Many species have already been imported. The most important ones will be described briefly here.

YELLOW-TAIL WRASSE, *Coris formosa.* Young specimens are dark- to black-red with three white, dark-edged, wedge-shaped spots. The dorsal fin has an oval black spot. One white band runs over the snout in front of the eye, and another short one behind the eye. The belly, ventral fins and anal fin are black. Adult specimens lose the vertical bands. Their bodies are brownish violet with large, dark patches. Two blue-green oblique stripes run along the gill plates. Maximum length: 16 inches. Range: Indian Ocean. (See photograph, page 251.)

GAIMARD'S RAINBOWFISH (Red Labrid, Gaimardi), *C. gaimard.* Often confused with the preceding species. Juveniles look very much like *C. formosa,* but lack the black patch on the dorsal fin. They have a white stripe on the front and sides of the head. The first white, wedge-shaped band reaches only halfway down the flank, whereas that of *C. formosa* reaches down to the belly. The body is also a lighter red. Adults have the same coloration as the *formosa*, but tiny blue spots edge their bodies. A few broad, blue-green, nearly horizontal stripes can be seen on the gill-cover. The tailfin is dark. Maximum length: 16 inches. Range: Pacific Ocean.

AFRICAN WRASSE, *C. gaimard africana.* This subspecies (sometimes considered a separate species, *C. africana*) occurs only in the western parts of the Indian Ocean. Juvenile specimens resemble young *C. gaimard* closely, but are lighter in color, ranging from orange-red to orange-yellow, and lack the black patch in the dorsal fin. Also, the white spot on the snout does not extend onto the sides of the head. The first white band on the body is shorter, as is the second band, which does not taper off into a point. The coloration of adults ranges from brick-red to violet-brown. They are marked with small bright green spots on the posterior parts and the tail. An oblique green stripe runs over the head through the eye, and three broader green stripes adorn the gill plates and the lower part of the head. Maximum length: 16 inches. Range: the western parts of the Indian Ocean.

CLOWN LABRID (Red-Throated Rainbowfish, Orange-Spot Wrasse), *C. angulata.* One of the most beautiful wrasses, which unfortunately grows quite fast and in no time is too big for the home aquarium. Young specimens are gray-white, with two large orange patches on the back. They appreciate bivalve flesh and crustaceans. Maximum length: 48 inches. Range: Red Sea, Indo-Pacific. (See photograph, page 47.)

SPANISH HOGFISH, *Bodianus rufus.* While adults are too large for most aquariums, the colorful and hardy younger specimens are most desirable. The latter act as Cleanerfish, but will pick on and kill small Crustacea. Length: up to two feet. Range: both sides of the Atlantic; in the western Atlantic from Florida to Brazil. (See photograph, page 215.)

CLEANERFISH (Bridled Beauty, Blue Streak), *Labroides dimidiatus* (formerly, *Fissilabrus dimidiatus*). These fishes are very slender. Juveniles have a deep, bluish black color enlivened by a blue band running along the back. In adults the forward portion of the body is whitish blue, while the posterior parts are darker blue. A black or bluish black band runs from snout to tail. These *Labroides* are called cleaners because they remove skin parasites from other fishes. (See photographs, pages 103 and 227.)

Stripe-Faced Unicornfish, *Naso literatus.*

The mature species lives in pairs in places on the reefs called *cleaning stations.* By moving up and down in a peculiar manner, the fishes attract the attention of other fishes, who respond by remaining motionless in the water, an upward tilted head indicating they wish to be cleaned. Other poses may be assumed as well. In any case, the fins will be extended to the utmost, and often the immobile fish slowly sink to the bottom while the cleaners perform their task. They also open their gill plates to allow a thorough cleaning of the branchiae. Even large predatory fishes, like the sea basses and morays, are among the patrons of these cleaners, opening their huge mouths wide for the cleaners to enter, often by way of the gills. *Labroides* not only eat skin parasites but also remove food particles, dead scar tissue and other nuisances. Naturally they play a very important role in reef life, taking care of hundreds of fish daily and thereby greatly improving the health of the reef population. Not only reef-dwelling fishes visit their stations; fishes from the open sea as well come regularly for treatment.

In captivity the Cleanerfish retains its natural behavior and tries to groom its tank fellows, who sometimes in turn invite him to do so. Fortunately this fish accepts normal, finely chopped food; otherwise it would very quickly die of starvation, since the aquarist tries to keep down parasites as much as possible. It probably eats parasitic crustacea as a mainstay. It is no guarantee against all parasites, however, since, so far as we know from aquarium observation, the Cleanerfish will not eat *Oodinium* and *Cryptokarion* parasites.

The external sexual characteristics are not yet identified, so if the aquarist wants to keep a pair, he will have to trust to luck. Actually it is best to keep just a single individual, though even a lone specimen may be lost to the bigger predatory fishes, especially the scorpionfishes. In buying *Labroides* be careful not to confuse them with "False Cleaners" (see below under blennies). The maximum length of the true Cleanerfish is four inches. Range: Indo-Pacific.

Other species of the genus *Labroides*, also considered "cleaners," are not commonly imported. These include: **BICOLOR WRASSE,** *L. bicolor;* **RED LIPPED WRASSE,** *L. rubrolabiatus,* and the **RAINBOW WRASSE** (Louse Eater), *L. phtirophagus.*

The **NEON GOBY,** *Elacatinus oceanops,* also acts as a cleaner.

Of the following species only the juveniles perform this service: the **BLUEHEAD**, *Thalassoma bifasciatum*; the **SPANISH HOGFISH**, *Bodianus rufus*; the **ROYAL GRAMMA**, *Gramma loreto*; the **FEATHER-FIN BULLFISH**, *Heniochus acuminatus*; the **PORKFISH**, *Anisotremus virginicus*; and many species of the butterflyfishes and angelfishes. Altogether, the cleaners comprise over twenty-five species of fish (distributed over eight families), six species of shrimp, one type of crab and even a worm.

BLUEHEAD, *Thalassoma bifasciatum*. In the males the head is deep blue and the body bright green. The females and young are yellow with a dark longitudinal band along the flanks. Juveniles are recognized and treated as cleaners by other fishes, but do not stay at special cleaning stations. Maximum size: six inches. Range: the tropical parts of the Atlantic and the Caribbean.

RAINBOWFISH (Moon Wrasse, Lyretail Wrasse), *T. lunare*. A beautiful, bluish green fish. On the head blue and red lines occur, and each scale has one tiny red vertical stripe. A bright yellow area marks the deeply forked tail. Easy to keep. Maximum size: 13 inches. Range: Indo-Pacific.

OLIVE-SCRIBBLED WRASSE, *Hemipteronutus taeniurus* (formerly classed in the genus *Novaculichthys* or *Xyrichthys*). Especially the juveniles are easily identified by the greatly elongated, first and second dorsal rays. Upon maturation this characteristic gradually disappears. The fish swims with snakelike undulations of the body. It commonly hunts for food under shells and stones, which it turns over. Young specimens suffer when forced to compete for food. Maximum length: twelve inches. Range: Indo-Pacific.

BLACK-BLOTCHED WRASSE, *Halichoerus gymnocephalus*. Frequently imported, usually from Singapore. The young live in schools, but adults are aggressive toward individuals of their own species. The fish, readily recognized by its grass-green body, is easy to keep and very lively. Maximum size: seven inches. Range: Indonesia and the Pacific.

SPLENDID RAINBOWFISH, *Halichoerus marginatus*. A beautiful fish, occasionally imported. Size: up to five inches. Range: from the Indian Ocean to western New Guinea. (See photograph, page 219.)

THICK-LIPPED WRASSE (Black-Eyed Thicklip, Half-

and-Half Wrasse), *Hemigymnus melapterus*. Juveniles of this species have a sharply defined color pattern. The front of the body is light while the posterior is much darker. Easy to keep. Maximum length: 15 inches. Range: Indo-Pacific.

Besides the above-listed wrasses, other species of the genera *Halichoerus*, *Thalassoma* and *Hemigymnus* and representatives of the genera *Stethojulis*, *Cheilinus*, *Gomphosus*, *Lepidaplois*, *Anampses*, *Pseudocheilinus* are regularly imported. Nearly all are relatively easy to keep, except for members of the genus *Stethojulis*. These have never been kept successfully in captivity; despite a healthy appetite they lose weight and die. They probably require a specialized diet. Species of the genus *Gomphosus*, the Birdmouth wrasses, should be fed with great care because of their elongated snouts. They require the same food as Long-Nosed Butterfly-fishes, and, similarly, suffer severely if forced to compete for food.

Parrotfishes

The Scaridae or Callyodontidae are noted for their highly specialized diet. Their fused teeth form a parrot-like beak, enabling them to crunch coral and crustaceans, although some species live exclusively on algae. A number of parrotfishes have been kept successfully in aquariums, where they have accepted all types of food, grown and remained healthy. The aquarist must take care, in every case, to include enough vegetable matter in their diet. By and large, they are suitable only for the experienced aquarist.

Some of the species that do better in captivity are: the **BLUE-BARRED ORANGE PARROTFISH**, *Scarus (Callyodon) ghobban*; **PRINCESS PARROTFISH**, *Scarus taeniopterus*; and the **BLUE-SPECKLED PARROTFISH**, *Leptoscarus vaigensis*.

Hawkfishes (Handfishes, Curlyfins)

Rather small, solitary fishes, the Cirrhitidae have adapted themselves perfectly to life on the reef. They do not swim in the open water, but rest on or among the corals, waiting for prey—which they catch with a quick, darting movement. The enlarged pectoral fins are used to grasp the coral branches firmly; the lowest rays are thick and elongated and project beyond the membranes connecting them. All have a characteristic tuft of fine "hair" on the spikes of the dorsal fin, the function of which is unknown. In general easy to keep, these fish tend to suffer when competition for food is severe.

RED-SPOTTED HAWKFISH, *Amblycirrhites pinos*. An attractive if not flamboyant fish, distinguished by darker and lighter green to brownish body-bands, a black band on the caudal peduncle and a round black spot at the top of the next to last bar. The head and dorsal fins are sprinkled with red dots. Range: Caribbean. (See photograph, page 183.)

SPOTTED HAWKFISH (Blotched Hawkfish), *Cirrhitichthys aprinus* (*aureus*). Identified by a pale body dotted with

Threadfin Butterfly, *Chaetodon* (*Anisochaetodon*) *auriga*, with Cleanerfish, *Labroides dimidiatus*.

angular, reddish brown spots arranged in three longitudinal rows. The Spotted Hawkfish lives in pairs and attacks individuals of the same species. Maximum size: four inches. Range: Indo-Pacific.

RING-EYED HAWKFISH (Arc-Eyed Hawkfish), *Paracirrhites arcatus*. The body is predominantly red or reddish brown with white longitudinal stripes. An orange-red crescent-shaped patch lies behind the eyes. Size: seven inches. Range: Indo-Pacific.

FRECKLED HAWKFISH, *Paracirrhites forsteri*. Has on its sides a broad dark band edged with yellow. The rest of the body is reddish brown. The head is bluish with black dots. Gill plates are adorned with red spots. Maximum size: twelve inches. Range: Indo-Pacific.

Jawfishes (Smilers, Monkeyfishes, Goggle-Eyed Cods)

The eyes of all species in this family (Opistognathidae) are large and mobile, their scales small. All are bottom dwellers. They dig holes, generally vertical, into the sand, hovering over them in a vertical or oblique posture while watching for prey. The ingress to the hole is often fortified with shell, bits of rock, and so on. Though some species live in colonies, specimens that live too close together constantly fight over these building materials. At dusk the fishes snuggle back into their holes and close the entrance with a shell or piece of stone. So far as is known, all species are mouthbrooders, removing the eggs from their mouths while hunting for food.

YELLOWHEAD JAWFISH, *Opistognathus aurifrons*. Also a mouthbrooding species, this fish has a beautiful bright blue body and a golden yellow head. This species has been bred in the aquarium, the male doing the incubating, but the young did not survive. It cannot compete readily for food and accepts only small prey or finely chopped mussels, fish or crab-meat. Small crustaceans are an absolute must in its diet. It is fairly easy to keep. The bottom must have sufficient depth to contain a burrow, and an ample supply of sand and fine pebbles should be provided for its construction. Maximum size: five inches. Range: Caribbean. (See photograph, page 246.)

Weevers (Grubfish, Smelts, Crocodilefishes)

Fishes of the family Parapercidae (Pinguipedidae, Mugiloididae) are rarely imported, although easy to keep and very attractive, due in part to their inquiring natures. They are slender, more or less cylindrical bottom dwellers, using their ventral fins for support while gliding over the bottom from hiding place to hiding place. Their mouths are relatively large with sharp teeth, and the top of the head is somewhat flattened. The larger species cannot be kept together with smaller fishes, but apart from this they are peaceful enough. They are heavy feeders and will accept all types of animal food.

Some imported species are the **FOUR-SPINED WEEVER,** *Parapercis quadrispinosa*, six inches; **SHARP-NOSED WEEVER,** *P. cilindrica*, nine inches; and **BAR-FACED WEEVER,** *P. nebulosa*, eight inches.

Blennies (Slimefishes, Combtooth Blennies)

Many tropical and subtropical species comprise the Blenniidae family. They lack scales, but possess a thick mucoid skin, which makes them slimy to the touch. The head is usually blunt and the body elongated. They inhabit shallow inshore waters, rocky coasts, dead coral reefs and the landward side of coral formations. Hidden under seaweed and rocks, many species wait out the receding tide, some staying on dry land for a considerable time. In the aquarium they make lively and inquisitive inhabitants, but need tight, preferably round, hiding places. Short lengths of plastic tube, camouflaged among rocks or corals, will be readily accepted as homes. Although often brightly colored and usually easy to keep, they are rarely imported.

STRIPED SLIMEFISH, *Petroscirtes temmincki*. This species has an elongated body with yellow and black longitudinal bands. Unlike most blennies it is free-swimming. In the wild it eats tiny prey, but in captivity will accept all kinds of food, though it is liable to weaken in competition for food. This species can be kept in a small school. Maximum size: six inches. Range: Indo-Pacific.

BICOLOR BLENNY (Two-Colored Slimefish), *Ecsenius bicolor*. A slender body, black in front and orange in back. Two small tentacles protrude from the head. An easy fish to keep if fed algae regularly, preferring to nibble it off stones and corals. It also accepts all kinds of animal food. If kept together with large or fast-eating fishes, it will remain shy and hide all the time. Does not swim freely. Maximum size: four inches. Range: Indo-Pacific.

FALSE CLEANERFISH, *Aspidontus taeniatus*. This fish closely resembles the true Cleanerfish (*Labroides dimidiatus*) and even imitates the characteristic swimming movements of the *Labroides* cleaners. It is, however, easily differentiated, as the False Cleanerfish's mouth is on the underside of the head. Also, its pectoral fins have a different shape and are located further towards the front, under the throat. Other fishes, mistaking *Aspidontus* for the true Cleanerfish, will allow it to approach or seek it out themselves. When quite close, the False Cleaner will lunge at the unsuspecting "patron," nipping bits of skin or fins. Dealers frequently mistake the False Cleanerfish for the genuine article.

Because of its feeding habits, it cannot be kept together with other fishes, although it is possible to keep specimens by themselves or in small groups. Though in inhabits cylindrical holes or the vacant exoskeletons of tubeworms, it should not be housed with tubeworms, since it will nibble at their tentacles. In captivity provide it with short lengths of narrow plastic tubing. Feed finely chopped meat, fish, mussels and small crustaceans. Maximum size: four inches. Range: Indo-Pacific.

BLUE-LINED BLENNY (Saber-Toothed Blenny), *Runula rhinorhynchus*. A very slender bluish black body with a yellowish white longitudinal band. It bears a superficial resemblance to *Labroides* and *Aspidontus* and is sometimes found among shipments of Cleanerfishes. It swims with swaying movements of the body. Like the two preceding species it inhabits empty tubes of tubeworms and close-fitting holes in corals. In captivity provide this fish with short lengths of narrow tubing sunk into the bottom. They are difficult to keep because they feed exclusively on the skin and fins of other fishes and the tentacles of tubeworms.

Maximum size: six inches. Range: Indo-Pacific.

Another species of the same genus, imported on occasion among *Labroides*, is the **VIOLET-BANDED BLENNY**, *Runula tapeinosoma*, which has a checkered pattern on its flanks.

Rabbitfishes (Spinefeet)

The shape and munching action of the mouth have earned Siganidae their popular name, rabbitfishes. They are also called spinefeet because when they dash frantically for caves, right under a disturbing wader's feet, the strong, sharp spines on the rays of its fins may penetrate the person's skin. Characteristically, the first spiny dorsal ray juts forward and is much smaller than the other dorsal rays; in some species, spines on the dorsal and pectoral fins are poisonous. The several schooling species which comprise this family feed mainly on algae.

VERMICULATED SPINEFOOT (Scribbled Spinefoot), *Siganus vermiculatus*. This species has a light body color marked with labyrinthine brown lines. In captivity it accepts animal food in addition to vegetable matter and algae. Maximum size: 16 inches. Range: Indo-Pacific.

BLACK SPINEFOOT, *Siganus rivulatus*. A greenish body, with a dark lateral line running parallel to and just below a matching top line. Flanking are nine golden stripes. Maximum size: 14 inches. Range: Indo-Pacific, Red Sea. It has also penetrated into the eastern Mediterranean via the Suez Canal.

BARRED RABBITFISH, *Siganus virgatus*. The silver white body is shaded yellow high on the back. An oblique brown band passes through the eye and a second band, parallel to it, passes behind the opercle. The dorsal and caudal fins are yellow. Maximum size: eleven inches. Range: Indo-Pacific.

FOXFACE (Badgerfish), *Lo* (*Siganus*) *vulpinus*. This rarely imported fish is easily recognizable by its tube-like, elongated snout. The coloration of the dorsal, caudal and anal fins, as well as the back, varies from yellow to orange. The rest of the body is bright yellow with a dark band on the side of the head. A wedge-shaped, dark marking extends from the opercle to the base of the pectorals. This fish is easy to keep since it eats vegetable matter in addition to animal food. Aggressive toward others of its species. Size: ten inches. Range: Indo-Pacific. (See photograph, page 98.)

Surgeonfishes (Tangs)

Acanthuridae, a small family, is found mainly in the tropics, with one or two species (e.g., *Acanthurus chirurgus*) also occurring in subtropical waters. Their outstanding physical characteristic is a series of lancet-shaped spines at the base of the tail. They can lock these spines at right angles to the body and use them to fight, usually with individuals of the same species, often ripping deep gashes in the opponent's skin. Like wrasses and parrotfishes, surgeonfishes swim with rapid movements of the pectoral fins. Most of them are schooling species, but in captivity they are mutually intolerant. All surgeonfishes feed on algae and, although they will accept animal food, they must eat vegetable matter to keep healthy. Too much animal food in proportion to flora will cause constipation and enteritis. Surgeonfishes are among the more difficult aquarium fishes, juveniles being easier to keep than mature specimens.

POWDER BLUE SURGEONFISH, *Acanthurus leucosternon*. One of the most beautiful of all coral fishes. The body is sky blue, the head black and the front white, while the dorsal fin and tail base are splashed yellow. In prime condition and at home, it is very mobile but, unfortunately, at the same time also very aggressive toward individuals of the same species. It requires a high proportion of vegetable food in its diet. Difficult to keep. Maximum size: twelve inches. Range: Indo-Pacific, particularly the Indian Ocean.

WHITE-CHEEKED SURGEONFISH (Lipstick Surgeon), *A. glaucopareius*. A particularly fine species. A roughly wedge-shaped white spot extending from the eyes to the corners of the mouth is characteristic. It has the same white band across the chin as does *A. leucosternon*, and its patterning is somewhat similar to that of *Naso literatus* (see below). Yellow zones which broaden toward the tail extend along the base of the red and black dorsal and anal fins. The tail fin is yellowish white with a faintly black edge. The body color is yellowish, but excitement causes it to turn violet or deep black. Fairly easy to keep. Maximum size: seven inches. Range: Pacific, Indonesia and the eastern part of the Indian Ocean—mainly the Philippines. (See photograph, page 239.)

CLOWN SURGEON (Blue-Lined Surgeonfish, Green-Line Surgeon), *A. lineatus.* An orange-brown body marked by a number of longitudinal blue stripes edged with black. The underside is usually bluish purple. Young specimens sometimes adapt themselves quite easily to conditions in the aquarium, but need a good deal of room when older. Maximum size: 7½ inches. Range: Indo-Pacific.

BLUE TANG, *A. coeruleus.* Juveniles are usually yellow but sometimes blue, while adults—marked with a large number of narrow, dark, longitudinal stripes—are invariably blue. Ill-at-ease adults turn grayish brown. Comparatively easy to keep. Maximum size: twelve inches. Range: Indo-Pacific.

PURPLE SURGEON (Ring-Tail Surgeonfish), *A. xanthopterus.* A purplish brown body, yellow fins and a white ring around the base of the tail. The dorsal and anal fins are marked with four blue longitudinal stripes. Maximum size: 24 inches. Range: Red Sea, Indo-Pacific.

CONVICT SURGEONFISH (Convict Tang, Five-Banded Surgeonfish), *A. triostegus.* Body color varies in the species from tan to olive-green. There are vertical black bars on the head and body and an incomplete bar on the caudal peduncle. Difficult to keep; even young specimens do not adjust readily to the aquarium. Maximum size: ten inches.

BLUE SURGEONFISH (Wedge-Tailed Blue Tang, Flagtail Surgeonfish), *Paracanthurus hepatus* (formerly *P. theuthis*). Of bizarre coloration, this fish has a blue body and a white or yellowish white underside. The head and dorsal fin are blue and the tailfin is yellow. A palette-shaped black marking extends from the eye to the caudal peduncle. Young specimens are fairly easy to keep. Aggressive toward individuals of the same species. Maximum size: ten inches. Range: Indo-Pacific. (See photograph, page 33.)

LONG-NOSED TANG, *Zebrasoma xanthurum.* Easily distinguished by its elongated snout. Specimens from the Red Sea are blue, from other places brown or brownish yellow. They have yellow or yellowish white tailfins. Fairly easy to keep. Maximum size: 16 inches. Range: Red Sea, Indo-Pacific.

SAIL-FIN TANG (Purple-Finned Sailfin Tang, Sailfinned Surgeonfish), *Z. veliferum*. This beautiful fish owes its name to the extended dorsal and anal fins. Its body color is highly variable with eight vertical bars. Adults do not adapt themselves easily to captivity, but juveniles can be acclimated. Maximum size: 15 inches. Range: Red Sea, Indo-Pacific.

YELLOW TANG (Somber Surgeonfish), *Z. flavescens*. The body is uniformly golden yellow with sail-like dorsal and anal fins. The snout is elongated. Maximum size: eight inches.

STRIPE-FACED UNICORNFISH (Smoothhead Unicornfish or Japanese Tang), *Naso literatus*. Like all *Naso* species, it is characterized by immobile spines on the caudal peduncle. The dorsal and anal fins are yellow, edged with blue lines. The pectorals are yellow, and the tailfin is bluish with a dark vertical band toward the rear. Fairly easy to keep. Maximum size: 22 inches. Range: Indo-Pacific. (See photograph, page 223.)

Tomato Clown, *Amphriprion ephippium*.

Other imported *Naso* species are the **SHORT-NOSED UNICORN TANG** (Short-Snouted Unicornfish), *N. brevirostris*, which has a short horn on the forehead, and the **LONG-SNOUTED UNICORNFISH** (Brown Unicornfish), *N. unicornis*, which sports a bump or short horn. Both species are fairly easy to keep. They occur in the Indo-Pacific.

Moorish Idols or Tobies (Zanclidae)

Bizarre fishes with long snouts and short, high bodies greatly compressed laterally. The most prominent characteristic of the Zanclidae is a high dorsal fin, the third ray of which is greatly elongated, trailing far behind the tail. They are very sensitive fishes and, when imported, must be in absolutely top condition to have a chance of survival.

While individual food requirements differ, these fishes all need a great variety of foods. In captivity they will do best if offered small crustaceans—especially living *Mysis* and algae—and provided with a great deal of swimming room. Since they do not tolerate drugs well, it is difficult to fight infectious diseases. Although they are apparently schooling fishes, they seem to be very aggressive in the aquarium within their species. There is only one genus—*Zanclus*—and probably only one species—*Z. cornutus.* (A second species, *Z. canescens*, is now regarded as the juvenile stage of *Z. cornutus.*)

The body of *Z. cornutus* is yellow, marked with two vertical black bands. A third black bar runs through the tail. On the face is a dark mask with a yellow triangular marking. Like many butterfly-, angel- and surgeonfishes, *cornutus* inadvertently eat many small crustaceans and other invertebrates while grazing on the vegetation covering corals and stones. They should therefore not be quarantined in "hygienic" tanks, but rather placed in an aquarium with extensive algae growths. If they refuse to eat, the best solution is to smear mussel flesh mixed with algae meal on a stone. (See Feeding, page 159). The aquarist should not keep these delicate creatures with other fishes, since they do not compete for food very well. Maximum size: ten inches. Range: Indo-Pacific. (See photograph, page 144.)

Turkeyfish, *Dendrochirus brachypterus*.

Gobies (Gobiidae)

This large family contains about four hundred species found in many parts of the world. Their pectoral fins join to form a sucker-disc with which they can adhere even to vertical, smooth surfaces. Most gobies inhabit shallow, coastal waters where they live on the sandy bottom, rocks or coral reefs or in banks of sea-weed. Nearly all are bottom dwellers; they do not swim about much and have a retiring temperament. They need hiding places, which they defend against other fishes including other gobies. When they adopt a defensive stance, their gill plates and fins are flared erect.

The females deposit the eggs in nests prepared by males, who safeguard them. Most species cherish solitude, but some form pairs or live in groups.

Gobies are generally easy to keep. They eat all sorts of animal food and require no special diet or care. Although there are many brightly colored tropical species, few are imported. This is a pity, because they are lively fishes, some maintaining an interesting type of symbiosis with certain pistol shrimps: these gobies stand guard at holes built by the shrimps; if danger threatens they take refuge in the holes, giving timely warning to the poor-sighted shrimps.

ISLAND GOBY (Eight-Banded Goby), *Cryptocentrus octo-fasciatus*. Found only around island shores and never mainland coasts. The green body is marked with eight transverse white bands; the head shows a pattern of red dots. Maximum size: three inches. Range: Indo-Pacific.

NEON GOBY, *Elacatinus oceanops*. Bluish black with a bright blue longitudinal band. Like *Labroides dimidiatus*, it cleans other fishes. In nature, Neon Gobies live in permanent pairs. They occasionally pair in the aquarium, but most home aquariums are probably too small to allow pairs to form within the group. When this does occur, the mated pair tries to drive off the others.

Successful hatchings have taken place in the United States. As a rule, the eggs are deposited in empty seashells, with both parents taking care of the eggs, which hatch within two weeks. The parents must be removed then, or they will eat the free-swimming fry. New-born Neon Gobies are transparent with a blue dot near the eye and a small blue spot on the caudal peduncle. For the first five days the larvae live on their egg sacs. The first month they should be fed the micro-organisms accumulating among flourishing algae growths, and powdered egg yolk. After a month they can eat newly hatched *Artemia salina* nauplii and other very finely chopped food. They attain one third of their adult size at three months and are mature at one year.

In the aquarium Neon Gobies will not perform cleaning services as energetically as do the *Labroides* and, as a rule, are interested only in larger species. Since they are bottom dwellers and cannot swallow large chunks of food, they are very sensitive to competition for food. Maximum size: 3½ inches. Range: Florida coast.

VARYING GOBY (Red Coral Goby), *Gobiodon rivulatus*. The body is greatly compressed laterally. The color varies individually from brown to red or a pinkish flesh-color. At times a pattern of red with irregular thin red lines is found. These gobies hide among coral branches and coral caves. Their natural food consists primarily of small worms and fish eggs. They are very sensitive to competition for food, since they hardly ever leave their hiding places to hunt for it. They are best kept together with other small fishes.

This species has spawned frequently in the Artis Aquarium. The males guard the eggs, which are deposited around thin coral branches. The larvae, like the larvae of most marine fishes, are pelagic (open-water swimmers). Maximum size: two inches. Range: Red Sea, Indo-Pacific.

LEMON GOBY (Goby), *G. citrinus*. Same description as the preceding species except for the color, which is yellowish with yellow markings on the head. Maximum size: two inches. Range: Red Sea, Indo-Pacific.

Scorpionfishes (Scorpaenidae)

These bottom dwellers are found in all seas. Most are solitary and live among stones, algae and corals. Some bury themselves completely or partially in the sand. A large head and wide mouth are characteristic. Many species have dermal flaps, loose bits of skin that hang in weird shapes from the body, head and fins. These, as well as the color pattern, provide excellent camouflage. Normally, scorpionfishes eat only living prey, which they swallow whole. Although it is sometimes difficult to persuade them to eat dead food in captivity unless it moves slowly down through the water, they can be gradually conditioned to eating it from the bottom. All species need hiding places in the aquarium. They must never be kept together with small fishes as they will eat these. The Scorpaenidae contain some of the most poisonous fishes of the world: the Lionfishes and the Stonefishes.

The hollow dorsal spines, capable of inflicting very painful wounds, carry poison sacs. A large amount of this poison in the system causes the same symptoms as a cobra bite and requires similar treatment. It is painful, although in general the amount of poison injected into the body is too small to have serious consequences. The best treatment is to hold the stricken part in the hottest water possible until the pain subsides. The spot where the spine has pierced the skin may remain sore for as long as four weeks.

Most suitable for the aquarium are three types differing in build and habits from the other scorpionfishes: the genera *Pterois*, *Dendrochirus* and *Amblyapistis*. Other family members make good aquarium fishes once they have learned to accept dead food, but they are of a retiring temperament, preferring to hide all day among rocks. Another reason they are not suitable for the mixed aquarium is that they allow faster eaters to snap up tidbits right under their noses.

LIONFISH (Turkeyfish, Red Firefish, Scorpionfish, Butterfly Cod, Peacock Lionfish), *Pterois volitans*. (See photograph, page 134.) Body and head red to pale red with a large number of

White-Cheeked Surgeonfish, *Acanthurus glaucopareius*.

alternating narrow white and broad brownish red vertical stripes. The upper pectoral rays, long and disjoined, are relatively larger in juveniles than in adults. Above each eye there is a long tentacle, which in juveniles exceeds the diameter of the eye; at maturity it all but disappears.

The *Pterois* species are not the least bit aggressive. They never attack of their own accord, but do turn their erect dorsal spines toward anything that threatens. Therefore transferring the fishes requires utmost care. Also, although *Pterois* will not purposely attack their tankfellows, a fish may be stung accidentally. Usually there are no ill effects, but if an eye is struck, it may swell and turn white, recovering after a few days unless a secondary infection by bacteria causes complications.

Pterois species normally eat live prey, which they slowly stalk and then capture by a sudden pounce and rapid inhalation of water which carries the hapless creature right down the Lionfish's gullet. In captivity they soon learn to accept dead food. Take care in the beginning to drop the food near their heads; later they will swim toward the sinking morsels. Soon they will become very tame and hang about the surface at feeding time, taking food from the owner's hand. They are heavy feeders and if offered a proper diet will be fully grown in 18 months. Like all scorpionfishes they are dangerous to smaller fishes, which they treat as prey. Even the *Labroides* (Cleaners) may be eaten if released suddenly into the tank. To be safe, introduce the Cleanerfishes in a separate compartment and give the scorpionfishes time to get used to them.

Adult *Pterois* live mainly on coral reefs. Juveniles are found mostly in brackish lagoons and estuaries as well as shallow inshore waters, where their favorite haunts are under fallen palm trees. Maximum size: 14 inches. Range: Red Sea, Indo-Pacific.

RUSSELL'S LIONFISH, *P. russelli.* Its build is more slender than that of the preceding species. On the head are short sharp spines instead of the conspicuous tentacles. The tail fin is longer and the black spots are absent. Maximum size: twelve inches. Range: Red Sea, Indo-Pacific.

SPOT-FIN LIONFISH, *P. antennata.* More compact build. Pinnate (feathery) tentacles above the eyes. Irregular bands across the body. Maximum size: eight inches. Range: Red Sea, Indo-Pacific.

WHITE-FIN LIONFISH (Regal Lionfish), *P. radiata*. The most beautiful of all the *Pterois* species. The dark, brownish red body is high and crossed by six thin vertical stripes, which split on the back. The long pectoral rays reach as far as the end of the tail. These may be white or pink, depending on the mood of the fish. Maximum size: eight inches. Range: Red Sea, Indo-Pacific.

TURKEYFISH (Scorpionfish, Butterflyfish), *Dendrochirus brachypterus*. In all species of this genus webs of skin join the pectoral rays together. Treat all *Dendrochirus* species the same as *Pterois*, and use the same caution; they are equally poisonous.

The red or reddish brown body of the Turkeyfish is marked with a pattern of dark spots, which sometimes coalesce into faint, transverse bands. The tentacles above the eyes are shorter than the diameter of the eye. Maximum size: six inches. Range: Red Sea, Indo-Pacific. (See photograph, page 236.)

DWARF LIONFISH (Zebra Lionfish, Zebra Scorpion), *D. zebra*. Brown transverse stripes mark an orange-red body. The tentacles above the eyes are twice as long as the diameter of the eye. This fish has large pectoral rays reaching as far back as the caudal peduncle. Maximum size: eight inches. Range: Indo-Pacific.

STONEFISH (Reef Stonefish, Devilfish), *Synanceja verrucosa*. The most poisonous fish in the world and therefore unsuitable for the home aquarium. It habitually lies half-buried in the bottom sand or hides among rocks, where, overgrown with algae, it is perfectly camouflaged. With its huge mouth it can eat even fairly large fishes. The poison glands at the base of the dorsal fin spines are clearly visible.

NAPOLEON, *Amblyapistis*. These owe their name to the shape of the dorsal fin, which resembles Napoleon's three-cornered hat. They are bottom dwellers, but more active than most scorpionfishes. As a rule, the body color is dark brown, marked with small white spots on the flanks and head. They are easy to keep if not put in with very lively and fast-eating fishes.

The most frequently imported species are *Amblyapistis binotatus*, *A. taenionotus*, *Tetraroge barbata*, and the laterally compressed **SWAYFISH** (Sailfin Leaf Fish), *Taenionotus triancanthus*. If danger threatens, this fish, which lives in seaweed waving in the current, will sway slowly back and forth with the swell of the water. It is more difficult to keep than other scorpionfishes.

Napoleons periodically slough off their entire mucoid skin.

Triggerfishes (Balistidae)

Characteristic of this family is the compressed form and distinctive head—enormous in relation to the rest of the body. They owe their name, moreover, to a most unusual mechanism: the first, large dorsal ray can be erected and locked into place by the second, much smaller one. The first spike cannot be released until the second ray is folded down. If danger threatens, triggerfishes withdraw into narrow coral crevices, where they erect their spikes, thereby wedging themselves tightly into the hole. When lowered, the dorsal spikes lie in a depression along the back. Triggerfishes normally swim with their spikes down.

They all have strong teeth, with which they crunch sea urchins, crabs and molluscs. They also attack other fishes, particularly sick or injured ones, usually aiming at the eyes, which they attempt to gouge. When resting, they adopt remarkable poses, such as standing on their heads among the corals or lying flat on their sides. Aquarists unfamiliar with the fishes' natural behavior are sometimes alarmed by these unusual resting positions. The fishes swim with undulating movements of their dorsal and anal fins. Some species are known to burrow shallow round depressions in the sand for spawning; the eggs are guarded by both parents. In the Artis Aquarium this spawning behavior has been observed in *Odonus niger*.

Nearly all triggerfishes adapt themselves well to captivity, but are very aggressive toward individuals of the same species. In the wild, too, adults at least remain solitary most of the time.

They must not be placed in an aquarium with smaller fishes, but will live peacefully with larger ones. They need plenty of hiding places. All sorts of animal food will be accepted, but hard-shelled food such as crabs, shrimps and mussels must be included to keep their teeth worn down. Invertebrates (especially echinoderms, crustaceans, molluscs and tubeworms) cannot be kept in the same tank, or they will be eaten.

STARRY TRIGGERFISH (Flat-Tailed Triggerfish, Varkvis, Varkenvis, Seevark—the latter three meaning, literally, hogfish), *Abalistes stellaris*. Most of the body, more elongated than that of other species, is grayish white; the brownish gray back is marked with a few oval white spots. The caudal peduncle is slender. Maximum size: 24 inches. Range: Indo-Pacific.

UNDULATE TRIGGERFISH (Vermiculated Triggerfish, Red-Lined Triggerfish, Orange-Green Trigger), *Balistapus undulatus*. A wavy pattern of orange lines marks a green body. This very aggressive fish will frequently attack its fellows. Maximum size: twelve inches. Range: Indo-Pacific.

CLOWN TRIGGERFISH (Yellow-Blotched Triggerfish, Big-Spotted Triggerfish), *Balistoides conspicillum*. The body of this fine-looking triggerfish is bluish black with large, round, white markings on the lower flanks and a yellow reticulated pattern on the back. A conspicuous orange band sets off the mouth. It is a temperamental species, more difficult to acclimate than other triggerfishes, but quite hardy once acclimated. Maximum size: 20 inches. Range: Indo-Pacific.

QUEEN TRIGGERFISH (Old Wife, Old Wench, Conchino), *Balistes vetula*. A very fine species with blue eyes and a golden body marked with two curved blue stripes across the face. The upper and lower lobes of the caudal fin and the upper lobe of the dorsal fin are extended in long filaments. One of the less aggressive species, it will grow large in the home aquarium and become a danger to small fishes. Maximum size: 20 inches. Range: Caribbean and the tropical Atlantic. (See photograph, page 175.)

BLACK TRIGGERFISH (Royal Blue Trigger, Red-Toothed Triggerfish, Redfang Triggerfish), *Odonus niger*. This schooling species has a blue body, red teeth and long tail filaments. In the aquarium it is not too aggressive and can be kept with other fishes of the same size. Length: 20 inches. Range: Indo-Pacific.

BLACK-FINNED TRIGGERFISH, *Melichthys ringens*. A black body with oblique rows of light dots. A peaceful species, which can easily be maintained with other fishes of the same size. Length: 20 inches. Range: Indo-Pacific.

PICASSO TRIGGER (White-Barred Triggerfish, Humu-humu-nukunuku-a-pua'a), *Rhinecanthus aculeatus*. Has a bizarre, very gaudy color pattern. Aggressive to individuals of the same species, as well as to fishes of similar size. Length: twelve inches.

Yellow Sweetlips, *Plectorhynchus albovittatus*.

Range: Indo-Pacific. (See photograph, page 161.)

BLACK-BANDED TRIGGERFISH (Humuhumu-nukun-uku-a-puaa), *Rhinecanthus rectangulus*. Distinguished from the previous species mainly by a large angular black marking on the back. The caudal peduncle is likewise black. Its behavior is similar to that of *R. aculeatus*. Maximum size: eight inches. Range: Indo-Pacific. (See photograph, page 14.)

BLUE-LINED TRIGGERFISH (Yellow-Spotted Trigger-fish, Brown Triggerfish), *Pseudobalistes fuscus*. Juveniles are yellow with an intricate pattern of thin blue lines. The bodies of older individuals are green or orange-brown, but the labyrinthine pattern remains. Very aggressive. Maximum size: 20 inches. Range: Red Sea, Indo-Pacific.

Other species sometimes imported are: **BLUE-FINNED TRIGGERFISH** (Spotted Triggerfish), *Balistoides viridescens*, a fairly peaceful species; **GREEN TRIGGERFISH,** *Pseudobalistes flavomarginatus,* also fairly peaceful; the aggressive **GOLDEN-FINNED TRIGGERFISH,** *Hemibalistes chrysopterus,* from the Indo-Pacific; and the **GREY TRIGGERFISH,** *Balistes carolinensis (capriscus),* from the Mediterranean, the tropical Atlantic and the Caribbean.

Filefishes (Monocanthidae)

Closely related to the triggerfishes, which they resemble in body form, filefishes are sometimes classified together with them as Balistidae. The rough skin of the filefish results in one popular name, leatherjacket. All species are laterally compressed. Ventral fins have given way to a simple, erectile spike connected with a collapsible skin fold. The first dorsal fin consists of one large erectile spine and a very small second spine by means of which the first spine can be locked in place. In the wild they live mainly on algae and coral polyps. In captivity they accept animal food, but definitely require regular additions of vegetable matter to keep them in good health. Most species are rather shy and suffer from competition for food, so should not be placed with lively, fast-swimming fishes. Many species have been imported. A few are listed below.

RAGGED FILEFISH, *Monacanthus spinosissimus.* Distinguished by the numerous branching dermal appendages all over its body. Maximum size: seven inches. Range: Indo-Pacific.

BLACK-SADDLED LEATHERJACKET (Valentini Mimic), *Paraluteres prionurus.* Similar in shape and coloration to the Puffer (*Canthigaster valentini*), it grasps a coral branch with its teeth at night and when resting. Maximum size: seven inches. Range: Indo-Pacific.

BEAKED LEATHERJACKET (Orange-Green Filefish, Long-Nosed Filefish), *Oxymonacanthus longirostris.* Green to bluish green with longitudinal rows of more or less oval orange spots. This sharp-nosed fish usually swims head down. Single specimens will pine away, so keep at least two. In the wild this

Yellowhead Jawfish, *Opisthognathus aurifrons*.

species feeds primarily on coral polyps, but in captivity accepts mainly small crustaceans and later chopped mussels, crabmeat and strips of fish. Filefishes can not be kept together with living corals, small anemones, crustaceans and tubeworms since they eat these. Maximum size: four inches. Range: Indo-Pacific.

Tripodfish (Triacanthidae)

Characterized by a single spine in place of the pectoral fins and by the large, strong first dorsal spike, these fishes, which resemble the filefishes, live in the open ocean, sometimes at considerable depths. They have small mouths and therefore need small prey or finely chopped food: they are weak competitors for food. Nevertheless these inoffensive little fishes are easy to keep if they do not arrive in an emaciated condition. The species most commonly imported is the **LONG-SPINED TRIPODFISH**, *Pseedotriacanthus strigilifer*, from the Indo-Pacific.

Trunkfishes (Boxfishes, Cowfishes, Cofferfishes)

Members of Ostraciontidae are unmistakable. Their bodies are enclosed in a solid sheath of fused hard scales, with openings for mouth, eyes, gills, fins and tail. The absence of ventral fins and the rigid shell make it awkward for them to swim, but they do remarkably well by waving their dorsal and anal fins and, to a lesser extent, their pectorals. They can turn with remarkable agility and are almost always on the move.

At first these bottom feeders will accept chiefly small crustaceans, but need green food as well. Because they can swallow only small morsels, they suffer in competition for food. Well-fed specimens have straight sides, which, in undernourished individuals, cave in.

Mutually intolerant, trunkfishes are never aggressive towards other species. In captivity they soon become tame and can be hand-fed. But not all species are easy to keep. The thin skin covering the shell is easily damaged and tends to become infested with skin parasites. At least some species are known to give off, particularly under stress, a substance poisonous to other fishes known as ostracitoxin. Also emitted when the trunkfish dies, this substance can kill off all the aquarium inhabitants. Peculiarly enough, ostracitoxin is somewhat toxic to the trunkfish itself.

BLUE TRUNKFISH, *Ostracion cyanurus*. The flanks are blue with black dots, the back is yellowish green and the cheeks are reddish brown. Juveniles are bright yellow all over, studded with black dots. In males the snout is convex, in females concave. This species has not been kept too often but seems quite hardy. Maximum size: six inches. Range: Red Sea.

BLUE-SPOTTED BOXFISH, *Ostracion lentiginosum*. The body is black to dark blue with a regular pattern of white dots. The upper part of the back and head in adult males is red. Maximum size: eight inches. Range: Indo-Pacific. (See photograph, page 36.)

BLACK-SPOTTED BOXFISH (Blue-Spotted Boxfish), *O. tuberculatus.* Juveniles have yellow bodies with black dots, making them look like swimming dice. Adults are yellow or yellowish brown with black spots edged in blue or bluish white. Maximum size: 18 inches. Range: Indo-Pacific. (See photograph, page 19.)

BOXFISH (Black-Blotched Turretfish), *Tetrosomus gibbosus.* The dorsal part of the shell is pointed, effecting a pyramidal form. The body is yellow to olive-brown marked with dark spots. Maximum size: twelve inches. Range: Indo-Pacific.

LONG-HORNED COWFISH (Cornutus Cowfish), *Lactoria cornuta.* The yellow body sometimes has blue markings in the center of the armor plates. Two long spines tilt forward in front of the eyes; another pair project under the long tail at the rear of the shell. Maximum size: 20 inches. Range: Indo-Pacific.

SCRAWLED COWFISH, *Acanthostracion quadricornis.* The body color varies from green to yellow or brown, with dotted blue lines and brown spots. A sharp ridge ending in a spine extends from the back of the outer sheath. Above the eyes two sharp horns tilt forward and slightly upward. At the rear of the shell under the caudal peduncle two spines extend backward. Maximum size: twelve inches. Range: tropical parts of the Atlantic as far as South Africa and the Caribbean.

Other species sometimes imported are the **TRUNKFISH,** *Lactophrys trigonus,* and the **SMOOTH TRUNKFISH,** *L. triqueter.*

Puffers (Boxfishes, Swellfishes, Sharp-Nosed Puffers, Tobies)

A small family, the Canthigasteridae contain a single genus of beautifully colored fishes which blow themselves into balls when excited; a sharp ridge or keel becomes visible on both back and belly in this inflated state. These fish are sometimes included in the Tetraodontidae (see below).

OCELLATED PUFFER, *Canthigaster margaritatus.* The

most frequently imported species. In the dorsal area it has a large bluish black ocellus (eye-like spot) edged with blue. The body is brown to brownish red with small blue spots, and the underside is white. In its natural surroundings it eats mainly coral polyps, but also small crustaceans and molluscs. In captivity it readily accepts all kinds of animal food. It is very aggressive toward individuals of the same species. Although it tolerates most other species, it does have a propensity for taking bites out of long fins. Maximum size: six inches. Range: Indo-Pacific. (See photograph, page 146.)

Other species occasionally imported are the **RETICULATED PUFFER,** C. *janthinopterus*, and **BENNETT'S PUFFER,** C. *bennetti*—both from the Indo-Pacific—and the **SHARP-NOSE PUFFER,** C. *rostratus*, from the Caribbean.

Blowfish (Puffers, Toados, Globefish, Pufferfish)

The Tetraodontidae are a large family of primarily tropical distribution, also found in brackish and fresh water. The bodies are usually round, with a few somewhat elongated or oval-shaped. They crunch crabs and molluscs with their strong, coalesced teeth. If danger threatens, they inflate themselves into large round balls by taking in air or water.

All species are easy to keep and eat anything, including green food. They are mutually very aggressive and like to take bites out of their opponents' undersides. In several species the male, during the spawning season, clings to the female's belly with its teeth. This family can not be kept with invertebrates or small fishes.

BROADBARRED TOADFISH (Stars and Stripes Toado), *Arothron* (*Tetraodon*) *hispidus*. Body olive-green to brownish gray marked with numerous blue or white round spots. A yellow circle surrounds the base of the pectorals, and yellow longitudinal stripes mark the underside. Maximum size: 20 inches. Range: Red Sea, Indo-Pacific.

RETICULATED BLOWFISH (Reticulated Toadfish, Lined Toado), *Arothron* (*Tetraodon*) *reticularis*. A dark brown body with light stripes on the underside and a light colored, reticulated pattern at the back end. Yellow rings surround both the base of the pectorals and the gill plates. Maximum size: 16 inches. Range: Red Sea, Indo-Pacific.

GOLDEN BLOWFISH, *Arothron citrinellus.* Maximum size: ten inches. Range: north of the equator in the tropical and semi-tropical waters of the Atlantic, in a broad belt stretching from Africa to South America. (See photograph, page 106.)

Amblyrhynchotus diademata. A dark gray body and a black mask across the face. Maximum size: twelve inches. Range: Red Sea.

Other species occasionally imported are: **DIAGONAL-BANDED TOADFISH,** *Arothron aerostaticus*; **BANDTAIL PUFFER,** *Sphaeroides spengleri*, an aggressive fish; and *Lagocephalus lagocephalus.*

Porcupinefishes (Burrfish, Balloonfish, Spiny Blaasops)

There is no mistaking the fishes of Diodontidae. They, like the puffers and swellfishes, have the ability to inflate themselves. Erectile spines cover the porcupinefishes' bodies, and stand out at right angles when the fish inflate. With their powerful, coalesced teeth they can crunch the hardest lobster and crab shells. They are fairly easy to keep in captivity, even though highly susceptible to infection by *Cryptokarion* and *Oodinium*—parasites which chiefly attack their large eyes. They can be fed all kinds of animal food, but their diet must include mussels (from time to time in the shell), freshwater snails, crabs and shrimps. Mutually aggressive, they tolerate other species, but should not be kept together with small fishes. Tempting as it is to show off their prowess, it is advisable to refrain from making the porcupinefishes inflate themselves since they often have some difficulty deflating. A lack of roughage in their diet may result in constipation and enteritis.

COMMON PORCUPINEFISH (Spotted Porcupinefish), *Diodon hystrix.* A grayish white body marked with brown spots. When the fish is not puffed up, the spines are folded back against the body. The fish inflates not only in reaction to danger and fright, but also in response to poor environmental conditions. In captivity it becomes very tame and can be hand-fed. Maximum size: 2½ feet. Range: all tropical seas; said to occur in the Mediterranean and Adriatic as well.

Yellow-Tail Wrasse, *Coris formosa.*

BROWN PORCUPINEFISH (Balloonfish, Long-Spined Porcupinefish, Freckled Porcupinefish), *D. holacanthus.* Does not grow as large as the preceding species. Can also be recognized by a number of brownish black bands across the back. Maximum size: 20 inches. Range: all tropical seas.

SPINY BOXFISH (Striped Burrfish), *Chilomycterus schoepfi.* This yellow-finned fish has a greenish body, marked with a series of undulated, olive-green, longitudinal stripes, and a few black ocelli on the flanks. The top of the body is somewhat flattened. The spines, immobile and kept in an erect position, are not as hard as in the preceding two species. Chiefly in juveniles, pliable tentacles protrude above the eyes. This species is not as likely to puff itself up as the *Diodon* species. When removed from the water, it produces croaking sounds. Maximum size: ten inches. Range: Atlantic and Caribbean. (See photograph, page 216.)

Anglers (Frogfishes, Anglerfishes, Estuarine Anglerfishes, Fishing Frogfishes, Toadfishes, Fishing Frogs)

Antennariidae are curiously built, highly specialized, bottom dwelling fishes. Hidden among corals or stones, they lie in wait for small fishes, which they lure into swallowing-range by means of a very flexible first dorsal spine. Like a fishing rod, this is elongated and projects just above the mouth. There is even a lump of flesh resembling bait at the end, and the angler wriggles this in a tantalizing manner when a prospective victim approaches. With huge mouths they gape to inhale and swallow their prey. The pectoral fins extend into leaflike limbs which, together with ventral fins mounted on leglike extensions, permit the fishes to waddle along the bottom on all fours or climb coral formations. The opercle (gill cover) is just inside the pectoral "legs."

Anglerfishes are difficult to keep alive in the aquarium for any length of time, but it is impossible to say why, since they are good feeders, as a rule. They can be offered live, freshwater fishes and live shrimps, but they will also rise to the bait if strips of fish are dangled in front of their mouths with a pair of tweezers. These fishes should be kept alone since they will eat fishes larger than themselves. Even Lionfishes have been known to fall prey to them.

The more frequently imported species are the **FISHING FROG,** *Antennarius polyophthalmus;* **MOTTLED ANGLER,** *A. oligospilos;* and **SARGASSUM FISH,** *Histrio histrio.* The latter species is usually found among clumps of floating weeds, but occurs on coral reefs as well.

Species for the Beginner

The aspiring marine aquarist is likely to be overwhelmed by the profusion of species available. He will do well to restrict his initial purchases to a few hardy species. It would be inadvisable for the beginner to buy, say, butterflyfishes, angelfishes or surgeonfishes, for all of which a great deal of experience is needed. The chances are that the beginning aquarist would lose these expensive beauties within a few weeks.

Some species that are easy to keep and which will enable the beginning marine aquarist to learn the ins and outs of his hobby are listed here.

Clownfishes:	*Amphiprion xanthurus, A. sebae,*
	A. ephippium, A. melanopus, A. percula
Damselfishes:	practically all Dascyllus species, for
	example:
	D. trimaculatus, D. carneus, D. aruanus
	and *D. reticulatus; Chromis xanthurus;*
	Pomacentrus species; *Abudefduf* species

Gobies
Many of the wrasses
Monodactylus argenteus
Scatophagus argus

VIII   Aquarium Invertebrates

A. General Information

Charming as a well-regulated marine tank with decorative coral fishes may be, an invertebrate aquarium is at least equally fascinating. An added extra is that a good many of these "lower" animals will propagate in captivity. What can be more enchanting than waking up one morning to discover a tiny starfish or a miniature snail or shrimp in the aquarium? The aquarist often finds small animals in the invertebrate aquarium whose presence he cannot at first explain. These creatures might have arrived from the tropics as larvae or tiny specimens in container water, or attached to larger invertebrates. If conditions suit them, they will mature unnoticed. In a tank containing fishes, this sort of surprise is improbable because the tiny interlopers would almost certainly be gobbled up by the fishes.

Banded Coral Shrimp, *Stenopus hispidus*

In general, the invertebrate aquarium is more difficult to maintain than a marine fish tank. Invertebrates are highly sensitive to changes in the composition of the water, particularly those most desirable because of their beauty or other unique qualities. In the main, the tiny cosmopolitan types of sponges, sea squirts and coelenterates give the least trouble; these also include many of the creatures which seem to appear spontaneously.

Most invertebrates are very sensitive to salinity changes, so acclimate them to a different type of water very gradually. When you arrive at home with your acquisitions, transfer them, together with the water in which they have been transported, into a glass or plastic basin next to the aquarium. Then allow a slow trickle of aquarium water to run into the basin using a siphon. The speed of the flow can be regulated with a screw clamp. From time to time, dip some of the water from the basin and pour it back into the aquarium (assuming, of course, that the water in which the animals were transported is of good quality). After a few hours the water in the basin will have the same composition as that in the aquarium, and the animals can be transferred.

Check the pH regularly. If it has dropped below 8.0, correct the acidity chemically or change part of the water. Since most invertebrates are harmed by high concentrations of nitrogenous, inorganic compounds, change some of the water regularly—and definitely more frequently than in the fish aquarium. Different groups and species vary widely in their sensitivity to such accumulations. Sea anemones, for example, tolerate almost the same concentrations as fishes, whereas most crustaceans do not. The defective formation of new exoskeletons by crustaceans kept in aquariums is probably due to this sensitivity. Scientific information about the exact environmental requirements of invertebrates in captivity is virtually non-existent. What we shall set down here is based solely on practical experience.

All invertebrates are extremely sensitive to high concentrations of heavy metals in the water. The doses of copper and zinc needed for killing skin parasites on fishes are fatal to most invertebrates. Though crustaceans are apparently not harmed by a few doses of copper, they, like molluscs, store copper in their body tissues, and may eventually succumb from the accumulation. Understandably, the aquarist is bound to encounter problems if he keeps fishes and invertebrates together. If the fishes are infected, the invertebrates must be removed or the treatment may destroy them along with the skin parasites. Quite apart from this, invertebrates frequently lose out in the competition with fishes for food. Moreover, many fishes gobble up the smaller invertebrates, or nibble them, or hinder them in other ways. In spite of this, certain invertebrates will do quite well in the fish aquarium—for instance, sea anemones, hermit crabs and cleaner shrimps (*Hippolysmata grabhami*). A few of the larger starfishes which, like sea anemones, can be hand-fed, can be maintained too, so long as fishes that prey on these invertebrates are not included. Hermit crabs, as well as the more robust species of brittle stars, make very good scavengers.

The best combination is obtained by putting invertebrates together with fishes harmless to them and that, because of their feeding behavior, can not be kept in a mixed aquarium. Seahorses, pipefishes, shrimpfishes and other plankton eaters come under this category. They can be kept together with tubeworms, brittle stars, starfishes, molluscs, sea urchins and the small crustaceans not likely to eat the larger fishes.

Water movement is of utmost importance, particularly to the sessile (permanently attached) and slow-moving invertebrates. Even more so than in the fish aquarium, a thick mantle of almost stagnant water must be kept from forming around the animals. (See page 53.) If the circulation is sluggish, sea anemones, for instance, will not properly get rid of the mucus which they continuously excrete from the surface of their bodies, nor the waste in the form of undigested food particles that pass from the stomach and settle on the oral disc. In sluggishly circulating water, sea anemones often remain closed and will not unfold their tentacles.

The water movement produced by circulation pumps and bubblers is different from the swell of ocean water. In the sea there is a constant back-and-forth motion, due to the washing of the waves. In the aquarium the water always flows in one direction, although it is possible to set up a complex flow pattern by installing several air releases, possibly combined with a circulation pump. Whether the absence of the natural swell has adverse effects is as yet unknown, but we do know that a constant flow in one direction is bad for several sessile animals. They frequently seem to atrophy on the side of the body or colony away from the impact of the current. The complex flow pattern set up by several bubblers will prevent such atrophy.

Purchasing Invertebrates

What should the aquarist look for when he buys invertebrates? The plain fact is that an invertebrate's health is more difficult to ascertain than that of a fish. A specimen which appears lively and shows a good appetite today may be dead tomorrow. A few warning symptoms, however, indicate whether a given individual is sick and perhaps dying. For example, a healthy sea urchin will continuously move its numerous tube feet even if it is not moving around; motionless or dangling feet indicate poor condition. Also, if it loses its spines, it is as a rule doomed.

A starfish must have a tautly stretched body. This can be clearly seen or, in case of doubt, felt. Avoid limp specimens with collapsed arms. Although broken-off arms can be regenerated, do not buy damaged starfishes, nor specimens with white blotches on the skin. Inspect the tips of the arms closely; in specimens infected by bacteria, degeneration will set in there first. If a starfish or sea urchin is grasped while underwater, it should close its mouth; if it does not, it is almost certainly dying.

Sea anemones, too, should be firm to the touch, since healthy ones can pump themselves full of water. Limp anemones may be sick or dying, so best leave them with the dealer, even though healthy specimens also may be limp as a rag. The same holds true for damaged anemones. Although their powers of recovery are enormous, animals injured during transportation have as a rule lost this regenerative faculty.

Before buying tubeworms, the aquarist should insist on seeing their tentacles fully extended. If the worms droop half out of their tubes or have left them altogether, they are dying. Ascidians must be fully inflated; they must deflate themselves when touched and close all their orifices. The condition of molluscs is difficult to judge, but they must close their shells upon being touched. The fact that they may remain closed, however, is no indication of their condition; they may merely be frightened. Crustaceans must be active, their shells undamaged and should have all their legs, though one damaged or missing leg is not cardinal. What is most important in selection are the numerous mouth parts; if they do not move them actively, they are not in good shape. Spiny lobsters should be watched for symptoms of loss of balance.

Quarantine

A quarantine period is advisable for invertebrates as for fish. Little is known about the diseases to which they are prone, but quarantine procedures will at least keep sick animals from bringing diseases into the aquarium. Also, if new acquisitions are isolated, the aquarist will be better able to observe whether they accept food. This is particularly important for species we know little about. Since drugs cannot be used, keep invertebrates in a "natural" quarantine aquarium (a procedure such as that recommended for fish: see page 137). A small tank with algae colonies is ideal for this purpose.

The Invertebrate Aquarium

Aside from the water requirements listed in the introduction to this chapter, invertebrates need flourishing algae colonies to protect them from high concentrations of ammonia, nitrites and

Green Mantis Crab, *Odontodactylus scyllaris*.

nitrates. If you plan to set up a separate invertebrate aquarium, best leave the aquarium fully operating but unpopulated until luxuriant algae growths have developed. Some invertebrates, such as certain burrowing starfishes, many crabs and shrimps and several sea anemones, need a fairly thick sandy bottom cover, which can best be provided by a layer of very fine coral sand. If this is not available, use finely grained hard river sand, preferably in combination with a reversed bottom filter.

Feeding

Invertebrates can be divided into plankton eaters, carnivores, herbivores and detritus eaters.

Among the plankton eaters are tubeworms, stone and horny corals, some sea cucumbers, bivalves, a few crustaceans, cylinder roses (Cerianthidae) and ascidians. All species which feed on minute plankton organisms can be offered a mixture of very finely pounded mussels (mussel milk) and algae or grass meal, to which has been added some fishmeal, egg yolk, bloodmeal and a little yeast. This substitute plankton should be carefully dispersed throughout the water, with the bubblers operating at peak capacity. After one or two hours, remove the excess by running a mechanical filter at high speed. This method does present problems. It is almost impossible to prevent overfeeding because an excess of organic matter may accumulate in the water, possibly with dire consequences. Good filtration is essential.

You can keep plankton eaters alive and thriving using this feeding method. It is questionable whether the plankton eaters eat the substitute plankton itself, since they often remain closed as long as the mixture is suspended in the water. It does seem probable, however, that the mixture does not sustain the animals themselves, but rather enriches the water so that after a while a microfauna develops on which the plankton eaters do feed. Once abundant microfauna is available, it will not be necessary to offer the substitute plankton quite so often. Just how often to carry out this messy operation is an individual matter, since each invertebrate aquarium is different.

Those plankton eaters capable of digesting larger organisms can be fed much more directly. An ideal diet for them is *Artemia salina* nauplii, supplemented by tiny bits of mussel flesh, waterfleas, *Cyclops* and minute slivers of fish. All these foods can be dropped right in front of the invertebrates by means of a fairly wide-mouthed pipette. Scrupulous bottom hygiene is not necessary in aquariums containing plankton eaters, since it is mainly there that the microorganisms that will serve as food for the plankton eaters will multiply.

Carnivorous invertebrates include practically all crustaceans (shrimps, crabs, hermit crabs, lobsters and spiny lobsters), most starfishes, serpent stars and brittle stars, sea anemones, octopi, many types of sea snails and worms. Depending upon their size, these carnivores can be fed smaller or larger pieces of mussel flesh, crabmeat, fish and lugworms. They can also be fed earthworms, shrimp, fish eggs and occasional bits of liver. Sea anemones should be fed individually. For other invertebrates distribute the food along the bottom. Mussels should usually be offered in their opened shells, although larger crustaceans and starfishes can deal with closed living mussels.

The herbivorous invertebrates include nearly all sea urchins, many molluscs and some sea slugs. The best food for them is algae, but if not abundantly available, supplement it with pieces of lettuce and an occasional soft weed, weighted down at the bottom. Sometimes these substitutes will not be eaten until they have been in the water for a long time and have almost disintegrated. Another possibility is to smear slabs of shale with algae meal mixed with a binding agent. Some herbivorous invertebrates, particularly sea urchins, will accept animal food in captivity, but this diet must be supplemented with vegetable matter.

The main representatives of the detritus eaters, finally, are the sea cucumbers. Many species spend the entire day drawing in sand at one end, sifting out the digestible organic matter in the intestine and passing out long "sausages" of clean sand at the other end. Therefore, sea cucumbers can only be kept in an aquarium with a good deal of bottom detritus. Keep them with plankton eaters.

Diseases

We know very little about most diseases among invertebrates in captivity, but assume they are generally caused by bacteria. Usually no outward symptom is visible. Once something abnormal shows up, it is probably too late.

Starfishes often manifest glassy blotches on one or more arms, or an arm will degenerate slowly from the tip. In such a case, it is best to amputate the arm with a very sharp knife or pair of scissors. The starfish will generally survive the operation, close the wound and start growing a new arm.

Lethargic behavior in crustaceans means they are either about to shed their shells or are sick. In the latter case good results have been obtained by placing the sick animals in antibiotic baths: streptomycin (concentrations of up to 100 mg/liter), aureomycin (3 mg/liter), or chloramphenicol (up to 20 mg/liter).

American clam farmers use polyvinylpyrrolidine-iodine complex (PVP–I) in concentrations of 50 mg/liter for a maximum of eight hours. Concentrations of 250 mg/liter for four hours were found to kill most bacteria, free-swimming as well as sedentary ciliates, and even parasitic *Cyclops*, without harming the young clams. This drug is worth trying on diseased invertebrates.

B. Invertebrate Groups

Sponges

Small species in particular, and the smaller specimens of large species, are fairly easy to keep. They feed on plankton organisms and organic particles suspended in the water. In older aquariums with much detritus in the sand and flourishing algae colonies, it is not necessary to feed the sponges, which filter enough food out of the water. They do not thrive, apparently, in the presence of many sea anemones—perhaps because the latter release poison from their stinging organs, or because the sponges absorb the ejected nematocysts of the anemones. Small cosmopolitan species sometimes develop in the aquarium from spores floating in the water.

Most sponges found at fairly great depths and in dimly lit places require dark corners in the aquarium so they will not become overgrown with algae. Some crustaceans, especially crabs, camouflage themselves with sponges, which they hold in place with their rearmost pair of legs. Sponge crabs and some spider crabs are always associated with sponges. Generally they place the sponges, as small growths, on their shells.

Coelenterates

These include the sea anemones, cylinder roses (Cerianthidae), hydroids, sea fans (horny corals) and stony corals. Most sea anemones adhere to rocks and other fairly flat surfaces by means of a foot-disc. Others dig themselves into the sand, leaving only the mouth and extended tentacles visible. When danger threatens, the latter withdraw into the sand. Most species can retract their tentacles and contract their bodies. Feed them fairly small pieces of food a few times a week. If too large a chunk is swallowed, it will as a rule be passed undigested the next day. Although sea anemones can do without food for a very long time, it is advisable not to deprive them too long. Not all species can be kept together, since the poisonous discharges of their nematocysts may be mutually fatal. Take care that unrelated species do not touch each other.

The symbiotic anemones are the most commonly imported. However, they are generally large, with diameters up to three feet and more, and rather difficult to maintain. They require intensive water circulation and do not tolerate too much infrared radiation, probably because of the amount of heat involved. Therefore, incandescent lamps can not be used. On the other hand, their light requirements are high, as nearly all species carry

Green Spiny Sea Star, *Protoreaster lincki.*

in their body tissues small algae (zooxanthellae), which play a role in the metabolic processes of their host.

Symbiotic anemones are easier to maintain without, rather than with, Clownfishes. Certainly it is ill-advised to keep more than two fish in one anemone. Too many "tenants" irritate them to the extent that they refuse food and soon die.

Symbiotic anemones (e.g., *Radianthus, Discosoma* and *Stoichactis*) prefer locations among rocks or corals, where they can withdraw from anticipated assaults. They will often wander about the whole aquarium before finding a suitable spot and settling down. They regularly change their body water completely. During this lengthy process, they are limp and unsightly, but when they pump themselves full again, they are as erect and firm as before. Sometimes their limp appearance signifies that a water change is overdue. Alternatively, it may be a sign that they have been overfed, although this does not happen easily, as symbiotic anemones are picky feeders. Those with long, thick tentacles are easiest to keep in this respect; they can be offered normal animal food. The genus *Stoichactis* have short thick tentacles, look like small rugs and are much more difficult to feed. In the wild they probably eat small plankton organisms or perhaps live on their zooxanthellae. The *Radianthus* species (see photographs, pages 13 and 162) also absorb food through the tips of their tentacles. You can observe this when offering them small pieces of *Tubifex*.

With the exception of the symbiotic anemones, nearly all species currently being imported are easy to keep. The transparent anemones of the genus *Aiptasia* are especially desirable for the aquarium. These are viviparous, the larvae developing in the digestive cavity of the female. They occur in all warm subtropical seas and are often brought into the aquarium by accident, together with other animals. They may reproduce to such an extent that they overgrow the whole aquarium and become pests. You can then use them to feed butterflyfishes (specifically, the *Chaetodon* species).

From the Caribbean come beautiful, fairly large anemones such as the **FLORIDA SEA ANEMONES,** *Condylactis passiflora*, which are easy to keep. The tips of their white tentacles are violet. *Barthelomea annulata*, with ringed tentacles, originates from the same area. As this species only accepts fairly small food morsels, it should be fed on water fleas, *Mysis* and similar fauna.

Another coelenterate is the hydroid, the polyp form of hydrozoan. It may occur in large numbers in the aquarium, covering stones, corals and glass panels with dense white "carpets." It lives on microorganisms and is harmless.

Sometimes polyps of the **MANGROVE JELLYFISH,** genus *Cassiopeia,* accidentally find their way into the aquarium. These polyps may continue to reproduce for a long time by budding off and, like the hydroid polyps, overgrow stones, corals and glass panels. At some time, however, the polyps produce tiny medusae —a process thought to be influenced, if not determined by, temperature. At any rate, it seems that a period of relatively high temperatures is conducive to medusa formation. These medusae, after a free-swimming period, attach themselves to the bottom with their mouth discs turned upward. Provided with enough food (*Artemia* nauplii) in captivity, they will grow into jellyfishes with a diameter of about five inches and remain more or less in one place. With pulsating movements of the body they carry plankton organisms to their mouths.

Occasionally polyps of other kinds of jellyfish will be introduced into the aquarium accidentally, but their medusae, being creatures of the open sea, cannot develop properly in the aquarium and will, as a rule, die after a few days.

Sea fans are imported fairly regularly. The skeletons of the colonies consist of a horny substance. The coral organisms look like tiny sea anemones. They are primarily active in the dark, when they extend their tentacles to trap minute plankton organisms. The colonies, which are either fan-shaped or dendriform (tree-shaped), are white, brown, red or yellow, according to the species. In general, they are fairly easy to keep if placed in an aquarium without any fish. They should be given a location away from the light. If they become overgrown with algae, they die. The imported species have not yet been scientifically identified.

The stony corals (the living corals of the genera responsible for the building of the vast reefs) are, as a rule, very difficult to keep, because they require extremely favorable environmental conditions. The best results in captivity have so far been obtained with species that have large polyps. These can be fed brine shrimp nauplii, water fleas and *Cyclops.* Feeding is not always an easy matter since the majority extend their tentacles only in the dark.

Stony corals are very sensitive to dirt settling on the colonies and to algae overgrowths. They should, therefore, be kept in dark areas or, better still, maintained in separate, small tanks. Stony corals are a great challenge to the experienced marine aquarist who may indeed be able to keep them alive—but only for a year or so.

MUSHROOM CORAL, *Fungia fungitis*, fairly frequently imported, has a large central oral cavity. It would seem, therefore, a fairly simple matter to feed them comparatively large morsels. Nevertheless, they live only for a few months in the aquarium. Mushroom corals form colonies which lie unattached about the sea bottom. In the aquarium, place them on a flat slab of stone a little above the bottom and see that no dirt collects on the colony.

Cylinder Roses (Cerianthidae) are closely related to regular sea anemones. All species live in tubes anchored in the sand. Usually imported without their tubes, they quickly build new ones in captivity for which they need a fairly deep layer of sand. Several organisms, such as shrimps and worms, live on and in these tubes in a commensal relationship. The tentacles of the Cerianthidae are very long, thin and flexible. These plankton eaters are generally very easy to keep. They will eat all sorts of finely chopped animal food (such as pieces of mussel flesh, finely shredded fish and crabmeat, pieces of lugworm or earthworm, water fleas, and so forth). The species imported so far have yet to be identified scientifically.

Tubeworms

Of the large group of segmented worms (Annelidae), only the tubeworms, which belong to the order of the bristle worms (Polychaeta), can be kept in the aquarium. They fashion their own tubes out of hardening mucus, calcium carbonate (lime) and grains of sand. At the head there is a crown of feathery tentacles, the precise shape of which varies with the species. These slowly revolving crowns trap small plankton organisms and, at the same time, perform a respiratory function. Tubeworms often react to unfavorable environmental conditions by shedding their crowns —for example, if suddenly transferred from one type of water to another. Under favorable conditions the crowns completely regenerate. Should danger threaten, the tubeworm will retract into its tube with lightning speed, and the crown of tentacles may be damaged in the process. Therefore, alterations in lighting, for example, should be gradual; otherwise tubeworms will startle and retract violently. For the proper diet for these plankton eaters, see page 259.

The finest species so far imported is *Sabellastarte indica*, found in all tropical seas. Its large double-crown of tentacles has alternating brown and purple stripes. Some species of other genera are occasionally imported, but so far none has been positively identified.

Crustaceans

The most commonly imported are hermit crabs (Paguridae), which protect their soft, uncovered hind parts by living in the empty shells of whelks or other gastropod molluscs. Naturally, as they grow, they have to abandon their shells and find new homes periodically. Hermit crabs almost always live in association with sea anemones, which they transfer with them. Most of these crabs are easy to keep and accept all kinds of animal food: they make excellent scavengers in the fish aquarium. While changing their armor, however, they are almost defenseless and often attacked and eaten not only by fishes or members of the lobster tribe, but also by their companions.

Easy to keep is the large **RED HERMIT CRAB,** *Dardanus megistos*, frequently imported from East Africa. (See photograph, page 267.) The smaller species of the genus *Diogenes* are also imported quite regularly.

Of the spiny lobsters (langoustes) the young of *Panulirus ornatus* is the species most likely to be imported. It is a beautiful species with white and blue bands and long, powerful, white antennae. If they arrive in good condition, they are fairly easy to keep, but grow very fast and soon may be too big for the home aquarium.

Crabs are treacherous animals in the aquarium. Although small crabs can not do much harm, large ones will prey on anything that comes near, including fishes, moulting individuals of the same species and other crustaceans. Swimming crabs of the family Portunidae are vicious predators. They can be recognized by the flattened plates on the last pair of walking legs, which are modified for swimming. Like many other crabs, they dig themselves into the sand to rest, leaving only their bulging eyes alert above the seabed. From this position a crab will pounce on passing prey. Species of the genera *Portunus*, *Callinectes*, *Scylla* and *Charybdis* have been imported occasionally. They should be maintained in a large tank set aside for crabs.

Many of the tropical species of spider crabs are suitable for the aquarium, but have rarely been imported. They are all slow-moving creatures with the deliberate gaits of old-age pensioners. Many species camouflage their carapaces (upper shells) and even their legs with bits of sponge, algae, shells or other available materials.

Phantom crabs, too, are eminently suitable for the aquarium. They are generally small, with very long legs. Imported fairly

Red Hermit Crab, *Dardanus megistos*.

regularly from the Caribbean is the species **DADDY LONG-LEGS** (Spider Crab), *Stenorhynchus seticornis*. The name speaks for itself.

Most mantis crabs (Squillidae) are extremely beautiful and very aggressive. These long-tailed creatures have strong, retractable pincers, which shoot out with whiplash speed to seize prey or ward off enemies. In doing so, they make a sharp cracking sound clearly audible through the glass of the tank. Mantis crabs excavate large holes in which they crouch, with only their eyes protruding—eyes which are mounted on stems and revolve continuously to spy out the surroundings. Mantis crabs can only be placed with big fishes (even then caution is required!) or with other species of large crabs in a spacious aquarium, not with other mantis crabs. They are mutually aggressive. They are such interesting creatures, however, that they fully deserve to be kept on their own in a small tank. Most frequently imported is *Odontodactylus scyllarus*, distinguished by a pattern of green, red and yellow. In captivity it eats all kinds of animal food. (See photograph, page 258.)

Neopetrolisthes oshiman, a little white crab adorned with red spots, is found on symbiotic anemones (*Stoichactis* spp.). It feeds almost exclusively on plankton. One of the pairs of legs near the rostrum is covered with long, thin hairs, with which it traps the plankton organisms. In captivity it can be fed *Artemia* nauplii.

Scores of mostly brightly colored little crabs live among the coral branches. These small creatures hardly ever move from their hiding places in the aquarium and must, therefore, be fed where they are if they are not to starve. Because of their retiring natures, they do not make very good aquarium exhibits and are only occasionally imported.

Shrimp

Two species of shrimp are imported fairly frequently: the **BANDED CORAL SHRIMP,** *Stenopus hispidus* (see photograph, page 254), and the **CLEANER SHRIMP,** *Hippolysmata grabhami*. The former is red with numerous white bands around its body and legs, and long, bright white antennae. They are very aggressive toward their fellows, so keep only one—or a pair—

per tank. They clean fishes at regular cleaning stations on the reefs and can be found in all tropical seas.

Cleaner Shrimps, widely distributed in the tropics, frequently share holes with moray eels and even groom them. They are peaceful animals and may be kept in small groups. Their body is a beautiful deep red marked with a bright white stripe along the back. The long antennae are also white. Both species can be put in with nonaggressive fishes, which they will clean regularly; the Cleaner Shrimp, however, is more active in this respect than the Banded Coral Shrimp. Both thrive on small bits of animal food and have survived in captivity for as long as three years. They will even accept *Mysis* and *Daphnia*, snatching them from the open water with quick, darting movements. (Photograph, page 138.) Specimens of the small shrimp, *Periclimenes brevicarpalis*, associated with symbiotic anemones, are occasionally imported. Their bodies are as clear and transparent as glass, with a few orange to yellow markings. They are difficult to ship, because their oxygen requirements are very high and, unless special precautions are taken, are often dead on arrival. Although mutually very aggressive, they live in pairs on one sea anemone.

Molluscs

Among the vast array of molluscs native to tropical waters are many interesting species highly suitable for the aquarium, but rarely imported. Molluscs, in general, are easy—even very easy—to maintain in captivity, with the exception of bivalves, which live on plankton and stirred-up bottom detritus. Among the gastropods are both herbivorous and carnivorous species. Some coneshell snails (Conidae), occasionally imported, are dangerous because of their movable, articulated poison spines, with which they ward off attackers and paralyze their prey. Even humans experience considerable discomfort on being stung by these creatures. They are carnivorous animals that are believed to attack, poison and eat even small fishes.

A very beautiful mollusc which is regularly imported and can be successfully maintained in the aquarium is the **TIGER SNAIL**, *Cypraea tigris*. When active, this large gastropod wears its mantle, bristling with short tentacles, turned outside over the shell. When the animal is resting, the mantle is partly or entirely retracted. The Tiger Snail is omnivorous and should be fed algae and lettuce as well as mussel flesh. Sea anemones are not safe from this heavy feeder. (See photograph, page 271.)

Smaller species of the cowrie family (Cypraeidae) that are sometimes imported are: *Cypraea histro*, *C. annulus*, *C. sulcidentata*, *C. carneola* and *C. eglantina*. In the Artis Aquarium *Cypraea tigris* and *C. histrio* deposited eggs after two years in captivity.

Among the predatory gastropods of the murex family (Muricidae) are many species that could be successfully kept if they did not feed exclusively on other molluscs. If supplied with plenty of mussels, they tend to leave their companions alone, but one can never be sure! A few imported species are *Murex cichoreus* and *M. ramosus* from the Indo-Pacific and *M. pomeum* from the Caribbean.

Representatives of the following families are also fairly easy to keep: Mitridae, Volutidae, Turbinidae and Bullidae—all of them carnivorous. *Lambis lambis* is a herbivorous sea snail which, although imported only occasionally, also appears to be fairly easy to keep. In captivity it accepts animal food as well as vegetable matter.

Bivalves are more difficult to keep alive since all are plankton feeders. Practically the only tropical species imported is the **FILE MUSSEL** (Flame Scallop), *Lima scabra*, from the Caribbean. This beautiful mussel with long red or white tentacles on the edge of its mantle is best placed with other plankton feeders. However, it seems to be very sensitive to accumulations of organic substances in the water and does not live long in captivity.

The shell-less **SEA SLUGS** (Nudibranchs), genus *Nudibranchia*, are beautiful little creatures. In some species the gills are fantastically shaped, highly colored extensions on their backs. Most marine slugs feed on coelenterates, particularly hydroid polyps and sea anemones. They are immune to the stinging cells of their prey and even store these in dorsal papillae (small projections like nipples), connected with the intestine and possessing a tiny slit opening to the outside. Apparently, sea slugs can use these stinging cells for their own defense. Since their diet is limited, they are difficult to maintain in the aquarium. A few species, however, feed on algae.

Tiger Snail, *Cypraea tigris*.

Echinoderms

This phylum contains five classes: sea lilies, sea urchins, star-fishes, brittle stars and sea cucumbers. The stalked forms of the sea lily are unsuitable for the aquarium.

Sea urchins are difficult to keep. First, they suffer badly during transport and are liable to arrive in poor condition. Second, almost all of them are herbivorous and need a great deal of algae; they feed, but reluctantly, on lettuce, spinach and soft weeds. (Although they accept animal food, they apparently can not live on it.) In large tanks with flourishing algae growths a single individual can be maintained successfully, but in a 'smaller tank it soon

271

exhausts the supply of algae. If you succeed in supplying your sea urchin with plenty of algae, it will make a rewarding charge.

Avoid bringing sea urchins out of the water, as air may become trapped under the shell, or the mouth parts destroyed upon return. As there is no way of knowing whether the animals were taken out of the water when caught, it is impossible to be sure of buying healthy specimens. If they start losing their spines or cannot right themselves after toppling over, they are dying. Many species camouflage themselves by attaching algae, shells or other materials to their spines. They may even make off with the thermometer in the tank. Among the species imported so far are *Tripneustes gratilla* and the **LONG-SPINED SEA URCHIN** (*Diadema* species).

The starfishes are less demanding than the sea urchins; they can be fed mussels, strips of fish and crabmeat. If kept with fishes, however, they will not, as a rule, survive, because the competition for food is too intense. Imported species that do well in the aquarium include the **RED SPINY SEA STAR,** *Pentaceraster mammillatus;* the **GREEN SPINY SEA STAR,** *Protoreaster lincki* (see photograph, page 262); the **CUSHION SEA STAR,** *Culcita schmideliana* and *C. novae-quinea*; and the **PICASSO SEA STAR,** *Leiaster leachi.*

The **BLUE STARFISH,** *Linckia laevigata*, is less easy to maintain because it is difficult to persuade it to eat. It is often infected with tiny parasitic molluscs (*Thyca ectoconcha*), which bore through the skin into the water vascular system of the starfish.

Contrary to what some authors maintain, brittle stars (serpent stars) are fairly easy to keep. Frequently hidden under stones or corals, they can also be seen moving through the aquarium with surprisingly fast gliding movements of their long arms. They also use their arms to pass small bits of food to the mouth. Like starfishes, brittle stars have tremendous regenerative powers.

In aquariums with a great deal of bottom detritus, sea cucumbers will thrive. Except for a few specimens of *Holothuria percivax* and *H. tubulosa*, they have seldom been imported. Neither beautifully colored nor particularly lively, sea cucumbers will appeal mainly to lovers of curious animal forms.

In thriving aquariums small ascidians (sea squirts, tunicates) of unidentified species sometimes develop unexpectedly. (The larval form is free-swimming and may arrive unnoticed in a shipment.) As a rule their colors vary from pink to brownish red. Tropical ascidians have apparently not been imported so far. They would not be difficult to keep in aquariums provided they arrive in good condition. Like sea urchins, they should not be brought out of the water when taken from the seabed.

Seahorse (Yellow), *Hippocampus kuda*. The Seahorse may not look like a fish, but that's just what he is.

Bibliography

Abel, E. F., 1960—Zur Kenntnis des Verhaltens und der Ökologie von Fischen an Korallenriffen bei Ghardaqa (Rotes Meer). Z. Morph. Ökol. Tiere 49: 430–503.

Axelrod, H. R. & W. Vorderwinkler, 1963—Saltwater Aquarium Fish. (T. F. H. Publications, Jersey City).

Beaufort, R. F. de et al., 1911–1962—The fishes of the Indo-Australian Archipelago. I- XI. (E. J. Brill, Leiden).

Breder, C. M., 1948—Field book of marine fishes of the Atlantic coast. (G. P. Putnam's Sons, New York—London).

Chlupaty, P., 1964—Schmetterlingsfische. (A. Kernen Verlag, Stuttgart).

—, 1966—Doktor- und Kaiserfische. (A. Kernen Verlag, Stuttgart).

Clark, J. R. & R. L. Clark (eds.), 1964—Sea water systems for experimental aquariums. Research Report 63. Fish & Wildlife Service. US Dept. of the Interior.

Fach, D., 1965—Die Kriechsproßalge Caulerpa prolifera. DATZ 18: 48–49.

Fogg, G. E., 1953—The metabolism of algae. (Methuen & Co, London).

Geisler, R., 1964—Wasserkunde für die aquaristische Praxis. (A. Kernen Verlag, Stuttgart).

Gelbhaar, R., 1961—Beitrag zur Korallenfischpflege. DATZ 14: 276.

Gosline, W. A. & V. Brock, 1960—Handbook of Hawaiian fishes. (University of Hawaii Press, Honolulu).

Graaf, Fr. de, 1957—Koraalvissen, lastige schoonheden. Artis 3: 90–95.

—, 1959—Koffervissen, bizarre dieren met een stevig huidpantser. Artis 5: 12–15.

—, 1964—Zeeanemonen en koraalvissen. Artis 9: 178–183.

—, 1965—Scheermesvissen. Artis 11: 5–9.

—, 1967a—Duveltjes in doosjes. Artis 13: 16–22.

—, 1967b—Poetssymbiose. Het Aquarium 37: 266–274.

—, 1967c—Wonderen der Zee. (De Geïllustreerde Pers, Amsterdam).

Grobe, J., 1966—Das Korallenaquarium. (A. Kernen Verlag, Stuttgart).

Herald, E. S., R. P. Dempster, C. Wolters & M. L. Hunt, 1962—Filtration and ultraviolet sterilization of seawater in large closed and semi-closed aquarium systems. Communications Ier Congrès International d'Aquariologie. Monaco 1960. Bull. Inst. Océan. Numero spécial IB: 49–62.

Hormann, J. R., 1963—Das Acrylglas-Aquarium. DATZ 16: 214.

Hückstedt, G., 1963—Aquarienchemie. (Franckh'sche Verlagshandlung, Stuttgart).

—, 1963—Aquarientechnik. (Frankh'sche Verlagshandlung, Stuttgart).

—, 1964—Pharmakologie des Meerwassers. DATZ 17: 121–123.

—, 1964—Praxis der Meerwasser-Aquaristik. DATZ 17: 146–148; 208–210.

Kawai, A. Y. et al., 1964—Biochemical studies on the bacteria in aquarium with circulating system.—I. Changes of the qualities of breeding water and bacterial population of the aquarium during fish cultivation. Bull. Jap. Soc. Sci. Fish. 30: 55–63.

Klee, A. J., 1964—A rebuttal to "Let's illuminate with Gro-Lux." The Aquarium 1964.

Knauf, H., 1964—Geklebte Vollglasbecken, aber diesmal ganz einfach. DATZ 17: 60–62.

Kühl, H. & H. Mann, 1951—Über die periodischen Änderungen im Chemismus von Seewasseraquarien. Verhandlungen Deutsche Zool. Ges. Wilhelmsh. 1951: 378–385.

—, 1956—Unperiodische Änderungen im Stoffhaushalt von Seewasseraquarien. Hydrobiologia 8: 66–78.

Ladiges, W., 1956—Tropische Meeresfische. (A. Kernen Verlag, Stuttgart).

Marshall, N. B., 1965—The life of fishes. (Weidenfeld & Nicholson, London).

Marshall, T. C., 1964—Fishes of the Great Barrier Reef and coastal waters of Queensland. (Angus and Robertson, Sydney).

Munro, I. S. R., 1955—The marine and freshwaterfishes of Ceylon. (Dept. of External Affairs, Canberra).

Plessis, Y. B., 1964—Marine aquarium procedures and techniques. In: Sea water systems for experimental aquariums.

Pringsheim, E. J., 1963—Die Ernährung der Algen. Die Naturwissenschaften 50: 146–150.

Probst, K., 1963—Meeresaquaristik. Teil III: Fische. (A. Philler Verlag, Minden).

Ray, C. & E. Ciampi, 1956—The underwater guide to marine life. (A. S. Barnes & Co., New York).

Saeki, A., 1964—Studies on fish culture in filtered closed system circulation aquaria. (Directorate of Scientific Information Services, D.R.B. Canada).

Schön, G. & H. Engel, 1962—Der Einfluß des Lichtes auf Nitrosomonas europaea Win. Arch. Mikrobiol. 42: 415–428.

Shilo, M., 1966—Predatory bacteria. Science Journal 2: 33–37.

Shilo, M. & B. Bruff, 1965—Lysis of gram-negative bacteria by host-independent ectoparasitic Bdellovibrio bacteriovorus isolates. Journ. Gen. Microbiol. 40: 312.

Simkatis, H., 1958—Saltwaterfishes for the home aquarium. (Lippincott, Philadelphia).

Smith, J. B. L., 1953—The sea fishes of southern Africa. (Central News Agency Ltd, Kaapstad).

—, 1963—The fishes of Seychelles. (Dept. of Ichthyology, Rhodes University, Grahamstown).

Stolp, H. & M. Starr, 1963—Bdellovibrio bacteriovorus sp.n. a predatory ectoparasite and bacteriolytic microorganism. In: Antonie van Leeuwenhoek 29: 212.

Straughan, R. P. L., 1959—The saltwater aquarium in the home. (A. S. Barnes & Co., New York).

Wachtel, H., 1963—Aquarienhygiene. (Franckh'sche Verlagshandlung, Stuttgart).

Wickler, W., 1962—Das Meeresaquarium. (Franckh'sche Verlagshandlung, Stuttgart).

Wood, E. J. F., 1965—Marine Microbial Ecology. (Chapman & Hall Ltd., London).

Fish Index

Page numbers in roman type indicate main entry.
Page numbers in italics indicate illustration.

Marine Tropical Aquarium Guide •

Frank de Graaf • ISBN 0-87666-805-8